D1246919

Critical Praise

"My cup runneth over with admiration for Scott and Murphy's *The Scouting Party*. The amount of primary research conducted by the authors is deeply impressive. But, even more important, they remind us that the Boy Scouts has been a whooping one-hundred-year success. Consider this scholarly book a gift to America."

—Douglas Brinkley, *New York Times* BEST-SELLING AUTHOR OF *The Wilderness Warrior: Theodore Roosevelt and the Crusade for America*

"Be Prepared! David C. Scott and Brendan Murphy have unsheathed their machetes and blazed a trail through the thickets of the fierce (and strangely delicate) masculine ideals that created the Boy Scouts. The story, with its subtexts of Anglo-Saxon superiority, chivalry, clean living, and military preparedness, explains much about the rough-rider ethos of American life in the early twentieth century. And for their handling of the colossal egos at the center of the story, the authors deserve merit badges in humor and fair play."

—Patricia O'Toole, BEST-SELLING AUTHOR OF *When Trumpets Call: Theodore Roosevelt after the White House* AND PULITZER PRIZE FINALIST, *The Five of Hearts: An Intimate Portrait of Henry Adams and His Friends*

"*The Scouting Party* is part history, part detective narrative as it uncovers and catalogues in rich detail the jealousies, intrigues, and earnest efforts of the men who created the Boy Scouts. Through careful research and vivid descriptions, Scott and Murphy have told a story that is fundamentally and uniquely American."

—Candice Millard, BEST-SELLING AUTHOR OF *The River of Doubt: Theodore Roosevelt's Darkest Journey*

THE
Scouting Party

THE
SCOUTING PARTY

PIONEERING AND PRESERVATION,
PROGRESSIVISM AND PREPAREDNESS
IN THE MAKING OF THE
BOY SCOUTS OF AMERICA

DAVID C. SCOTT &
BRENDAN MURPHY

RED HONOR PRESS
DALLAS, TEXAS

Published by Red Honor Press.

Red Honor Press and colophon are trademarks of Red Honor Ventures, Ltd.

Copyright © 2010 by David C. Scott

First Edition 2010

Red Honor Press publications are available at special discounted rates for volume and bulk purchases, corporate and institutional premiums, promotions, fund-raising, and educational uses. For further information, contact:

Red Honor Press
P.O. Box 166677
Irving, Texas 75016
specialsales@redhonor.com

www.TheScoutingParty.com

Book design and layout by Publications Development Co.
Cover design by Matthew Simmons.

Printed and bound in the United States of America.

LCCN: 2010905890

ISBN-10: 0-9789-8363-7
ISBN-13: 978-0-9789-8363-5

Get informed & inspired at

www.redhonor.com

10 9 8 7 6 5 4 3 2 1

For Aimee Regmund Scott
And in memory of William Buerk Scott

ACKNOWLEDGMENTS

The Scouting Party began as a research project by David into the origins of American Scouting and over time developed into a collaborative effort with Brendan, to whom David had turned for help delving into the Daniel Carter Beard Papers in the Library of Congress in Washington. Between that research and the initial drafts of the book, Brendan became as fascinated as David with the strong and often idiosyncratic personalities who launched the Boy Scouts of America and their disagreements over issues small and large that ranged from insignia to clashes over pacifism versus preparedness in the early days of World War I.

Over several years of research, writing and editing, we spent many hours on the phone between Dallas and Washington discussing these compelling individuals and their foibles—often times sharing a laugh over pungent remarks by Dan Beard or ripostes by Ernest Seton as they contended for recognition as the founders of Scouting, though at times allied against the distant and lofty Robert Baden-Powell.

In the very beginning, David received critical encouragement from the late Gene Stone, then Scout Executive of Circle 10 Council, Dallas, who talked up the project to BSA Director of Properties Haynes Harbaugh, who in turn put David in touch with BSA lawyers David K. Park and Richard John Mathews. They provided David with access to the BSA National Archives for in-depth research, in particular into correspondence between BSA founders and early managers, and kindly granted permission to quote from those letters. Many thanks to them, and to Connie Adams, Pat L. Wellen, Tracy Anderson, and BSA Museum Archivist Steven Price. As research progressed and some chapters stalled, former Scout Executive Jim Stevenson and wife Bea reminded David to start setting and hitting more self-imposed deadlines.

We want to thank museum archivists around the world who helped us unearth documents and photos: David L. Witt, Seton historian at the Academy of the Love of Learning; Seth McFarland, former curator of the Seton Museum and Library and the Philmont Scout Ranch in Cimarron, New Mexico; and Colin R. Walker, founder of the remarkable Scouting Milestones website in the United Kingdom. Insights into British Scouting came from archivists Paul Moynihan and Chris James of the British Scouting Association at Gilwell Park, England, and English Scouting historian John Ineson. Robert Peterson, author of a history of the Boy Scouts of America that was published on the occasion of the organization's 75th anniversary, provided David with copies of his numerous interview transcripts before his untimely passing. Warm thanks as well to the always-helpful archivists in the Library of Congress Manuscript Division, and the genial staff in the John Adams Building reading room.

Scholarly advice in the early stages came from Dr. William V. Kahler, Dr. Roger Schustereit and Robert Reitz, curator of the Harbin Scout Museum in Dallas. Counsel came as well from David and Lynne Jones, Bill Bliss, David D. Durrett, Hank Arndt, Fred Flores, Dana Smith, and Dr. Robert Lee Edmonds. Discussions with Dr. John Dizer, an authority on the creation of children's literature and *Boys' Life* magazine, offered important insights into the little known history of this genre. Our appreciation to Caryle Murphy for her reading of the manuscript and advice on how best to tell the story.

Janice Petterchak, the author of *Lone Scout*, and Dr. Edward L. Rowan, author of *To Do My Best*, provided David with insights on BSA incorporator William D. Boyce and Chief Scout Executive James E. West. Archivists at many libraries worldwide helped us acquire key documents: Susan M. Kooyman and Jim Bowman of Canada's Glenbow Museum, Ann Goddard and Rob Fisher of Canada's National Archive in Ottawa, Jodi Aiko of Trent University Archives, and researcher Betsey Baldwin. Danelle Moon of the Yale University Library, Eleanor Corridan and Dr. Paige Roberts of Springfield College's Babson Library, Dagmar Getz of the Kautz Family YMCA Library, Joe Milato of the University of Texas at Dallas Library, Lauren Gurgiolo of the Harry Ransom Center at the University of Texas, and Marje Schuetze-Coburn of the University of Southern California Libraries provided invaluable aid.

Thanks also to the family of Ernest Thompson Seton, including R. Dale Barber and his wife, the late Dee Seton Barber, and their children, who granted permission to quote from Seton's correspondence and copyrighted works, as well as Seton's granddaughter, Pamela Forcey. Ronald Edmonds, an officer of the Ernest Thompson Seton Institute, helped us establish contact with them. Before her passing, the Hon. Betty Clay, daughter of Robert Baden-Powell, offered insights into her father's personality through correspondence with David that he incorporates into speaking engagements to this day.

We cannot forget the wonderful work performed by our production team at Publications Development Company in Crockett, Texas, who made this book a reality. They include Matthew Land, Elizabeth Chenette, Pam Blackmon, and Celeste Johns. Our cover designer, Matthew Simmons, deserves kudos for his fine work. And finally, hearty thanks go out to our impeccable, detail-oriented publicist, Stephanie Barko, who put this manuscript onto the desks of many, resulting in valuable review, comment, and endorsement.

Do you fear the force of the wind?
The slash of the rain?
Go face them and fight them;
Be savage again!
Go hungry and cold like the wolf,
Go wade like the crane;
The palms of your hand will thicken,
The skin of your forehead, tan;
You'll be ragged and swarthy and weary,
But you'll walk like a MAN!

—*Hamlin Garland*

CONTENTS

INTRODUCTION
AT THE WALDORF-ASTORIA

I f not for the artificial trout stream running through its lobby, the Waldorf-Astoria Hotel on Fifth Avenue might have seemed an improbable setting in which to launch an institution dedicated to improving boys in the great outdoors. But in September 1910, this crossroads of social, political, and financial life was entirely suitable as a venue to assemble the affluent and the eminent to this purpose as the Gilded Age of excess tarnished and the Progressive Era of reform took shape.[1]

One contemporary scribe noted that "if you stopped long enough there everybody in the world that is worth knowing would eventually happen along . . . the real men of affairs who hold court . . . for their satellites and issue to minions orders that have much bearing upon the affairs of the world."[2] It was in a suite at the Waldorf-Astoria that financier J. Pierpont Morgan, industrialist Andrew Carnegie, and other Wall Street powers agreed in 1901 to create the United States Steel Corporation in what was then considered the "deal of the century." The hotel served as U.S. headquarters for Philippe Bunau-Varilla, the

1

French engineer and promoter whose dexterous lobbying and force of persuasion convinced President Theodore Roosevelt in 1902 to choose Panama over Nicaragua for a canal linking the Atlantic and the Pacific oceans.

The financiers, philanthropists, social workers, educators, and clergymen who filled the Astor Gallery ballroom on this evening of September 23 were drawn by social purpose and a measure of curiosity.[3] The drawing card was British Lt. Gen. Sir Robert S.S. Baden-Powell, renowned as the Hero of Mafeking for his courage and ingenuity leading an out-manned and outgunned garrison in the Boer War siege of the British colonial outpost.[4] More recently Baden-Powell had launched a movement called Scouting by which he proposed to shape the character of boys for the challenges of the modern age. For this elite audience, it seemed a promising way to prepare American youth for future greatness.

But there was also a political dimension to this event. Incorporated seven months earlier in Washington by Chicago newspaper publisher William Dickson Boyce, the Boy Scouts of America was standing itself up in the world. Already, though, competition loomed in the American Boy Scouts of publisher William Randolph Hearst, whose *New York Journal American* defined jingoism. So BSA was eager to have Baden-Powell's endorsement as the sole legitimate American expression of the Scouting movement he had launched in Britain.

Amidst the clink of porcelain, the clash of silverware, and the murmur of conversation, heads craned for a look at Baden-Powell. New Yorkers familiar with the light opera works of Gilbert & Sullivan might well have concluded that Baden-Powell, a lean, mustachioed man of fifty-three, was "the very model of a modern" British general. In fact, as a young subaltern stationed in India with the 13th Hussars, Baden-Powell had diverted himself and his fellow officers by staging garrison productions of the *Pirates of Penzance*.[5] Baden-Powell had a dramatic flair that served him well as he talked up Scouting across the Empire and beyond—the role he had perfected for this purpose was simply to be himself.

Though slight in stature, Baden-Powell was self-possessed as might be one who had received the adulation of the entire British Empire for holding off 5,000 Boer attackers with a garrison a quarter that size from October 1899 to May 1900. This feat of arms shot Baden-Powell from brevet colonel to major general, and on his retirement from the military at the age of fifty afforded him a position from which to muster support for his project from the great and the good.

He was seated at the head table next to the event's chairman John D. Rockefeller, Jr., son of John D. Rockefeller, the founder and chief shareholder of Standard Oil Co., whose name was a byword for ruthless business practices. But Rockefeller senior through his scion had also become the leading U.S. philanthropist, rivaled only by the steel magnate Andrew Carnegie.[6] Among the beneficiaries of Rockefeller largesse was the Young Men's Christian Association, under whose wing BSA had been taking shape over the past several months.

At Baden-Powell's side were two men who had helped shape his concept of building youthful character through the experience of nature. Next to him at the head table sat Ernest Thompson Seton, another Englishman, though expatriate, whose fanciful books about the lives of animals had earned him a small fortune that enabled him to pursue interests including Indian lore and the development of boys into men. Nearby sat Daniel Carter Beard, an Ohio-born artist known for illustrating Mark Twain's political fable *A Connecticut Yankee in King Arthur's Court.* Seton and Beard had launched youth organizations of their own before Baden-Powell brought forth Scouting. Seton established the Woodcraft Indians in 1902 on his Connecticut estate. Beard three years later launched the Sons of Daniel Boone, later renamed the Boy Pioneers of America to resolve a dispute with a magazine sponsor. The men behind BSA hoped Seton's Indians and Beard's Pioneers would before long come around to be Boy Scouts.

But Baden-Powell by far overshadowed Seton and Beard in the public eye. The organizers and business backers of the Boy Scouts of America considered his stamp of approval indispensable to brush aside competitors, Hearst in particular. The press baron saw Scouting as a quasi-military outfit that would train recruits to defend and expand U.S. interests. Though Baden-Powell's movement had military trappings, including khaki uniforms, he called his recruits "peace scouts," aware that many Britons and Americans in this era of progressive politics and ascendant trade unionism were averse to regimentation and conscription. His presence this evening in effect endorsed the U.S. branch of a movement aimed at promoting good citizenship, moral fiber, and other virtues through robust encounters with nature. Patriotism was the expected byproduct of such activities—but it would not be Hearst's populist brand if its organizers had anything to say about it.

Though absent from this gathering, pleading an overburdened schedule, Theodore Roosevelt, who had left the White House in March 1909, was the Scouting movement's unofficial patron. He powerfully influenced its value system with his gospel of manly striving and established the future terrain of its activities as the champion of conservationism, having established fifty-one National Bird Reservations in seventeen states and various territories by Executive Order during his presidency and placed 234 million acres of land under federal protection, an area nearly half the size of the Louisana Purchase.[7]

But the organizers saw to it that Roosevelt and Baden-Powell had a face-to-face meeting in New York. Seton and Beard had greeted Baden-Powell that morning on his arrival from Canada by train and escorted him to Roosevelt's office at *The Outlook,* an influential progressive magazine that had become Roosevelt's bully pulpit after the presidency. But this was no workaday editorial engagement: at *Outlook* Roosevelt held forth from a replica George Washington desk in a finely appointed three-room suite.[8]

Just three months before this September of 1910, Roosevelt had returned from an East African safari during which the avatar of U.S. conservationism cut a wide swathe through the animal kingdom with the purpose of collecting specimens for the Smithsonian Institution. Roosevelt and his son Kermit dispatched 17 lions, 20 rhinoceroses, 8 hippopotamuses, 9 giraffes, 47 gazelles, 29 zebras, and 9 hyenas, among other trophies, shipping home to the National Museum 8,463 vertebrates, 550 large and 3,379 small mammals, and 2,784 birds.[9] Roosevelt returned to the United States through Norway where he accepted the Nobel Peace Price for his role in ending the Russo-Japanese War in 1905, making another stop in England to rub shoulders with seven kings at the funeral of King Edward VII.

Unassailable as senior U.S. statesman, Roosevelt nevertheless found himself in a politically ambiguous position. Having become president in his first term following the assassination of President William McKinley, Roosevelt retained the option of seeking the office again, but, bowing to tradition, declined to seek a third term. He groomed Secretary of War William Howard Taft as his successor but became displeased with Taft's drift away from the reforms he had instituted. Roosevelt as president had reconciled progressive and conservative Republicans; Taft, to his displeasure, surrounded himself with businessmen and snubbed those who, like Roosevelt, saw government as the essential arbiter of economic justice and a countervailing force to industrial combines and Wall Street financiers.

At *The Outlook,* Roosevelt had planted himself at the heart of the progressive movement. The magazine's offices were in the United Charities Building, which one later chronicler described as the "social reform mecca of America."[10] At hand were pioneering intellectuals such as Paul Kellogg, editor of *The Survey* magazine, a major voice on industrial reform. Roosevelt's charisma was as effective here as it had been in politics. One colleague described him as "great fun; a warm-hearted, affectionate, companionable giant who makes everybody that knows him his friend."[11]

Introduced to Baden-Powell, the former Rough Rider lost no time bonding with his fellow soldier and proponent of the robust life and of character as the ultimate manly virtue. No doubt they compared notes on Africa and may have traded hunting stories—one of Baden-Powell's earliest publishing efforts as a young captain in the 13th Hussars was titled *Pigsticking or Hoghunting.*

Roosevelt expressed regret that he could not attend the gathering at the Waldorf-Astoria that evening. But he had prepared a note for Seton, which he instructed him to read to the gathering later on:

> I believe in the movement with all my heart, . . . The excessive development of city life in modern industrial civilization which has seen its climax here in our own country, is accompanied by a very unhealthy atrophy . . . of essential virtues, which must be embodied in any man who is to be a good soldier, and which, especially, ought to be embodied in every man to be a really good citizen in time of peace.
>
> Your movement aims at counteracting these unhealthy tendencies. Your especial aim is to make the boys good citizens in time of peace and incidentally to fit them to become good soldiers in time of war; although the latter inevitably follows, being what might be called a byproduct of the former.
>
> I heartily wish all success to the movement.
> Sincerely yours, Theodore Roosevelt.[12]

Such encomiums are common at the launch of institutions with high purposes and grand objectives. What lent Scouting unique appeal was its evocation of the saga of Western migration and settlement at a time when the closure of the frontier was a relatively recent event, albeit one on which the Harvard historian Frederick Jackson Turner was already delivering influential lectures.[13]

Americans since the late nineteenth century had been coming to grips with the end of a certain way of life, a certain way of thinking about themselves. Nostalgia and mythologizing were common responses. Publishers and impresarios marketed frontier accounts and spectacles that were as fanciful as they were factual, even as intellectuals like Turner contemplated this watershed in American life and others warned of the ongoing and accelerating destruction of the wilderness.

Roosevelt's presidency fostered the growth of organizations uniting those who believed America's essence to derive from the wilderness, threatened by the later stages of Western expansion. Years before an assassin's bullet elevated him to the presidency, Roosevelt brought together like-minded, well-heeled associates in the Boone & Crockett Hunting Club while those of more modest means—including Seton and Beard—grouped under the banner of the Camp Fire Club, which was also more vocal in its call for the preservation of nature for its own sake.

Some notion of the sentiment prevailing among these men can be gleaned from some lines contributed by Captain Jack Crawford, the "Poet Scout," to an evening organized by the Camp Fire Club in December 1909 at the Hotel Astor, New York, in honor of Charles Jesse Jones, known as "Buffalo" Jones for his work in rescuing the American bison and other much-publicized exploits:

> *The Buckskin days! The Buckskin days!*
> *How memory 'round the old time plays;*
> *The days out in the great West land*
> *When life was carried in the hand.*[14]

American Scouting found its footing in this milieu and drew its strength from the notion of the frontier scout as the personification of strength, resourcefulness, and virtue, "full of self-reliance in his own ability to meet and overcome any unlooked-for difficulties," as proclaimed a 1900 show program for Buffalo Bill Cody's Wild West and Congress of Rough Riders of the World.[15]

The indefatigable scout was a staple of American folklore and literature. The memoirs of Daniel Boone, published in 1784, related his cutting of a track into "an howling wilderness, the habitation of savages and wild beasts."[16] The scout blazed his mark on American fiction in 1826 with *The Last of the Mohicans* by James Fenimore Cooper, whose Natty Bumppo, or Hawkeye, possessed a "singular compound of quick, vigilant sagacity, and of exquisite simplicity, that by turns usurped the possession of his muscular features."[17] After the Civil War, the scout's terrain of employment shifted to the Great Plains and the Indian Wars. Before treading the boards, Buffalo Bill made his name by killing 4,280 American bison in the space of eight months from 1867 to 1868, contributing to the species' near extinction in supplying meat to the work crews building the first transcontinental railroad, and later serving as Chief of Scouts for the Third Cavalry in the Plains Wars.[18]

Baden-Powell was not impervious to such myths.[19] During a 1903 run of the Wild West Show in London's West End theater district, he went backstage to pay his respects to Cody. They were mutual admirers: upon learning that the siege of Mafeking had ended, Cody cabled congratulations to Baden-Powell, telling him that "all American soldiers and sailors are today singing your praises."[20]

But Baden-Powell's main personal experience with the American scout was with Frederick Russell Burnham, anointed "King of Scouts" by Fleet Street for his work on behalf of the British military in Southern Africa. He was, wrote war correspondent Richard Harding Davis, "as unlike the scout . . . of the Wild West Show, as it is possible for a man to be."[21] The Los Angeles native set out to learn the craft of scouting across the Southwest and Mexico. He "guarded bullion on stage-coaches, for days rode in pursuit of Mexican bandits and American horse thieves" and contracted his services in range and mining wars.[22] Burnham struck out for South Africa in 1893 seeking his fortune in gold, but found employment with the British military instead when Matabele warriors rose up against mostly British settlers in Rhodesia. Burnham earned tabloid fame riding through enemy territory seething with warriors to summon relief for an encircled—

and ultimately doomed—detachment. When the Matabele rebelled again in 1896,[23] Burnham joined Baden-Powell and taught him the finer points of scouting, earning a place in *Aids to Scouting,* which Baden-Powell published as a military handbook in 1899 and which became a British best-seller as the Mafeking siege stretched on.

"Riding with a really trained scout, such as Buffalo Bill or Burnham, you will notice that while he talks with you, his eyes scarcely look you in the face for a moment, they keep glancing from point to point of the country round from sheer force of habit," Baden-Powell wrote. "As you move along, say, in a hostile country, your eyes should be looking afar for the enemy or any signs of him; figures, dust rising, birds getting up, glitter of arms, etc."[24]

The notion of the scout wove through Baden-Powell's career. The phenomenal success of *Aids to Scouting* demonstrated its powerful appeal to boys, perhaps leading Baden-Powell to take the name of his new venture from the pages of "penny dreadful" pulp novels for young readers. Thus fact and fiction mingled in Scouting's origins, as elsewhere—Roosevelt's celebrated Rough Riders had, in shaping up for their role in the Spanish-American War and the battle of San Juan Hill, taken their name from Buffalo Bill Cody's Wild West Show.

This was potent marketing material for the crowd at the Waldorf-Astoria. After reading Roosevelt's note to the room, Seton noted the presence of Buffalo Jones, who received a standing ovation. Jones had recently returned from his own African safari during which, disdaining the use of firearms, he lassoed animals including a female lion which he presented to the New York Zoological Park.[25] The Buffalo Jones's African Expedition had included two cowboy ropers, ten New Mexico ponies, and a motion picture photographer.[26] Jones premiered his film at the New York Press Club the evening before the dinner at the Waldorf-Astoria. Guest of honor Roosevelt offered an endorsement that went straight into lecture promotion leaflets. "Buffalo Jones's work with wild animals is beyond anything ever recorded in the annals of time," the former president declared with typical exuberance. "My hunt sinks into insignificance compared with it."[27]

Rockefeller Junior called Jones "the man who did things," a remark that also found its way into Buffalo Jones's lecture advertisements. Posters added that the intrepid Buffalo Jones "also teaches Knowledge, Wisdom, Self Reliance, Humanity, Brotherly Love, Virtue, Honor, Justice and Mercy."[28]

Yet Jones was not universally admired. Some considered him a charlatan, one associate remarking his "well-known tendency to stretch the blanket."[29] Writing a month before this dinner to an investor in one of his ventures, Jones confided: "I am building an air ship that will raise itself straight up into the air . . . I have a full size airship nearly completed and will set it going within the next 30 days. I have two patents on it, so I may yet be of some use to mankind."[30]

Yet Jones had done some of the things he claimed to have done, and looked every inch the plainsman, "a slenderly built man, with piercing gray eyes, a firm jaw, and a slouching gait, as if he had spent much of his time on horseback."[31]

As his name implied, Jones had a long association with the buffalo. Striking out for Kansas from his native Illinois, Jones joined the slaughter of buffalo for meat and hides in the 1870s.[32] By the end of that decade, this livelihood was gone with the great herds. Jones founded Garden City, Kansas, became its mayor and won election to the Kansas Legislature.[33] He graced Main Street with the Buffalo Block of limestone buildings topped by a stone buffalo. The theme developed as Jones gathered a herd of buffalos from survivors in the Texas Panhandle and other remote areas. He said he wanted to atone for his "wickedness" in helping destroy the Plains herds.[34] But he also hoped to make money crossing buffalo with cattle to produce the "cattalo," a beast suited to harsh open-range winters while yielding a superior steak.[35] But the male cattalo tended to be sterile, and a recession helped drive his American Buffalo & Land Co. out of business.[36]

Undaunted, Jones in 1899 published an autobiography entitled *Buffalo Jones' Forty Years of Adventure,* which helped him secure appointment in 1902 as game warden of Yellowstone National Park. Jones established a buffalo herd there, but fell out with Acting Superintendent John Pitcher, a U.S. Army major. Jones made enemies higher up the chain of command when he told a lecture audience in 1906 that the average soldier was "good for nothing" in protecting wildlife. Pitcher told his superiors that Jones had done "very good work" implanting the herd of buffalo in Yellowstone, "but here his usefulness . . . ended absolutely."[37]

Having angered the Army and alienated local staff, Jones resigned, but his fame spread. A 1907 lecture at the Camp Fire Club in New York captured the imagination of a former semiprofessional baseball player and Brooklyn dentist named Zane Grey who had an itch to write. Grey tagged along with Jones and a cowpuncher through the Arizona high country later that year as they lassoed and captured a mountain lion.[38] Grey went on to perfect the Western pulp novel with *Riders of the Purple Sage* and other genre classics. He would later write that, "The like of Buffalo Bill, Wild Bill, Buffalo Jones, and many other famous frontiersmen will never be met with again in this world."[39]

For the financial and social elite at the Waldorf-Astoria, Jones's colorful persona combined two important strands in Scouting—American frontier heritage and conservationism. The latter unified men as dissimilar as Roosevelt and Seton and lent a scientific burnish to the enterprise. In this respect, no creature was as iconic as the buffalo. Some of those at the Waldorf-Astoria this evening belonged not only to the Boone and Crockett Club, but also to the American Bison Society, dedicated to protecting and promoting the resurgence of the noble beast.

This represented a sea change in American thinking. No less a conservationist than Roosevelt could write in 1884 in his *Hunting Trips of a Ranchman* that the destruction of the buffalo "was the condition precedent upon the advance of white civilization in the West."

Wiping out the buffalo herds, the basis of the Plains Indian economy, "was the only way of solving the Indian question." So, Roosevelt
wrote, "From the standpoint of humanity at large, the extermination
of the buffalo has been a blessing." Yet he simultaneously acknowledged that its near-extinction "has been a veritable tragedy of the
animal world."[40]

Though Jones was popularly credited with saving the buffalo, its survival as a matter of U.S. policy owed more to the work
of William Temple Hornaday, who in the late 1880s published a
series of articles warning of the animal's impending doom. He informed readers of *Cosmopolitan,* a journal of opinion: "At last the
game butchers of the great West have stopped killing buffalo. The
buffalo are all dead!" Hornaday confessed that he was "guilty of
killing buffalo in the year of our Lord 1886." But under happier
circumstances "nothing could have induced me in such a mean,
cruel, and utterly heartless enterprise." Between leaving them to be
killed by "care-for-naught cowboys" and "killing them ourselves for
the purpose of preserving their remains, there was really no choice,"
he wrote.

"Perhaps you think a wild animal has no soul," said Hornaday, a
taxidermist by training, "but let me tell you that it has. Its skin is its
soul, and when mounted by skillful hands, it becomes comparatively
immortal."[41]

At the time, he was conferring such comparative immortality on
six of the threatened species, *Bison americanus,* which in March 1888
were to be unveiled at the National Museum in Washington. He was
convinced that these six buffalo—stuffed, mounted, and displayed in
a case sixteen feet by twelve—might well be the only means by which
the American public and future generations could encounter the buffalo in its fullest physical dimensions.[42]

Hornaday had launched on this undertaking in early 1886, by which time the extermination of the buffalo "had made a most alarming progress." His contacts informed him that "the destruction of all the large herds, both North and South, was already an accomplished fact."[43] Many assumed a few thousand buffalo still roamed remoter areas of the northern high plains. But in fact "the actual number remaining in the whole United States was probably less than three hundred."[44]

Hornaday signaled this "alarming state of affairs" to Smithsonian Secretary Spencer Baird, who "determined to send a party into the field at once to find wild buffalo, if any were still living," and if so, to collect specimens.[45] Hornaday heard from an army officer that buffalo might still exist at the head of the Powder River in Wyoming and in two locations in Montana. The secretary of war ordered army posts in the region to provide Hornaday with what transportation, equipment, and escorts he would need. Railroads gave Hornaday's party free passage that May from the nation's capital to Miles City, Montana.

Inquiries there and at nearby Fort Keogh brought a discouraging word: "There are no buffalo any more, and you can't get any anywhere."[46] Hope revived when a rancher told Hornaday buffalo might be found between two tributaries of the Missouri River—Little Dry Creek and Big Dry Creek. Hornaday headed north from Fort Keogh on May 13 with two fellow Smithsonian naturalists, six mules, a teamster, and a Fifth Infantry escort of six troopers. After eighty miles they hit Little Dry Creek and followed it in north to Big Dry Creek, setting up base camp just to the west on yet another tributary of the Missouri.

Buffalo remained elusive for ten days, until two bulls were found on Little Dry Creek. After bringing one down, Hornaday realized it was the wrong season for collecting specimens: the animal was still shedding its matted winter coat. "It was therefore resolved to leave the buffaloes entirely unmolested until autumn, and then, when the robes would be in the finest condition, return for a hunt on a liberal scale."[47] Hornaday returned to Washington with an adopted buffalo calf, setting the young animal to graze on the Smithsonian's front lawn.

Hornaday returned to Miles City in late September 1886. The commander of Fort Keogh again set him up with equipment, six mules to haul supplies for two months, and a soldier to cook and guard the party's camp. Hornaday also recruited three cowboys adept at scouring canyons and ravines for lost cattle. He focused his search along Sand Creek, which fed into Big Dry Creek near their base camp. On October 13, a cowboy bringing in supplies spotted a herd of seven buffalo in a deep ravine coming off a high plateau. "He fired upon them, but killed none, and when they dashed away he gave chase and followed them two or three miles" but with his horse tiring and night approaching he gave up the pursuit.

Hornaday and his wranglers set out at dawn the next day and found the herd, now comprising fourteen beasts, after hours of riding through miles of crumbly soil and crevices that made treacherous going. Fired upon, the buffalo "sprang up and dashed away at astonishing speed," into tortuous ravines. Following a "most exciting and likewise dangerous chase" over rugged terrain pocked with prairie-dog holes, the expedition killed two bulls, a two-year-old male, and one female. Through the end of October they managed to fell another eight bison.

In early November, snowflakes flying, Hornaday shifted camp to the southern slopes of the high plateau, where better water was to be had. While he worked on specimens in the new base camp, his cowboys rode south toward the aptly named Buffalo Buttes, where they killed another five animals, bringing the expedition's count to nineteen. Hornaday, arriving with a wagon, shot a solitary bull, "a very fine specimen, measuring five feet six inches at the shoulders."

This twentieth specimen fulfilled the objective he had set before leaving Washington.

By then a blizzard had descended upon the party and Hornaday was "anxious to get out of that fearful country." A trooper named West set out for Fort Keogh to request a relief party. The storm peaked on November 25 as the temperature plunged to minus sixteen degrees Fahrenheit. By early December, the blizzard had passed, but there was no sign of rescue. Hornaday, undaunted, headed back to the Buffalo Buttes and collected two more specimens. When his party got back to its original camp on Big Dry Creek, a rancher told them that West had wandered the badlands for days before fetching up at a sheep camp where he and his horse were provided with food, fodder, and shelter. On reaching Fort Keogh, West set right out again with a mule team to bring the expedition to safety. Soon Hornaday was boarding an eastbound train with twenty-five examples of *Bison americanus* plus buffalo grass and sagebrush to lend verisimilitude to the diorama within which, fifteen months later, his mounted group would be presented to the nation.[48]

Ernest Seton provided drawings for a fuller report on the extermination of the buffalo which the Smithsonian later published. Hornaday sent him photos of his mounted group, from which Seton produced illustrations. "The drawing of the old bull has just arrived and is fine," Hornaday wrote to Seton in May 1889. "The head, shoulders and general anatomy is [*sic*] very finely worked art, and your treatment of the hair is simply marvelous. It is a great satisfaction to a lover of exquisite detail to see an animal's nose and mouth so clearly and distinctly and correctly drawn." Hornaday added a postscript: "The scrotum is O.K."[49]

He was more effusive in 1896 in his praise of the story Seton had published in a national magazine about his hunt in the New Mexico high plains for a wolf that he gave the name of Lobo. "It is a Great Story!" Hornaday enthused. "We have all enjoyed it immensely; & I have read it twice."[50] Somewhat as Hornaday had slain buffalo to immortalize the beasts, Seton had snared Lobo and given him a literary afterlife in *Wild Animals I Have Known.* Through this collection of stories and his naturalist pursuits, Seton acquired the sobriquet of "Wolf," reflecting his image as a Bohemian—albeit one who moved in the upper circles of New York society. To some degree this was an affectation, but Seton was decades ahead of his time in conceiving and preaching an holistic relationship between man and nature.

By September 1910, Seton had become the creative engine of Scouting. Even Baden-Powell was in his intellectual debt, though Seton would always remain in the general's shadow. In April 1910, the *New York Times* had run a feature spread on the burgeoning movement with the headline "Baden-Powell's Boy Scout Plan Invades America." A smaller photograph of Seton was included, over the caption: "Ernest Thompson-Seton, Who Contributed Much to the Plan."[51]

At the Waldorf-Astoria event, Seton shared the limelight with Baden-Powell, though as master of ceremonies, not guest of honor. Few of those in the room that evening could have imagined the resentment Seton felt over what he considered to be the usurpation of his place in the movement. But he mastered his feelings and stuck to the script written by BSA senior management. For that evening at least, Seton seemed content to bask in reflected glory, and Baden-Powell deferred to Seton and Beard, referring to them in his remarks as Scouting's "fathers."

But Seton continued to believe Baden-Powell had lifted key ideas from his *Birch-Bark Roll of the Woodcraft Indians* and folded them into his best-selling *Scouting for Boys.* His complaint was not unfounded, but his obsessive pursuit of those claims alienated many who might have supported them. And the simple fact was that Baden-Powell had set his seal on world Scouting, and nothing Seton said or did could ever change that.

Other than their nationality and interest in Scouting, the two men shared little. Baden-Powell's identity and outlook were shaped by the late Victorian values and closely entwined with the expansion of the British Empire. Born into an upwardly aspiring middle-class family, Baden-Powell went out to India, Afghanistan, and Southern Africa to defend and add to British possessions, earning distinction and favor. Scouting for him was about patriotism, character, service. Seton's voyage through life was one of discovery, as much of himself as the natural world that he observed, sketched, and described. Uprooted from Britain at an early age, he came to maturity in Canada at a distant remove from the mother culture, finding his interests and aspirations in nature and art, developing his intellectual framework in the free-thinking hothouse of Paris in the 1890s before launching his youth training experiment.

Beginning in 1906, Seton had shared his ideas freely with Baden-Powell as he attempted to export his Woodcraft Indians to England, hoping that Baden-Powell would throw his influence behind the organization. But the Hero of Mafeking was not one to join another's parade. Seton would later regret having proffered ideas that he believed formed the essential kernel of *Scouting for Boys* and, in his mind, largely accounted for the tremendous success of Baden-Powell's Scouting.

The day after the dinner at the Waldorf-Astoria, Baden-Powell boarded the *S.S. Arabic* for his return to England. Before the liner sailed, he jotted a note to Seton to thank him for his hospitality. "I cannot leave without telling you how very sincerely gratified I have been by the exceedingly generous reception which has been accorded to me by yourself and those connected with the organization of the Boy Scouts movement in the United States." He added: "I am, from the personal point of view, most deeply grateful—and from that of the movement I feel confident that it's in the hand of such capable workers."[52]

Seton must have received these lines with mixed emotions. He had to acknowledge that Baden-Powell had ignited British and American enthusiasm for Scouting in a way he had never been able to do with his Woodcraft Indians. Seton hoped to put his own stamp on the American version—but the backers of the U.S. offshoot had a vision of Scouting quite different from Seton's.

Even his closest associate in the Scouts, YMCA executive Edgar Robinson, a pivotal figure in launching the U.S. movement, saw Scouting in terms of building character rather than promoting oneness with nature, and thought that its success would be closely tied to American national defense. "If here in America we could have another Gen. Baden-Powell, like Theodore Roosevelt . . . take an interest in promoting the idea, and if Japan, let us say, threatened an invasion, making an analogous military situation to that prevailing in England, the Boy Scouts idea would sweep the country like wildfire, as it has abroad," he said.[53]

Seton did not yet understand, or perhaps could not admit even to himself that Baden-Powell's iteration of Scouting had absorbed all it needed of his Woodcraft Indians and been embraced by the U.S. establishment. Outmaneuvered from his first meeting with Baden-Powell in 1906, unwilling to compromise on what he saw as matters of principle, and often egocentric in attitude, Seton would never be able to infuse the U.S. movement with the naturalist and nonconformist creed he taught his young Indians. But it was never a fair match: Baden-Powell's military career and fame gave him the organizational acumen and connections he needed to make Scouting an international phenomenon. Seton at first did not understand this and then refused to accept it, urging the U.S. Scouting movement to integrate values antithetical to those of its conservative sponsors: Indian lore rather than the pragmatism of the frontiersman; naturalism rather than conservationism for the sake of hunting bags; individual spontaneity instead of organizational structure;

and idiosyncratic animism over mainstream religious sentiment and practice.

Such differences, combined with his bitterness over what he stopped just short of publicly calling plagiarism by Baden-Powell, undermined his relations with BSA senior management. Moreover, Seton was often indiscreet in expressing his disapproval of American expansionism in Mexico, the Philippines, and in Cuba. This in time would render him vulnerable to those who opposed Scouting's dalliance with the pacifist movement in the early days of World War I, Roosevelt among them.

Pacifism versus preparedness would become the first major test for the Boy Scouts as an American institution. BSA's board of directors in those first years, bringing together gimlet-eyed Wall Street lawyers with idealistic social reformers, eschewed partisanship and declined to choose one path or the other, leaving the matter to the conscience of each member. America was inescapably pulled into the conflict, but BSA avoided becoming a tributary of one political camp or another—though its members would throw themselves into the war effort from April 1917 onward, transforming the organization into a national institution that was not of the Republican Party or of the Democratic Party or even of Roosevelt's own Bull Moose Party, but remaining, quite simply, the Scouting Party.

The story of those early years is in many respects the story of Ernest Seton, who though overstating his grievance against Baden-Powell was unquestionably the mainspring of American Scouting in its formative period. His open-minded, questioning philosophy has much to offer the present-day Boy Scouts of America, under fire from liberal critics, its ranks dwindling year to year, and its leadership walled up in a fortress of traditional—one might say conservative—values that seem increasingly detached from the simple frontier self-reliance and generosity that gave rise to Scouting in the late nineteenth and early twentieth centuries. A backward look as BSA marks its one-hundredth year in existence provides useful guidance as Scouting moves into its second century of shaping American youth.

CHAPTER I

BLACK WOLF

It was an eclectic group of New Yorkers and visitors that gathered for lunch on the afternoon of Saturday, November 14, 1896, at The Players, a gentlemen's club in a Greek revival townhouse looking onto Gramercy Park in Manhattan. The meal was in honor of Scottish writer James M. Barrie, who had yet to bring forth a timeless stage play called *Peter Pan* but had already established a reputation for his sketches of Scottish country life. First among equals at the table was New York City Police Commissioner Theodore Roosevelt, a former state legislator on his way to bigger things in Republican national politics. He was fresh from a Midwest campaign swing during which he had helped William McKinley and running mate Garret Hobart into the White House. Roosevelt's 1880's interlude as a cattle rancher in the Dakotas lent him credibility with heartland voters who might otherwise have thrown their votes to Democratic contender William Jennings Bryan, an advocate of an expansive monetary shift from the gold standard to a currency based on more abundant silver, thought to favor farmers and mechanics over financiers.[1]

The gathering had a distinctly Western theme: other guests included artist Frederic Remington, known for his dramatic renditions of cowboys, Indians, and soldiers, and Hamlin Garland, a chronicler of American farming life.[2] Born to a Wisconsin farming family, Garland made his name with a collection of stories called *Main-Traveled Roads* that portrayed rural life with a grim realism. The eminent critic William Dean Howells had high praise for these accounts so "full of the bitter and burning dust, the foul and trampled slush of the common avenues of life: the life of the men who hopelessly and cheerlessly make the wealth that enriches the alien and the idler, and impoverishes the producer."[3]

As an agrarian populist, Garland would have sympathized with Bryan's call for economic reform favoring farmers, small business people and laborers over Wall Street tycoons. Yet Hamlin and Roosevelt somehow found as many points of agreement as of difference. Still Republican to the core, Roosevelt's probing intellect, natural charisma, and Western experience charmed Hamlin, who found the thirty-eight-year-old politician a man "of great energy, of good impulses, and undoubted ability . . . strong physically, full of talk, always interesting . . . a man of powerful prejudices and intense dislikes but manly and just in his impulses."[4]

Hamlin's interest in Roosevelt was matched by his curiosity about another guest, British-born Canadian naturalist, artist, and writer Ernest Thompson Seton, introduced by their host, Scribner's editor H.I. Kimball, as "Wolf" Seton. During lunch, Seton upstaged the slight and retreating Barrie with anecdotes of outdoor life. He was, Hamlin noted, "the most picturesque guest at the table," weathered, voluble, and engaging, with an unruly shock of black hair and a full moustache. As coffee was served, Hamlin took Barrie aside to express admiration for his work, but Kimball soon interrupted their conversation to say Seton was about to tell one of his trademark wolf stories. His performance, Seton recalled with satisfaction, "made such a hit that it put me on the social map with the company present."[5]

Roosevelt, a serious amateur naturalist, had encountered wolves during his relatively brief career as a rancher in the Badlands, and was impressed enough to invite Seton to attend the annual dinner of his Boone and Crockett Club, an elite group of outdoorsmen. At the Metropolitan Club on an early December evening soon after, Seton justified his growing reputation as a raconteur.[6] "In particular," he later noted, "I enlarged on the Wolf Telephone or Odor Posts, by which means the wolves communicate with each other throughout the region they inhabit."[7]

Seton had been in contact with Roosevelt some time previously through the Smithsonian Institution, to which both contributed bird skins and from which, in recompense, they received specimens not required by the Institution. The meeting at the Players gave the relationship a more personal basis. Just a few months after Seton's appearance at the Boone and Crockett Club, as he was preparing a visit to Yellowstone National Park, which President Ulysses S. Grant had established in 1872, Roosevelt wrote on Seton's behalf to the park's superintendent, Captain George L. Anderson of the U.S. Army, recommending Seton as "a man who knows more about wolves than anyone else I have ever met."[8]

Seton's reputation as an expert on wolves was based on years of observing the species in nature. But his personal bond with wolves dated from 1882 when, on a train crossing Western Canada, he spotted a lone timber wolf fighting a pack of dogs. "In the instant of identifying with the wolf, Seton began to change his own self-image," a biographer writes. Emotionally bruised by a domineering father, the young man who perceived himself as "vulnerable and abused by an insensitive world" now felt "untamed [and] contemptuous" of that world. Seton "became obsessed with the need to know more about wolves, to understand them, to track them down and inevitably to pit himself against them."[9]

As an art student at the Académie Julian in Paris, Seton spent many hours at the Jardin des Plantes sketching a wolf in captivity. His painting "Sleeping Wolf" won favorable notice at the Grand Salon, a showcase for young talent. Seton had found a personal identity and a motif; he adopted the sobriquet of "Wolf" and began sketching a paw print next to his signature at the bottom of letters.[10]

By the late 1890s, though, his reputation was based on an encounter with a particular wolf in the wild. The episode took place three years before his meeting with Roosevelt at The Players. Seton became acquainted in Paris, and eventually traveled from France to the United States by ship, with the daughter of a wealthy man by the name of Louis Fitz-Randolph whose interests included a ranch in New Mexico that was losing an inordinate number of cattle to wolves. Seton proposed to hunt down and eliminate the predators.[11] In October 1893, Seton arrived at the L Cross F Ranch near Clapham, New Mexico, where he drew his sights on a large male wolf that had frustrated all attempts to poison or snare him. Lobo, as Seton named the animal, led the wolf pack that had been making the deepest inroads on local herds. Seton finally snared Lobo in January 1894 by trapping his mate, to whom he had given the name Blanca; Seton arranged her carcass in such a way that Lobo in his grief would step into a series of steel traps set for him.

"Poor old hero, he had never ceased to search for his darling," Seton wrote of Lobo's downfall in an article published by *Scribner's* magazine that November, "and when he found the trail her body had made he followed it recklessly, and so fell into the snare prepared for him." Captured alive, Lobo died the next day to the admiration and regret of the thirty-three-year-old naturalist, providing the basis for the story with which Seton would become most intimately associated.[12]

The $1,000 bounty set on Lobo by local cattlemen financed Seton's return to Paris later that year.[13] Aboard ship he met yet another attractive young woman of means. Grace Gallatin, daughter of a California industrialist, was in the company of her mother, a divorced Chicago socialite. Grace's father, Albert Gallatin, was president of the Huntington-Hopkins Company, which had been deeply involved in building the transcontinental railroad and developing hydroelectric power in California.[14] Seton helped the Gallatins find lodgings in Paris, then courted Grace and married her in June 1896 on their return to the United States. Seton was starting to make a name for himself as a writer. But he needed a $1,500 loan from Grace's mother Nemie to purchase their home in New Jersey, a thirty-room mansion called Sloat Hall on 235 acres of land.[15] The couple moved in elite social circles in Manhattan and kept a studio apartment on Fifth Avenue near Greenwich Village. Grace edited Seton's writing as he completed a reference work entitled *Art Anatomy of Animals* and advised him on the development of his now-burgeoning career.[16]

Seton's greatest success lay just ahead. In 1898, Charles Scribner's Sons brought out a collection of animal stories that Seton had earlier published in magazines, called *Wild Animals I Have Known*. It became a cross-generational publishing phenomenon. Lobo the Wolf King of Currumpaw, Silverspot the Crow, Raggylug the Cottontail Rabbit, Bingo the Dog, Redruff the Partridge, and other Seton creations captivated children and adults. From distant Russia, Count Leo Tolstoy called the tale of Lobo "the best wolf story I have ever read." At Roosevelt's Sagamore Hill retreat on Long Island, the children of the (by then) Undersecretary of the Navy named a rooster and hen Lobo and Blanca.[17]

Seton had established credentials as a naturalist-artist, but the publication of *Wild Animals I Have Known* established him nationally as a popular writer. His intimate knowledge of the secret life of animals, gathered through years of study and field observation, allowed him to portray them not only authentically but with deep empathy. Seton gave his subjects names and voices, bringing out their particular traits without suspending the harsh law of the wild.[18]

"These stories are true," he assured readers in the introduction to his book. "Although I have left the strict line of historical truth in many places, the animals in this book were all real characters. They lived the lives I have depicted, and showed the stamp of heroism and personality more strongly by far than it has been in the power of my pen to tell . . . The fact that these stories are true is the reason why all are tragic. The life of a wild animal *always has a tragic end.*"[19]

Seton saw animals as kin to men. "Man has nothing that the animals have not at least a vestige of, the animals have nothing that man does not in some degree share." Because animals are "creatures with wants and feelings differing in degree only from our own, they surely have their rights."[20] The contradiction between his defense of animals and pursuit of them for science or gain, as in the case of Lobo, merely bolstered his popular appeal. "In an atmosphere of growing public guilt and gradual awakening to the danger of the extermination of wildlife," writes a biographer, his confession about Lobo "met with a sympathetic audience."[21]

Though highly successful with the mass reading audience, Seton's unorthodox accounts of animal life drew criticism from those whose esteem he most desired: the U.S. community of scientific naturalists. His great success with *Wild Animals* and subsequent books inspired imitators whose knowledge of the animal world was greatly inferior to his own. The genre became known as the "realistic animal story," but many such works made bad literature and even poorer science.

The realistic animal story became a Canadian specialty; his main competitor for readers was Charles G.D. Roberts, who credited Seton with establishing this literary niche and encouraging him to forge into it. The minister's son had grown up on a farm in New Brunswick where like Seton he developed youthful skills in woodcraft. He had the utmost respect for Seton, once writing that, "If there be one man, since St. Francis of Assisi, whom all the kindreds of the wild have cause to bless, it is Ernest Thompson Seton."[22] He found Seton's work "untainted by that excess of sentimentality" which flawed many other accounts of nature.[23]

Seton biographer John Henry Wadland argues that the two men brought the readers of the time an understanding not only of animals but of the wilderness, which "continued to dominate the North American continent." Both had grown up close to the wilds. "For them it did not constitute some remote fantasy world to which they could escape from reality, or onto which they could project their own idealism. Having lived in the wilderness, Seton was quite firmly convinced that the wilderness now lived within him, demanding articulation." Seton, taken aback by the lukewarm reception of his earlier work on birds, "diverted his attention to the mammals, using the animal story as a vehicle for exploring the uncharted territory of behavior analysis. Despite his abrasive exterior, his lack of formal scientific training constantly undermined his self-confidence. Here he was at least secure in the knowledge that there were no qualified experts."[24]

But Seton's imputation of psychological motivations to animals, as opposed to simple instincts, raised the hackles of some eminent American naturalists, and the emergence of far less knowledgeable imitators undermined his position. One was William J. Long[25], a Congregationalist minister in Stamford, Connecticut, who for instance "alleged that he had seen a woodcock with a broken leg fashion a splint from roots and grass fibers," secured to the fracture with mud.[26]

Twaddle like this drew a scathing attack from the eminent naturalist John Burroughs, a patriarchal figure with close ties to Roosevelt. He published an article entitled "Real and Sham Natural History" in March 1903 in *The Atlantic Monthly,* slamming not only Long but Seton and Roberts too. He was most severe with Long and Seton, qualifying them as "sham" naturalists in whose works "the line between fact and fiction is repeatedly crossed." Seton "says in capital letters that his stories are true, and it is this emphatic assertion that makes the judicious grieve. True as romance, true in their artistic effects, true in their power to entertain the young reader, they certainly are; but true as natural history they certainly are not. Are we to believe that Mr. Thompson Seton, in his few years of roaming in the West, has penetrated farther into the secrets of animal life than all of the observers who have gone before him? There are no stories of animal intelligence and cunning on record, that I am aware of that match his . . . those who know the animals are just the ones Mr. Thompson Seton cannot fool."[27]

Seton, said Burroughs, twisting the knife, should have entitled his book, "*Wild Animals I Alone Have Known.*"[28]

The critique was devastating. Burroughs, sixty-six, was the dean of American naturalists. Following an early career at the U.S. Treasury, Burroughs had escaped at age thirty-six to a small farm ninety miles up the Hudson from New York to contemplate and describe nature.[29] Now he accused Seton of seeking to "profit by the popular love for the sensational and the improbable."[30]

Multimillionaire philanthropist Andrew Carnegie poured oil on the waters of scientific controversy three weeks later, though, bringing Seton and Burroughs together at his annual literary dinner. The recollections of Carnegie's guests differ as to how the two naturalists wound up sitting next to one another, but according to Seton's memoirs his extensive rebuttal brought Burroughs around.

"Mr. Burroughs, did you ever make a special study of wolves?" Seton demanded.
"No," Burroughs responded.
"Did you ever hunt wolves?"
"No."
"Did you ever photograph or draw wolves in a zoo?"
"No."
"Did you ever dissect a wolf?"
"No."
"Did you ever live in wolf country?"
"No."
"Did you ever see a wild wolf?"
"No."

"Then by what rule of logic are you equipped to judge me, who have done all of these things hundreds of times?"[31]

As Seton reconstructed the exchange, his irrefutable logic revealed to the eminent naturalist the error of his ways: Burroughs broke down and wept. Though Seton biographer Betty Keller notes that "no one else present . . . seems to have seen Burroughs in tears," the naturalist did temper his criticism in another *Atlantic* essay. "Some are nature students, dryly scientific, some are sentimental, some are sensational and a few are altogether admirable. Mr. Thompson Seton, as an artist and a raconteur, ranks by far the highest in the field; he is truly delightful."[32]

Unfortunately, before this conciliatory piece could appear, Roosevelt weighed in endorsing Burroughs's first broadside, denouncing "nature fakirs" and "yellow journalists of the woods."[33] Roosevelt had praised the story of Lobo after it appeared in *Scribner's*. But even when a mutual friend urged Roosevelt to make clear he did not regard Seton as a "nature faker," Roosevelt insisted "he should draw the line more clearly between his fiction and his zoology."[34]

Ultimately, Seton was mollified by this private communication, particularly as Roosevelt never criticized him by name, and more vociferously attacked Long, who qualified Roosevelt as a "bloodthirsty hunter." Seton remained above the fray and emerged from the fracas with even more lecture engagements.[35]

Readers packed Seton's public appearances, enthralled by his tales of the lives and deaths of animal protagonists as appealing as any human character.[36] Audiences found Seton Indian-like, "tall, active and sinewy, with dark eyes and hair," as one observer noted; continual exposure to the elements had "burnt his skin to a deep copper color." On his feet were moccasins, and he never wore a hat.[37] Telling the story of Johnny Bear to a Toronto audience, "children, carried away by their unusual surroundings, began to copy the calls and Johnny's whining yelps came from all over the hall. Then other children, who were anxious to have the lecture proceed, would shout 'Order,' 'Silence,' 'Hush,' until the hall was filled with a good-natured roar." His lecture continued "amid a perfect Babel of laughter, animal cries and the impromptu efforts of juvenile lecturers."[38]

Wild Animals also made Ernest Thompson Seton a wealthy man. The editors at Scribner's had initially been skeptical, but Seton, confident in the potential of his work and often in his life financially astute, proposed to take no royalties on the first two thousand copies sold, thereafter receiving a 20 percent royalty instead of the typical 10 percent. Three weeks after the book hit stores the first printing of two thousand copies sold out; by Christmas 1898 it had gone through three more press runs. By the turn of the century, Seton's royalties and lecture fees amounted to some $200,000, the equivalent a century later of around $4 million.[39]

These literary spoils gave Seton the means to create a personal environment suited to his interests. In the countryside of Connecticut forty miles north of New York, he purchased 100 acres of fields and woods in Cos Cob, an artists' colony.[40] "Here at last," he exulted, "were trees . . . a sparkling brook . . . rocky hills, sloping green banks, noble trees, birds in abundance, squirrels in the woods, fish and turtles in the pond, a naturalist's paradise in truth and all was mine."[41]

Seton had achieved most of the goals he set in March 1881 while still living precariously in Paris as an art student. "In 1890 I shall marry an English woman, or of English extraction. In 1905, I shall by God's help, have made a comfortable fortune by my pen and pencil, also in part by judicious speculation. I shall then return to England, buy a small estate in Devonshire and a house in London." His bride was American, his estate was in Connecticut, his urban residence was in Manhattan, and Seton would never receive the knighthood to which he aspired in his "Plan of My Life." But for the most part he had achieved the life he had envisioned as an aspiring youth.[42]

The man who was to become Ernest Thompson Seton was born Ernest Evan Thompson on August 14, 1860, in South Shields, England, a manufacturing town and seaport that served the Newcastle coal center nine miles up the River Tyne. His ship-owner father, Joseph Thompson, loomed as a fearsome authority figure. By Victorian standards, he was not exceptionally strict or harsh, but to Seton his father was an implacable despot who beat his sons with a riding crop or slipper for the least perceived disrespect, at least according to Seton's recollection.[43]

His mother, Alice Snowden Thompson, was of a sweeter temperament. This dutiful Victorian wife had borne eleven children. During her last pregnancy, in the hopes that her child would have "better gifts than the common," she plunged into the Edward Bulwer Lytton novel *Ernest Maltravers,* about a country gentleman, hunter, and naturalist.[44] When Joseph Thompson's shipping concern suffered a series of reverses—a vessel captured and burned by pirates off the West African coast, the failure of a business associate whose notes Thompson had co-signed—he liquidated his interests and took his family to Canada for a fresh start.[45]

In Lindsay, Ontario, Seton made his first connections with nature. Developing an interest in ornithology at the age of thirteen, he bought a manual on the birds of Canada that he soon revised based on his own observations. Years later, Seton would publish his own reference on the subject, *Key to the Birds of Canada.*[46]

In late 1876, Ernest Thompson, six feet tall and rail thin at age sixteen, earned his first fees as an artist sketching local businesses. His animal drawings impressed a local painter who took him as an apprentice. He studied nights at the Ontario School of Art and drew attention for his sketches and oil painting. Joseph Thompson urged his son to pursue his studies in London and the family provided him a $25 monthly stipend.[47] He gained admission to the Royal Academy School of Painting, though only on a second attempt, and read widely, soaking up the reflections of Henry David Thoreau and the nature writings of John Burroughs. "I had thought that all naturalists were dead; that none had taken up the torch when it fell from the aged hands of Audubon," he would later recall.[48]

Reality intruded upon his return home in 1881. His father presented him with a bill for $537.50, the amount calculated to have been spent on him since his birth. Interest would thenceforth accrue at an annual rate of 6 percent. Seton was "staggered," but presentation of the debt "focused his attention on making a living."[49] The next March he boarded a train in Toronto for the frontier settlement of Carberry, Manitoba, with sixty dollars and a letter of invitation from his older brother Arthur, who was homesteading there. Ernest Thompson also brought sixty hens, four turkeys, four geese, and "my energy, my hope, my belief in the future and in myself, my eagerness for life, life, life in its fullest abundance."[50]

His brother had settled under a Canadian government program that offered 160 acres to anyone over the age of eighteen prepared to build a home and raise crops. In Manitoba, Seton started a detailed journal of his observations of local birds and animals. Though he would later call this his "Golden Age," the isolation of the Canadian West was not to his taste on a long-term basis.[51] He decided to head for New York City, arriving in November 1883 with three dollars in his pocket. He soon found work as an illustrator and his wildlife drawings caught the eye of *Century Magazine* art manager, W. Lewis Fraser. Before long Seton was mining his journals to write, illustrate, and publish stories about the animals he had observed in *St. Nicholas* and other leading family magazines.[52]

In 1883, on reaching the age of twenty-one, Ernest Evan Thompson legally changed his name to Ernest Evan Thompson Seton. As family lore would have it, a forebear had abandoned the name of Seton in the eighteenth century after taking the losing side of Charles Edward Stuart—Bonnie Prince Charlie—in an uprising by Scottish Jacobites against England's Hanoverian rulers transplanted from the Netherlands to ensure Protestant dominance. The eponymous ancestor fled south to England after the Jacobite defeat at Culloden in 1746, suppressing a name that might cost him his head. Genealogists considered the line of Seton, Earl of Winton, to be extinct, but that did not matter to Seton, who was already busy creating a personal mythology.[53] But he did, at the request of his mother, wait until after her death in 1897 to start using the Seton name publicly.[54]

In the 1880s, Seton gravitated between New York and the Canadian wilds. He returned to Manitoba in 1884 to stake a land claim deeper in the wilderness where farming had not displaced nature. With him went the "battered and tattered greasy old journal" from which, over the years, was to flow an impressive portfolio of artistic and literary works. Seton built a log cabin eight feet by twelve feet and came into closer contact with Indian culture.[55] He learned to track animals from a Cree named Chaska he met while hunting deer. Six feet tall, wrapped in a blanket over leggings, Chaska wore his black hair braided and embellished with brass rings. He carried a fire bag, a knife, and a gun. "There was an indefinable charm about his quiet dignified manners, and I knew that he could teach me much about woodcraft," Seton would later write.[56]

After establishing a homestead, Seton returned to Toronto in early 1885 to work on a book called *The Birds of Manitoba*. He never returned to the cabin and his claim expired. The austerities of frontier life held little appeal for him, and he had also concluded that "the pioneer who ploughed up the land and drained the swamps was anathema to the naturalist."[57] With *Birds of Manitoba* in progress,

Seton went back to New York to pursue his career as an illustrator. His drawings of birds caught the attention of ornithologist Elliott Coues, who helped him secure a commission to produce a thousand animal drawings for the *Century Dictionary* at five dollars each. Seton's work brought the interest and acquaintance of other prominent naturalists at the Smithsonian Institution and the Museum of Natural History in New York. Upon completing the massive group of illustrations for *Century,* Seton traveled north again and settled on a brother's property on Lake Ontario outside Toronto, where his family had relocated. He stayed for two and a half years, completing his *Birds of Manitoba* and writing more animal stories. The collapse of his brother's resort business impelled him to take ship to England and on to Paris where in 1890 he studied art at the Académie Julian and fatefully encountered a somnolent wolf in the nearby Jardin des Plantes.[58]

Having achieved financial independence with *Wild Animals I Have Known* and acquired property in Cos Cob, Seton in 1900 reshaped his estate into a nature preserve where he could pursue his interests within commuting distance of Manhattan. He called it Wyndygoul, Scots for "Windy Gulch," after an estate it pleased him to believe his Jacobite ancestors had inhabited. On a clear day he could see across the nearby Long Island Sound to Roosevelt's Sagamore Hill estate.[59]

Seton dammed a stream to turn a swamp into a lake that "furnished the central beauty spot to a little paradise of birds and wildlife." He built a cabin pending the construction of a mansion, and ringed his land with a fence topped with barbed wire. This did not endear him to local youths who had become accustomed to freely roaming those woods.[60] They responded by drawing "shocking pictures" on his fence. "I was an outsider, an interloper," he recalled.

Seton continued to repaint the fence, and repair the repeatedly van-
dalized gate. "One Saturday morning late in the summer I was busied
painting out an array of dreadful pictures on my gate, when a gang
of the boys went by. I turned to them and said: 'Now, boys, I don't
know who has painted this gate, and I do not wish to know. But
if you know, I wish you would ask him to stop.' The boys giggled,
snickered, whistled with much significance, and passed on. The next
morning the gate, the posts, and the adjoining trees and rocks were
decorated with a new array of the most shockingly improper pictures,
with inscriptions to give them a personal point for me, all showing
the . . . modes of thought, and the same master hand."[61]

Seton reflected on his problem over the winter. In the late spring
of 1901, he obtained permission to address students at the local
school and invited all its boys over the age of twelve to an Easter
weekend outing on his estate. He had expected twenty but twice as
many showed up. They swam in his lake and devoured the food he
supplied, then listened around a campfire to his wilderness and Indian tales. His antagonists were hooked, spending the night in teepees
after electing chiefs and councilors. Seton—Black Wolf—became
their medicine man.[62]

The naturalist had stumbled onto a new vocation: the development of youth by sharing his knowledge of the wilderness, animals,
and Indian lore. But Seton had always meticulously planned his ventures, and the camp was no exception. Since his return from Paris in
1896, Seton had been absorbing a heady mix of notions about the
American frontier, Indians, the nature of human society, and child
development. In freethinking Paris, he had associated with noncon-
formists like American painter Robert Henri, a self-professed anarchist, and James Mavor, a Canadian socialist. Mavor introduced
Seton to the Russian anarchist Prince Peter Kropotkin in Toronto in

1897; funding from Tolstoy had allowed Kropotkin to export 8,000 Dhoukobor agrarian pacifists to Canada.[63] Such influences shaped Seton's thinking on man, society, and nature. The process continued in New York, where Seton maintained a studio residence in the Beaux Arts Studio Building on West 40th Street, built by another Paris friend, portraitist A.A. Anderson. At the Players Club, he met Garland, who shared his interest in Native Americans.

Seton believed Western writers and artists formed a distinct school of thought: Men like Bret Hart and Mark Twain "write, paint or speak because they have a story that they burn to tell," he wrote. He identified the Indian as the source of Western virtue, finding a parallel to socialism in the communal ownership of land by Native Americans.[64] He borrowed from anthropologist Lewis Henry Morgan, founder of the Grand Order of the Iroquois, a secretive society of white men who saw in the Indian the basis of America's greatness. Seton developed a friendship with Canadian poet Pauline Johnson, half Iroquois, who so admired a Seton wolf painting in 1893 that she called him a "Medicine Brother." Johnson introduced Seton to the figure of Tecumseh, the Shawnee chief who fought for the British-Canadian side in the War of 1812.[65] Seton admired his "personal prowess, his farseeing statesmanship, his noble eloquence, and lofty character." He immersed himself in Indian history, anthropology, music, and folklore. He befriended Dr. Charles A. Eastman or Ohiyesa, a Minnesota Santee Sioux who took a medical degree at Boston University, treated casualties at Wounded Knee after the 1890 U.S. Army massacre there, represented Indian tribes in federal proceedings, and cared for Indians on the Crow Creek, South Dakota, reservation from 1900 to 1903. From White Swan, a Crow who had scouted for General George Armstrong Custer before the soldier's defeat in detail at Little Bighorn, Seton learned Indian sign language, on which he would later publish an authoritative work.[66]

Seton's research and interviews with Indian survivors of the Plains wars led him to conclude that official U.S. treatment of the Indians had been "an unbroken narrative of injustice, fraud and robbery." He wrote in a letter to the *New York Herald* that "for every drop of righteous blood spilled" at Wounded Knee, "a fearful vengeance is being stored and will certainly break on us."[67]

Such eclectic strands gave rise to a highly idiosyncratic conception of man's relationship to nature and to the divine—for him increasingly a pantheistic notion. As he reshaped his estate into an idealized wilderness, Seton also transformed his interior landscape, taking the bond with nature that he had established as a child to a higher philosophical and spiritual plane. Seton would always characterize his Indian camp for boys as a serendipitous accident. But his standoff with the youth of Cos Cob also provided the means for him to experiment with these new ideas. Edward Bok, the editor of the *Ladies' Home Journal*,[68] had heard from Rudyard Kipling about Seton's desire to publish a book on woodcraft based on Indian lore, and invited the British-Canadian to produce a wilderness page in that magazine targeting boy readers. Seton accepted Bok's offer in 1901 and by the following year, he would later recall with some embellishment, he had "commenced a series of articles destined to launch America's largest youth movement."[69]

Seton was particularly influenced by the work of G. Stanley Hall, a pioneer in child psychology. Hall embraced the theory of recapitulation, the notion that "the stages of a child's development repeat those through which the (human) race has passed."[70] Hall's call for education to be "full of the spirit of the field naturalist observer" resonated profoundly for Seton and informed his experiment in new ways to educate boys emphasizing nature's lessons and Indian wisdom.[71]

Seton set up Indian camps in his Village of the Standing Rock complete with Sioux, Blackfoot, and Cheyenne teepees and Algonquin canoes.[72] Tribal events unfolded around a council blaze. "Inspired by a Navajo sand painting, the fire was encircled by a necklace of stones to symbolize the Great Spirit," writes a Seton biographer. "Equidistant around its circumference four arms extended to represent spirit, mind, body and service. At the end of each arm was attached a lamp, with three rays, each symbolizing the laws of woodcraft."[73]

Seton's Indians elected Head, Second, and Third chiefs, a Wampum Chief to manage tribal possessions, a Chief of the Painted Robe to keep the Law Book, the Record of Camps and Seasons, and the Feather-Tally of coups—exploits meriting recognition—and a Council Fire Chief, who alone was empowered to make the fire but had to do so without matches. These, together with the Medicine Man, formed the Council of Twelve, the ultimate tribal authority.[74]

Seton created a sense of drama and occasion and made it all fun with games he made up or to which he imparted a fresh spin. One of those listening to Seton around the fire at Wyndygoul was Julian Salomon, who read about the Woodcraft Indians and formed a tribe in New London, Connecticut. He and friends explored local woodlands and learned from a Mohegan how to chew birch bark and brew it for tea. Salomon made his way to the estate in Cos Cob to begin a long association with Seton, "an absolute genius [and] a born teacher." The Indian recruit recalled many years later the "great thrill to learn what a blue jay was and to tell the difference between a white-throated sparrow and an ordinary sparrow."[75]

Seton's contact with the campers was "very informal and very irregular." On mornings when camp was in session, the Woodcraft founder crossed the lake to join his Indians, leaving them to their own devices for the rest of the day under the supervision of the older boys. His Indians understood that Seton had other obligations: Grace Seton would come across the lake, "rowed over by a footman because they had two or three servants in those days, and take Seton away from us, just gather him up, you know, and take him home."[76]

Besides running Seton's column, the *Ladies' Home Journal* also serialized a tale that Seton published in book form in 1903 as *Two*

Little Savages. Set in his transplanted hometown of Lindsay, *Savages* recounts the experiences of Yan and Sam as they learn the North American Indian crafts and rituals. Seton's readers learned along with them through diagrams and explanations. "Seton continues to weave the Indian and nature study themes together, creating a sense of their mutual interdependence," a biographer writes. "By the end of the book, Indian, animal, child and wilderness have been combined in purest innocence."[77]

Seton's tribe spawned others locally and nationwide and by 1903 there were between fifty and sixty. Seton organized a Confederation or Nation under which a League of Seton Indians would coordinate policies. The phenomenon drew the attention of journalists who further spread word of the movement.[78]

Seton's initiative impressed Charles Fletcher Lummis, a former classmate of Roosevelt at Harvard (though he dropped out in his senior year). Lummis became the city editor of the *Los Angeles Times* before a stroke partially paralyzed him. He moved to New Mexico to recover and among many other pursuits became an advocate for Indian rights. Introduced to Seton in the 1890s, Lummis visited the Indian camp on what he described as "a wonderful natural woodland of hemlock, chestnut, oak and other New England trees with great granite ledges and a pretty little lake. I think it is the prettiest place I ever saw in New England. He has a big costly house on the finest point overlooking the Lake and in the thick trees; and lives in baronial fashion." Lummis had supposed that the Indian camp was "a lot of wealthy boys paying about $20 a week for the privilege of camping under his expert direction." But, Lummis recorded, "On the contrary, he gives his money and time to them each year without a cent of recompense, and teaches them not only to be hunters, fishers, swimmers, and wrestlers, but to be Men. To rely on their strength and courage and to be reliable in their word."

Lummis took part in some camp games that July morning, then lunched with his hosts and went fishing. Later, with Seton and another guest named Walcott, he observed the Grand Council ceremonies around the campfire. The self-governing Indians "fined their own chief for leaving a tin can and a piece of paper visible—it being a cardinal virtue to keep the camp spotlessly clean." Walcott told the boys about photographing a grizzly "in action," then Lummis was called upon to share his knowledge of Indians.[79] "I talked for about an hour and the poor boys stood for it." Upon concluding his visit, "The gaudy footman drove me down to the station at Cos Cob and I escaped by the noon train to New York."[80]

Conservationist Hornaday also approved of Seton's latest venture, writing to President Roosevelt that the naturalist "has got hold of a big thing" in his camp. "I have been there once and much impressed with it all, and with good results to the boys that are sure to follow from this scheme. All the boy's wild energy and love of deviltry are turned to new channels, and he is taught woodcraft and natural history and Indian lore in a most fascinating way. I really think it well worthy of your attention and encouragement," Hornaday told the chief executive.[81]

Seton had drawn on many sources to create his Indians, eventually wrapping them all into something he called woodcraft—achieving harmony with nature and learning to exist within it as the Indians had, unleashing youthful imaginations through play. He believed his movement could break social barriers and establish in young minds "a finer kind of humanity, a real understanding that the important thing is the association of the human spirit."[82] Traditionally structured schools, disconnected from nature, could not accomplish this, he maintained. Well ahead of his time, Seton—Black Wolf—asserted that "if the young people of this nation can be so trained that they will grow to look upon Nature with eager interest, if they become familiar with her traditions, her kindness, her discipline, her beauty, her tragedies, they will find themselves held together by a bond of sympathy that no superficial social structure can ever obliterate."[83]

CHAPTER 2

SONS OF DANIEL BOONE

Ernest Seton was not alone in promoting the outdoor experience in the United States at the turn of the century. Generations of Americans had lived in proximity with nature on the frontier and on farms. But in the late 1800s, camping out as a recreational pastime as opposed to an uncomfortable necessity came into its own. Initially it was associated with Presbyterian and Methodist camp meetings that drew families with the necessities of life loaded onto their wagons for a week of sermons and songs. The emergence in the late 1800s of the Chautauqua lecture and entertainment circuit, named for the lake in upstate New York where the first such gathering was held for Sunday school teachers, broadened camping's appeal. On-site concessionaires rented tents and sold provisions to Chautauqua-goers.

Among the first to see educational value in camping itself was Frederick Williams Gunn, founder of the Gunnery School for Boys in the northwestern Connecticut town of Washington. During the Civil War, summer-term students eager to emulate Union troops "were given opportunity to roll up in blankets and sleep outdoors on the ground."[1] Pennsylvania physician Joseph Trimble Rothrock established his North Mountain School of Physical Culture in 1876, proposing to take "weakly boys in summer out into camp life in the woods" for exercise and study.[2] Summer camp as a distinct institution emerged in 1881 when Dartmouth student Ernest Balch, observing the "miserable condition of boys belonging to well-to-do families in summer hotels," established Camp Chocorua on Asquam Lake in Holderness, New Hampshire.[3] But by 1888 Balch had piled up debts of $8,000—no small sum at the time—and was forced to close his innovative camp on Burnt Island.

Camping became a key element of "boys' work" programs of the Young Men's Christian Association, which in that era proposed to rescue "boys from the better homes" rather than street urchins and slum children, citing a "preventative and character-building" purpose.[4] Camping offered "healthful recreation without temptation" and satisfied "the natural desire for a free and easy life out of doors" while at the same time developing a "manly Christian character."[5]

Seton's Indians were little inclined to Bible study, but he could see that the YMCA might be a useful channel to spread his wilderness gospel. Seton's gift for sparking young imaginations impressed fellow Canadian Edgar M. Robinson, a YMCA executive in charge of programs for boys. Seton walked into Robinson's office one day at noon, introduced himself, and invited the social worker to lunch and "a talk about camping" in the Waldorf-Astoria Hotel dining room. Robinson accepted "with alacrity," recalling the meal as "a memorable occasion."[6] Seton could be very engaging, and the two men had much in common. Robinson grew up in a remote eastern Canadian district where Indians traded for merchandise in his father's dry goods store, but Robinson did not share Seton's romantic vision of Indians. "I saw nothing in them to inspire the boyhood of a nation to worthy achievements."[7] But Robinson was intrigued by Seton's experiment.

Invited soon after that to visit Wyndygoul, Robinson found Seton and twenty boys assembled for a round of "Hunt the Deer," one of their most popular games. The "deer" was made of chicken wire, straw, and burlap and a bull's-eye of rings painted over the heart of the mock quarry. Seton strapped irons to his feet to leave hoof marks, setting off down a dirt road and through the woods, setting the "deer" under some hemlock branches, all but concealing it. Circling back to the starting point, Seton and Robinson observed as the boys picked up the trail. Once they had found the deer, the would-be Indians took turns shooting arrows at it.

"One cannot, in relating the incident, inject into it the zest, enthusiasm and excitement of those who participated," Robinson remembered. "The game had been so clothed with drama, so full of tense expectancy, so intensely active, that every boy was on his toes, physically and mentally every minute. For the moment, he had practically forgotten who he was, or where he was, for his whole attention was concentrated on tracking an elusive deer, and his mind was filled with anticipation of achievement." Seton had the ability to "lift a group of boys . . . out of a prosaic white man's world (into an) ideal Indian's world."

But Robinson wondered if this experience could be duplicated by YMCA social workers without Seton's knowledge and gifts. His friendship with Seton and interest in Woodcraft were tempered by his understanding of the conservative YMCA culture. As a youth, Seton had rebelled against organized religion and his spiritual beliefs now tended more to animism than Christianity, a vision which "appealed to some as a new and unique contribution to the realm of character education for boys [but] to others it was a puzzle, a mystery, with a vague appeal to submerged instincts." For some, Seton was a "master hypnotist who could cast a spell over a group of boys and onlookers and make the unreal seem real for the time." But others felt Woodcraft was too much bound up with Seton's personality and his enthusiasm for nature and

Indian lore. "Some disapproved and thought the whole thing degrading," noted Robinson, "some were skeptical and some saw only the visible and heard only the vocal, missing the spiritual significance that even a minimum of insight might have apprehended."[8]

Yet Seton's ideas made their way into YMCA programs. Organizers needed ways to enrich time spent out of doors. Woodcraft offered a way to take YMCA camping culture beyond pitching a tent, building a fire, and cooking dinner. One YMCA camp in New Jersey organized "White Man vs. Indian" games while a Massachusetts group organized a "Pawnee Indian Camp." In Roanoake, Virginia, YMCA organizers built a program around Seton's book *How to Play Indian,* while in Racine, Wisconsin, nine Bible clubs were formed as Indian tribes.[9]

Success breeds imitation, and in the spring of 1905 it came to Seton's attention that he had competition. The conservationist magazine *Recreation* had established an organization for boys not unlike his own, called the Sons of Daniel Boone. Its founder was *Recreation* editor Daniel Carter Beard, known in literary and artistic circles as an illustrator of works by Mark Twain, in particular the anti-industrialist fable *A Connecticut Yankee in King Arthur's Court.* He had dabbled in Progressive politics and published political tracts in the early 1890s. But like Twain, he fell on hard times and turned back to an earlier sideline: writing and illustrating books for boys. His *American Boy's Handy Book,* brought out in 1882, continued to sell strongly in reprint, and Beard published a stream of new titles for boys including *Field, and Forest; The Outdoor Handbook.*

Beard and Seton had intersected earlier in life at the Art Student's League in New York, and had a number of friends in common. On a visit to Beard's studio in Fulton Street in the Lower Manhattan printing district, Hamlin Garland dashed off some verses that Beard displayed there long after the paper had yellowed with age:

Do you fear the force of the wind?
The slash of the rain?
Go face them and fight them;
Be savage again!
Go hungry and cold like the wolf,
Go wade like the crane;
The palms of your hand will thicken,
The skin of your forehead, tan;
You'll be ragged and swarthy and weary,
But you'll walk like a MAN![10]

Now Seton tracked Beard to *Recreation's* offices off Fulton Street. After refreshing their acquaintance, Seton expressed his concern that the Sons of Daniel Boone was infringing on his territory. Beard ought to be careful, he joked, or his Indians would dispatch the Sons of Daniel Boone. Beard retorted that the Indians had far outnumbered the pioneers in Daniel Boone's time, and the latter-day Sons of Daniel Boone would deal with Seton's Indians like their forebears.[11]

This touched a nerve with Seton, immersed in Indian culture and all too aware of the continued oppression of the Native American tribes.

"Go to hell," he flung at Beard, storming out.[12]

The encounter foreshadowed the complex relationship that would develop between the two men in the years to follow. The feisty Beard gleefully made hay of the confrontation in the very next issue of *Recreation*. "The news of the great and growing popularity of the new order of the Sons of Daniel Boone has reached the wigwams of the Seton Indians and their chief," he informed his readers. "Mr. Ernest Thompson Seton called on the Founder the other day to smoke the pipe of peace with him. He seemed worried, but we told him that unless his redskins put on paint and went whooping on the warpath, the Boone Boys would not molest them. We also told him that the notches in our tally guns stood for good deeds and not for scalps and that if his Indians wished to become good citizens the Sons of Daniel Boone were ready to devote themselves to teaching their savage brothers how to build houses and be good."[13]

Beneath the jocosity hot rivalry simmered. The two men would within a few years become close collaborators—and at times fierce antagonists. Both had gained a measure of public recognition. Beard wandered the American heartland for years before settling in New York, and as an artist his path was not so different from Seton's. But they were very different in temperament and outlook—though they shared a predisposition to tetchiness. Beard did not have Seton's intellectual depth, but was nonetheless imaginative and resourceful. He was, by one later account, "an iconoclastic traditionalist, a combatant Quaker, an individualistic organizer, an urban pioneer, a revolutionary conservative, a practical idealist, an inquisitive anti-intellectual, a school-hating educator, and a genial dogmatist."[14] In short, he was contrary by nature but his flaws were redeemed by a deep underlying generosity and a fundamental good nature, traits formed and informed by a quintessential American upbringing.

Daniel Carter Beard was born on June 21, 1850, in Cincinnati, Ohio, fourth son of artist James Henry Beard and Mary Caroline Carter Beard. The self-taught James H. Beard had earned a national reputation with frontier themes like "North Carolina Emigrants, Poor White Folks," depicting a threadbare family moving through the wilderness in search of the American dream. He painted portraits of famous Americans: Daniel Webster, General William Sherman, General George Custer, and two presidents.[15] On a reading tour of the United States, Charles Dickens commended Beard's "first rate" rendition of Fagan, the thief-master in *Oliver Twist*.[16]

The family's American roots ran deep. Beards fought in the French and Indian Wars, signed the Declaration of Independence, and took up arms in the American Revolution. They were Puritans and

Quakers, farmers and preachers, ship's captains and doctors, judges, governors, and cabinet members.[17] Daniel's oldest brother read law in the firm of Rutherford B. Hayes, U.S. president from 1877 to 1881. Beard senior associated with Texas patriots Sam Houston, Jim Bowie, and Davy Crockett, and painted the San Jacinto battle flag that flew on the battlefield where the soldiers of the Republic of Texas defeated the forces of General Santa Anna on April 21, 1836, winning that War of Independence.[18]

Ten years old when Abraham Lincoln and Stephen Douglas contested the presidency, Dan Beard joined the throng that greeted Lincoln as his barouche rumbled through Cincinnati following his election in 1860. "As I ran alongside the carriage, men were also running with me and reaching up to shake hands with the tall man whom the other occupants of the carriage were steadying to keep him from falling. Turning to me, Abraham Lincoln looked down and smiled."[19]

Too young to fight in the Civil War, he closely followed the experiences of his brother Harry, a Union officer who besieged Vicksburg, and Frank, a traveling artist for *Harper's Weekly*. But the young Beard did not entirely miss the war. In 1862, he took up a shovel with the region's able-bodied men to build earthworks and trenches to protect Cincinnati from Confederate attack.[20] He worked as an orderly in a military hospital, experiencing "awe and admiration" when irregular scouts in gold-piped uniforms, buckskin gauntlets, and ostrich-plumed hats would "appear suddenly from nowhere and disappear in as mysterious a manner."[21]

Near the end of the Civil War, the Beard family's center of gravity shifted to New York City. By early 1864, James H. Beard and Dan's brother Frank were living in rooms on lower Broadway and pursuing careers in art and publishing. An uncle, William Holbrook Beard, was known for animal subjects evoking human foibles.[22] James also painted animals along domestic and sentimental lines. Frank made fifteen dollars a week as an artist for the *New York Illustrated News*.[23] By 1866, James Beard and Frank were joined by eldest son James Carter Beard, also an artist. By 1869, Frank was married and living in Brooklyn, commuting by ferry across the East River to Manhattan past the rising Brooklyn Bridge to draw cartoons at the *Comic Monthly* on Nassau Street.[24]

The Beards were often short of money. James the elder was striving for recognition and financial security as his wife and other children fretted in Covington, Kentucky, across the Ohio River from Cincinnati. Harry Beard, in business in Cincinnati, sent a reproachful letter to his father chiding him for neglectfulness. But he, too, made his way East in 1874, writing often to Dan.

Daniel established his own connection with New York in 1874, securing employment with the Sanborn Map Company in Pelham, New York, which sold detailed maps of cities and towns across the country to insurance companies that used them to assess risk and price coverage. The maps indicated not only locations but building firewalls, sprinkler systems, and roof materials. Daniel's engineering background and drawing skills qualified him well for such work. But the job was tedious and required constant travel.[25] By the summer of 1876, he was expressing weariness to Harry, who advised him to save his money to go into business for himself to "be independent of any impertinence or ill humor of an employer."

In 1878, Dan sold a drawing of a fish to the Century Company, a top New York publisher, and left Sanborn behind. He lived with his parents in Flushing and worked in his brother's studio on Fulton Street, in lower Manhattan, illustrating children's fiction for *St. Nicholas* magazine, drawing animals for *Forest and Stream,* and sketching items for retail catalogues.[26] In 1882, he published *The American Boy's Handy Book: What to Do and How to Do It.* Organized seasonally, the volume taught kite flying in spring, small boat rigging in summer, dog training in autumn, and snow-shoeing and ice-fishing in winter. Highly successful for decades, the book is still in print today.

Beard's earnings funded night classes at the Art Students League. He rubbed shoulders with Frederic Remington and successful illustrators such as Charles Dana Gibson, creator of the Gibson Girl.

As the League's recording secretary, he offered advice to younger artists including a Canadian named Ernest Thompson Seton.[27] He led a faction of "radical" night-school students, championing art for humanity's sake.[28] Artists, he wrote, should "despise . . . that great, slow-moving, conservative old soul called the public." Beard ran for League president in 1883 and was defeated, but then was unanimously elected vice president.[29]

Beard in his early thirties became attuned to Progressive politics. He was strongly influenced by Henry George, a former journalist who achieved national prominence in 1879 with a book called *Progress and Poverty,* "an inquiry into the cause of industrial depressions and of increase of want with increase of wealth."[30] George blamed poverty on the concentration of wealth in the appreciated value of land held by a monopolistic rentier class, proposing to redress this with a tax on unearned gains in property, earning the nickname Single-Tax George."[31]

When George ran for mayor of New York in 1886, Beard campaigned for him as a street-corner speaker and poll-watcher.[32] But his candidate with 31 percent of the vote lost to Democratic reformer Abram Stevens Hewitt, an industrialist and New York congressman. Theodore Roosevelt placed third with 28 percent. Soon after, George launched a progressive weekly newspaper called *The Standard.*[33]

Beard built a reputation as an illustrator with a political edge. His illustrations for a *Cosmopolitan* article on Chinese Empress Wu Chih Tien brought an inquiry from Mark Twain's New York business manager, inquiring whether he might be available to illustrate Twain's next novel.[34] The inquiry was highly flattering and financially promising. After establishing the publishing firm Charles L. Webster & Co. with a nephew by marriage, Twain enjoyed successes with *The Adventures of Huckleberry Finn* and the memoirs of Ulysses S.

Grant. But his finances were in poor shape after he poured thousands of dollars into developing an innovative but ultimately unworkable automated typesetting machine.[35]

Twain's latest work, *A Connecticut Yankee in King Arthur's Court*, marked a departure into fantasy: Hartford, Connecticut, machinist Hank Morgan sustains a concussion and is transported to the England of King Arthur and the Knights of the Round Table.[36] Morgan's sharp wits and mechanical abilities bring him power and he tries to reshape feudal English society. Aiming to relieve the downtrodden through technology, Morgan achieves a Pyrrhic victory as he mows down armor-clad opponents with Gatling guns, then succumbs to a spell cast by Merlin.

Many interpreted *A Connecticut Yankee* as a fling at the British (a conclusion also reached by many London critics), but at heart it was a fable of the industrial era. For Beard, steeped in the progressive ideas of Henry George, the commission was not only flattering, but also highly appealing. Moreover, Twain's instructions transmitted through his business agent afforded Beard the greatest possible artistic freedom.[37] "Tell Beard to obey his own inspirations, and when he sees a picture in his mind put *that* picture on paper, be it humorous or be it serious . . . They will be bullier pictures than if I mixed in and tried to give him points on his own trade."[38]

Beard produced 260 drawings that went beyond illustration of the novel to provide a gloss on economic and political issues Twain had only hinted at in his prose. Beard drew on personalities of the time for inspiration, borrowing features of actress Sarah Bernhardt for Sandy, Morgan's love; those of financier Jay Gould, for a brutal slave driver; and British and Prussian royalty for Twain's noble "chuckleheads." Hank Morgan first appears in Arthurian times as a vulgar promoter in a checked suit. By the end of the novel, he is a goateed, striped-trousered Uncle Sam bestriding a book labeled "Common Sense" with a quill pen pointed "like a lance at the midriff of a bloated aristocrat suggesting Henry VIII."[39]

Some felt Beard went too far in some respects while falling short in others. His illustrations "constituted a drastic reading-in of radical doctrines only faintly suggested or not suggested at all, in Mark Twain's text," one scholar would later write.[40] Twain voiced no such reservations. Citing Beard's caricature of financier Jay Gould, he told the *New York Times* that he was "delighted at the way the artist has entered into the spirit of the book in executing the illustrations." He wrote to Beard in August 1889 upon first viewing his submissions: "I have examined the pictures a good many times, and my pleasure in them is as strong and fresh as ever."[41] Twain again praised Beard's work that November as the book went to press. "Hold me under permanent obligations. What luck it was to find you! There are a hundred artists who could illustrate any other book of mine, but there was only one who could illustrate this one. Yes, it was a fortunate hour that I went netting for lightning bugs and caught a meteor. Live forever!"[42]

Beard's satisfaction with *A Connecticut Yankee* was soon overshadowed by grief at the death of his brother Harry, overcome by gas in a hotel room in what a newspaper later described as a suicide.[43] Beard left the studio he had shared with Harry and set up in a Flushing *atelier* lined with dusty books and curios to help conjure up "poetry, romance, pathos and humor."[44] Four years later, his father succumbed to pneumonia at the age of eighty on April 4, 1893. The elder Beard had become a fixture of city life, the *Times* once noting his "tall, gaunt form, his masses of long dark hair, his kindly, furrowed face, and his scintillating gray eyes under shaggy eyebrows [which] gave him a Kentucky air."[45]

At forty-three, Beard was all but formally engaged to a woman fifteen years his junior. Beatrice Alice Jackson was the daughter of a diamond merchant who regarded the artist as an unsuitable match. Samuel Jackson withheld his blessing and Allie would not marry Dan without it; it was only upon Samuel's death that her mother assented. They eventually married in 1894.[46]

Beard turned his hand to writing as well as illustrating along po-
lemical lines with *Moonblight*,[47] a novel published in 1892 by Twain's
firm. It was reminiscent of *A Connecticut Yankee*. The main character,
a rich, indolent mine owner visiting a poor Pennsylvania coal town,
falls under the spell of arcane books found in his hotel room, acquiring the power to see "things as they really are." He realizes the error
of his ways and tries to establish a utopian community but is caught
up in a strike engulfing the region. Hit on the head in a street battle
between miners and Pinkerton detectives, the hero wakes up in the
home of his lovely fiancée.

Beard illustrated other Twain works, including *Tom Sawyer
Abroad*,[48] a flight of fancy in which Tom tours Europe and the Near
East aboard a dirigible with his friends Huck and Jim. It was not a
commercial or critical success. Beard provided sketches for articles
Twain dashed off for the *New York Herald* to fend off ruin in the early
1890s. But his efforts were in vain: Webster & Co. failed in 1894
after bringing out *Pudd'nhead Wilson*. The next year Twain went on
an international lecture tour to restore his finances. But his daughter
Susie's death in 1897 at his Hartford home while he was in Europe
initiated a final period of decline.

When Henry George ran for New York mayor again in 1897,
Beard joined his Party of Thomas Jefferson. George told voters that
industrial machines had been "turned like captured cannon, against
the ranks of labor."[49] But the frenetic pace of the campaign soon
exhausted the fifty-eight-year-old social visionary. In late October,
Beard welcomed a faltering George to a stage in Flushing. George
"took a few steps, found the side of the stage, looked upward for a
moment, and raising his right hand as if addressing someone over-
head, said, 'Time and tide wait for no man.' His arm fell to his side,
his head fell forward, the chin on the breast, and he stood as though
lost in thought. Presently he roused, turned to the audience and said:
'I have only time to come, take a look at you and go away.'" Eventually he stirred himself and delivered something more like a campaign
speech.

After a Manhattan appearance, the candidate returned to his hotel, dined on oysters and milk, and retired. He rose in the small hours, complaining of an upset stomach. His wife found him in the next room of their suite. "He was standing, one hand on a chair, as if to support himself. His face was white; his body rigid like a statue; his shoulders thrown back, his head up, his eyes wide open and penetrating, as if they saw something; and one word came—'Yes'—many times repeated, at first with a quiet emphasis, then with the vigour of his heart's force." A doctor diagnosed stroke. "The great heart had worn out the physical body, and a thread in the brain had snapped." The doctor comforted the widow, "then in utter helplessness . . . cast himself face downward upon the floor. For at that moment, Henry George's spirit was answering the call of the All-Father."[50]

Dispirited by George's death following those of his brother and his father, and disillusioned with politics, Beard became convinced that his work for Twain had damaged his career. "I grievously offended parties unknown, and was constantly boycotted for about ten years," he later wrote. Some editors—John Ames Mitchell at *Life* and John Brisbane Walker of *Cosmopolitan*—gave him work, though.[51] He eked out a living with assignments from them as well as *Harper's Weekly* and the *Ladies' Home Journal.* But at the age of fifty Beard was past the prime of his career as a political illustrator—his style had become outdated—and seemed on the downslope of life.

Returning to juvenile publishing, Beard brought out two works for boys in 1900: *Playground, Field & Forest; the Outdoor Handbook,* and a manual crafts guide called *Jack of All Trades.* In 1905, a former studio assistant named William Annis who had purchased an outdoor magazine called *Recreation* asked Beard to become editor-in-chief. Beard readily accepted the offer, averring an "all-absorbing love for nature."[52] The publisher wanted to increase *Recreation*'s appeal to young readers, and Beard at his urging worked up something called "The Sons of Daniel Boone," announcing its creation in the July 1905 issue. "The youths of today are the powers of tomorrow," he declared. "To them future generations must look forward for the preservation of game, fish and forest. To carefully educate and guide the young minds aright in this direction is (the) principal object."[53]

The Sons of Daniel Boone would "strengthen the love all boys have for the out-of-doors," promoting the conservation of nature and "all that tends to healthy, wholesome manliness," its constitution declared. Its aims included the passage of "laws prohibiting the sale of guns."[54] On the other hand, boys launching a Sons of Daniel Boone chapter, called a "Fort," were urged to acquire an old, unloaded rifle and cut notches in the stock to keep track of good deeds protecting forests and wildlife. While doing so they were instructed to chant: "Cut a notch, cut a notch, cut a notch soon, for we are the Sons of Daniel Boone."[55]

Between July 1905 and March 1906, Beard published ten columns under the heading, "Dan Beard and the Boys, Sons of Daniel Boone." Forts were chartered once the founder received a roster of members and elected officers. The president of a Fort held the title "Daniel Boone," the secretary received the honorific "Davy Crockett." The boy elected treasurer became "Kit Carson," while the recorder of "notches" went by the name of "Simon Kenton." Beard set broad guidelines in his columns, but in reality his Sons of Daniel Boone were pretty much on their own. There were no dues, but Fort members signed a good-conduct pledge.[56]

His columns elicited interest from adults, too. Some regretted not having had such an activity when they were young. Others offered suggestions for improving the concept. "The Sons should not only be an incentive to study the lives and adventures of the pioneers of this country, but (should keep boys) amused so that they will not be hanging around saloons," offered one Arthur Mead.[57] But trouble was brewing at *Recreation*. In October 1905, Annis told Beard he could no longer afford his editor's salary, but asked him to keep writing the column for a nominal fee and leave his name on the masthead. Beard finally resigned in March 1906.[58]

He found a new home for the Sons of Daniel Boone at the *Woman's Home Companion.* At the instigation of editor Arthur Vance, Beard sought and secured a meeting in the White House with President Theodore Roosevelt, who authorized the institution of a "top notch" in his name for "deeds of heroism and daring," for instance "protecting women and children from injury or abuse; saving property from fire and flood, or in times of riot; or standing up to some noted bully or tough when the interest of peaceable citizens demands it."[59]

Beard wrote to Buffalo Bill Cody at the East Twenty-Second Street offices of his Wild West organization seeking his endorsement of a notch for "pioneering" skills including camping, hunting, firearms handling, construction of log houses, and "breaking wild horses to drive and ride." The notch would encourage a Son of Daniel Boone to "be true to yourself and others, as the Lord is true to you." The showman was "pleased very much to see that the names of the old pioneers and scouts are to be kept fresh and green with the rising generation."[60] Beard asked Twain for permission to create a "Moral Courage Notch" in his name. Twain's secretary sent a note saying the writer had no suggestions for the boys—"that matter he will have to leave to you," implicitly giving permission.[61]

Although the Sons of Daniel Boone primarily existed in the columns of the *Woman's Home Companion,* a few thousand active members came forward and Beard recorded their names and addresses on three-by-five-inch index cards.[62] That was about all the organizational structure there was to the Sons of Daniel Boone, later to become the Boy Pioneers, but it gave Dan Beard impeccable credentials in the emerging field of outdoor work with boys.

Despite his initial skirmish with Beard, it is not clear if Seton saw the Sons of Daniel Boone as much of a threat to his Woodcraft

Indians. He could see that Beard's creation was largely a magazine marketing endeavor, nor did Beard have the luxury of dedicating himself more or less full time to building a national organization, as Seton did. His relationship with the YMCA held the potential to become a formal partnership, providing a robust administrative infrastructure.

Seton was, in addition, looking to expand internationally. He had reestablished ties to Britain, an important overseas market for his books and lectures. In 1904, he started promoting his Woodcraft Indians there, and in the summer of 1906 he started to plan another trip to Britain in the fall, not only to talk up Woodcraft but to promote a new book, *Biography of a Grizzly*. Never shy about self-promotion, Seton wrote to Lord Roberts, British commander-in-chief in the Boer War, to ask for introductions to men who might get behind his Woodcraft Indians. Roberts suggested he contact Robert Baden-Powell, a renowned but retired army general with an interest in training youth. Seton mailed a copy of the *Birch-Bark Roll* to Baden-Powell that July, initiating a relationship that would turn out to be as problematic for the two men—in particular for Seton—as it was to be beneficial to the youth of the world.[63]

CHAPTER 3

THE HERO OF MAFEKING

Ernest Thompson Seton sent off his *Birch Bark Roll* to Robert Baden-Powell in hopes that he might, in the Boer War hero, secure a highly influential sponsor for his movement. The name of Baden-Powell resonated powerfully for Seton, as it would have with any other Briton of the time. Only six years had passed since Baden-Powell led the defense of the South African colonial outpost of Mafeking for seven months against thousands of Boer besiegers with far fewer defenders, earning the epithet of the Hero of Mafeking.

Like many other British expatriates, Seton was much distressed in 1899 at the humiliation of Britain's military at the hands of Boer irregulars in the war that had just broken out in Southern Africa. It was the second war between Britain and the Boers in two decades, but the British army was not prepared. Its hidebound tactics gave an advantage to Boer militia who were at ease on the sweeping *veld* and steep *kopjes.* They were "big, bearded men, loose of limb, shabbily dressed in broad brimmed hats, corduroy trousers, and brown shoes" whose rusticity concealed a "dormant fierceness."[1] With help from Germany, the Boers armed themselves with Mauser rifles more accurate than British standard issue Lee-Enfields, and fired Creusot artillery pieces, Krupp howitzers, and English-made Vickers-Maxim rapid-fire naval guns.[2] From December 10 to 17, 1899, known thereafter as "Black Week," Britain sustained heavy losses at Stormberg Junction, Magersfontein, and Colenso with a thousand British troops taken prisoner at Ladysmith and the diamond town laid siege by eight thousand Boers.[3] The Empire was humiliated by this "mauling at the hands of bewhiskered farmers," one U.S. paper of the time commented.[4]

Following these developments with dismay, Seton wrote to fellow writer and countryman Rudyard Kipling, enclosing five pounds sterling for a patriotic fund Kipling had launched for the needy families of soldiers.[5] Though Seton was by disposition and conviction a pacifist, he urged Kipling to put his money toward a Maxim gun, "or for other purpose . . . as you deem best."

But his patriotism only went so far. "There (are) hundreds of us, yes thousands, in this country, only awaiting the time when England shall really need us to come back home and join the flag," he told Kipling. "But we that have families and business responsibilities do not feel that we should go until the unexpected emergency shall arise." The setbacks would "work double good for England, first in showing England what she needs in the way of an army. Second in showing the world how concrete the British Empire is."[6]

The Anglo-Boer conflict elicited more mixed feelings among Americans, who felt a cultural affinity with the British but sympathized with the Boers as settlers resisting colonial overreach. The Boer War embodied an implicit reproach to the American government, pursuing its own colonial ambitions in the Philippines where the U.S. Army was brutally putting down rebels led by Emilio Aguinaldo. Mark Twain observed the uncomfortable parallel between the United States and England, which had "sinned when she got herself into a war in South Africa which she could have avoided." President McKinley took the British side, while press lord William Randolph Hearst unleashed anti-Boer propaganda in the pages of his newspapers.[7]

South Africa was of strategic interest to Britain because it controlled the Cape of Good Hope sea route to India, the jewel in the imperial crown. Britain wanted to keep rival powers, Germany in particular, from getting a foothold in Southern Africa.[8] The British had succeeded the Dutch in South Africa, taking possession of Cape Colony in the early 1800s following the Napoleonic Wars. The Boers, of Dutch and French Huguenot blood, chafed at rule by Britain. After it outlawed slavery there in 1834, Boer *Voortrekkers* headed northeast on horseback and ox wagons looking for a piece of Africa where London's writ did not run. Clashes inevitably followed, leading to a first war between Britain and the Boers in 1880–1881. Britain fared poorly and conceded self-government to the Boers.

But the discovery of gold in the Transvaal in 1886 undermined relations as British fortune hunters poured in. Fast outnumbered in the Transvaal, the Boers refused political rights to the *Uitlanders*. Agitation by British newcomers and machinations by politicians and financiers in 1895 produced an armed raid into the Transvaal by Leander Starr Jameson, a physician and Rhodesian colonial administrator. The abortive sally merely heightened Boer suspicions of British expansionist intentions. A diplomatic crisis flared as British Colonial Secretary Joseph Chamberlain protested discrimination against Britons in the Transvaal. Talks between Transvaal President Paul Kruger and British High Commissioner Alfred Milner yielded no solution.[9] Milner demanded voting rights for those who had lived in the Transvaal for five years—in effect a demand that the Boers cede political control. Kruger offered concessions, but Britain was by then intent on annexing the Boer republics and consolidating its regional holdings.[10]

In early September, the British Cabinet voted to send 10,000 troops to reinforce its position in the Cape. In early October, the Boer republics mobilized their citizen-soldiers and issued an ultimatum that Britain speedily rejected. The Great Anglo-Boer War ensued on October 12, 1899.

War with the Boers broke out just as Robert Baden-Powell was beginning to make his mark in the British military. Born Robert Stevenson Smyth Powell in London on February 22, 1857, he was the fourth son of an Oxford professor, the Rev. Baden Powell, and his considerably younger third wife, Henrietta Grace Smyth, daughter of a British admiral, who was to bear him three more sons by the time he died in 1860. Nine years later, in honor of her late husband, Henrietta, attuned to social nuance, changed the family name to Baden-Powell.[11]

From an early age, Robert displayed a quick humor, a talent for sketching, and a gift for theatrics that would serve him well in military postings. He attended the Charterhouse School in Surrey, thirty miles southwest of London. The school was bounded on one side by a wood known to students as the Copse, where, Baden-Powell acquired "the invaluable habit of Observation and Deduction."[12]

Completing his studies at Charterhouse in 1876, Baden-Powell unsuccessfully sought entry to Oxford. He did better in military exams, placing fifth and seventh, respectively, in tests for the infantry and cavalry.[13] Sub-Lieutenant Baden-Powell was sent to Lucknow, India, garrison of the 13th Hussar Regiment.[14] He spent two years in the dust, sweat, and boredom of Indian post duty before going home to recover from a bout of ill health. In 1880, he followed his unit to Afghanistan.

At the 13th Hussars' encampment near Kandahar, revolvers were kept handy throughout a production of the *Pirates of Penzance* in which the subaltern took a leading role. In Quetta, India, he orga-nized more theatrical productions and found diversion in the pursuit of wild hogs on horseback. "To the uninitiated," Baden-Powell wrote in one of his first books, "the term 'pigsticking' conveys but a very feeble idea of the nature and qualities of the pursuit, which, were they more widely known, would prove attractive to a more extended circle of sportsmen than at the present."[15]

He impressed his commander, Colonel Sir Baker Russell, and in early 1882 became his adjutant. He drafted twenty training lectures for enlisted men, which were published in book form as *Reconnais-sance and Scouting.* "Scouts are the eyes and ears of the army," he wrote, "and on their intelligence and smartness mainly depends the success of all operations."[16]

Home on leave in 1885, Baden-Powell refreshed family ties and fretted over what seemed a stalled career. He sought a move to army intelligence, undertaking freelance espionage in Germany and Rus-sia, which mainly provided fodder for a later book entitled, *My Ad-ventures as a Spy.*

His next assignment came about through family connections: his uncle, commander-in-chief of Cape Colony, engaged Baden-Powell as aide-de-camp. He sailed to South Africa in December 1887, the year after miners struck a reef of gold in the Witwatersrand. He won distinction for his role in putting down a Zulu uprising in Natal Colony in 1888. But in 1890 he was obliged to follow his uncle to Malta, from which he gathered intelligence in the Eastern Mediterranean.[17]

After uneventful duty with the 13th Hussars in Ireland[18] in 1894–1895, he was posted to the Gold Coast of West Africa where incursions from the Ashanti region were disrupting local trade. Baden-Powell raised 800 local troops and set out for Kumasi, capital of the Ashanti ruler Prempeh. The potentate declined to fight, and was exiled to the Seychelles, his kingdom annexed.[19] Back in London, Baden-Powell received the Ashanti Star campaign medal and promo-tion to brevet lieutenant colonel. He provided London newspapers columns and sketches, and dashed off an account of his campaign entitled *The Downfall of Prempeh.*

Baden-Powell's career was in full flower. His deft management of the Ashanti expedition earned him the confidence of Army Commander-in-Chief Lord Garnet Wolseley. After a brief stint in Belfast, Baden-Powell was sent back to Africa to help Rhodesian authorities put down an uprising by Matabele tribesmen displeased with colonial appropriation of their land and cattle.[20]

The rebellion closely followed the ill-fated Jameson Raid. That operation had involved members of the Rhodesian constabulary who remained in Boer hands or were deported, presenting the Matabele a tactical opportunity. Warriors attacked settlers across the country in March 1896, killing hundreds of whites and laying siege to Bulawayo. Baden-Powell reached that town in June as staff officer to the commander of a relief force, soon after that taking part in a cavalry charge against a Matabele *impi,* or regiment, sending the rebels into retreat in the moonscape of the Matopo Hills where Baden-Powell organized their pursuit.

From London in early 1897, he headed out to India to take command of the 5th Dragoon Guards, consolidating his reputation as a forward-looking officer with a method for training military scouts. In mid-1898, he became acting major general of the regiment and by 1899 was set for promotion to brigadier-general.[21] But the brewing conflict in South Africa intervened, and in the summer of 1899, while on leave in London, Baden-Powell was called into the War Office by Wolseley, who told him to leave in days for South Africa to see to the defense of Mafeking, an obscure but strategic rail depot on the line from Cape Town to Rhodesia.

Mafeking was not much to look at—a thousand-yard-square rectangle of tin-roofed houses and offices of sun-baked mud. Its

1,700 European inhabitants were keenly aware of the standoff between Britain and the Transvaal Republic starting eight miles to the east. Railway workers and idlers at the Mafeking depot that July took note of a small group of Britons arriving from Cape Town. Though dressed in civilian clothes, their bearing was military, and it soon became an open secret that they constituted an advance military party sent to prepare Mafeking against Boer attack. The identity of their compact senior officer also became known: Brevet-Colonel Robert S.S. Baden-Powell.

His orders from Wolseley were: "To raise two regiments of mounted cavalry; to organize the defense of the Rhodesia and Bechuanaland frontiers; as far as possible to keep forces of the enemy occupied in this direction away from their own main forces."[22] These instructions did not call for Mafeking's fortification and defense. But as Baden-Powell considered the likely balance of forces and the rugged terrain favoring the mobile Boers, as well as Mafeking's strategic value, he concluded that a defensive posture was the most sensible option.[23]

But it would not be easy to protect Mafeking against a determined assault. He pushed out the town's defenses to create a more effective field of fire against Boer attackers and discourage sniping, resulting in a five-mile perimeter of eight-foot-deep trenches manned by around 1,000 troops, including local recruits.[24]

As much as these preparations, Baden-Powell's self-possession bolstered local morale. "He is eminently a man of determination, of great physical endurance and capacity, and of extraordinary reticence," wrote Angus Hamilton, correspondent for the *London Times*. "Outwardly, he maintains an impenetrable screen of self-control, observing with a cynical smile the foibles and caprices of those around him. He seems ever bracing himself to be on guard against a moment in which he should be swept by some unnatural and spontaneous enthusiasm, in which by a word, by an expression of face, by a movement, or in the turn of a phrase, he should betray the rigours of the self-control under which he lives."[25]

The first contact with the enemy came on October 14 with a skirmish several miles north of town. A small detachment of British scouts exchanged fire with the enemy, then fell back. After shelling Mafeking for three hours, Boer commander General Piet Cronje sent a messenger under a white flag to demand its immediate surrender "to avoid further bloodshed." Baden-Powell's officers gave the envoy a beer and sent him back to the Boer lines.[26] At least initially, Boer artillery proved ineffective. Some days later, Baden-Powell sent a messenger through the Boer lines to Bulawayo, several hundred miles to the northwest.

"All well," he reported. "Four hours' bombardment. One dog killed."[27]

The London newspapers seized on this laconic reply as an exemplar of British understatement and fighting spirit. The town was well on its way to becoming an obsession with the public. Readers hungered for details about the colonel leading its defense.[28] As 1899 closed, Mafeking had assumed outsized importance for British public morale, deflated by early military setbacks. Mafeking's defense became, for Fleet Street, a symbol of indefatigable British will, focusing the attention of the Empire on its commander.

The siege of Mafeking would last for 217 days. Baden-Powell did all that he could do from the outset to take the fight to the enemy. His aggressive stance in the initial stage deterred Cronje from launching a determined frontal assault on paper-thin defensive lines. In October-November 1899, Baden-Powell sent out seven raiding parties at a fairly high cost in casualties.[29] He bluffed Cronje into believing the garrison and fortifications were stronger than they actually were. He built dummy forts and guns, and the town's sole searchlight was rushed back and forth along the perimeter, discouraging a night assault.[30] Boys organized as "cadets" carried despatches to the front lines on bicycles and otherwise assisted the defense.

Eventually Mafeking settled into the grim realities of life under siege. Despite the large food stocks Baden-Powell had piled up before Mafeking was encircled, rationing went into effect in November for the 1,708 European men, women, and children. Meat supplies were replenished with animals "killed by shellfire or other enemy action," reported the *Mafeking Mail,* the town's newspaper.[31]

Yet as sieges went, Mafeking was hardly a desperate struggle for survival. Six months into the siege, a friend of Baden-Powell was captured trying to approach the town with a relief column. Under a white flag, Baden-Powell sent amenities to the prisoner including "cocoa, wine, a soft mattress, hairbrushes, books, mosquito curtains, eau de cologne, soup, lemonade, stamps, stationery and money."[32]

The siege seemed close to being lifted by early May 1900.[33] One column of relievers was moving up from the south; another approached by a circuitous route through present-day Mozambique into Rhodesia (destined to become Zimbabwe in 1980), picking up a train in Bulawayo to a point 60 miles north of Mafeking.

On May 16, the town's defenders heard shots far off as the relievers clashed with the Boer siege force. Baden-Powell received confirmation by carrier pigeon that the column was in striking distance.[34] Around 2:00 a.m. on May 17, British scouts galloped into the main square, soon followed by the main force.[35]

Baden-Powell[36] sent a telegram to Queen Victoria later that morning. "Happy to report . . . Mafeking successfully relieved today. Relieving forces marched into Mafeking this morning at nine. Relief and defense forces combined, attacked enemy laager, shelled them out, and took large amounts of weapons and stores. Townspeople and garrison . . . heartily grateful for their release."[37]

The Queen instantly promoted Baden-Powell to major general. "I and my whole Empire greatly rejoice at the relief of Mafeking after the splendid defence made by you through all these months," the Empress of India wrote.[38]

The news spread through London on May 18. At Mansion House, a large colored image of Baden-Powell hung from a balcony, the Lord Mayor read a declaration and thousands burst into "Rule

Britannia," "God Save the Queen," and "Soldiers of the Queen."[39] The celebrations in England lasted five days, adding a new word to the language: "mafficking," or riotous celebration.[40] Euphoria ensued around the Empire. Canadian towns "went wild with patriotic fervor." Australians fired guns, rang bells, and poured into the streets.

Some of Baden-Powell's fellow officers did not share wholeheartedly in the national joy. "To burrow underground on the very first shot being fired in a campaign, and to commence eating his horses, seemed to me the strangest role ever played by a cavalry leader"[41] remarked one cynic. But Major-General Robert Baden-Powell at the age of forty-three had the world at his feet.[42]

Baden-Powell's fame took particular hold among British schoolboys, who had devoured *Aids to Scouting for NCOs and Men,* the pocket-sized book published under his name during the siege. Baden-Powell finished correcting proofs soon after arriving in Mafeking in July 1899, sending revisions back to his London publisher, Gale & Polden, with the terse instruction, "Publish it."[43] The manual's red cover noted the author's precarious situation in Mafeking, informing readers that "The Corrected Proofs of this Book accompanied the last Despatches that got through the Boer Lines." Though intended for soldiers, sales were brisk to boys eager to emulate the intrepid Mafeking commander.[44] The *Illustrated News* reported in mid-siege that the book "touches the imagination and really makes one eager to join the hazardous profession of scout."[45]

When Baden-Powell returned to England in 1901 on sick leave, several boys' groups had already arisen in his name: the Baden-Powell Boys of Greenock, the Baden-Powell Brigade of the Primitive Methodists' Sunday School Union, and the Baden-Powell Anti-Cigarette League. The press attributed to him a special connection with youth. In September 1900, four months after Mafeking's relief, one Cape Town journalist would write somewhat fulsomely that Baden-Powell's "love for children is perhaps his ruling passion. He is never happier than when surrounded by them and joining in their amusements."[46]

Baden-Powell's triumph fired up sales of *Aids to Scouting*. A magazine called *Boys of the Empire* secured serial rights, publishing the first installment near the end of 1900. Although the British captured Johannesburg just two weeks after relieving Mafeking, and annexed the Transvaal in September 1900, a guerrilla war dragged on through May 1902, sustaining interest in the manual.[47]

"Scouting is a thing that can be learnt but cannot be taught," Baden-Powell advised readers of *Aids to Scouting*. "A man must pick up much of it for himself by his own effort," he cautioned, but those who are determined "not only take to it with the greatest keenness, but [become] quite equal to many of the colonial scouts bred and trained on the prairie." The language could not have been better calculated to appeal to a youthful sense of adventure. The British scout had to be superior to all others, "because he is called upon to act not only against civilized enemies in civilized countries . . . but he has to take on the crafty Afghan in his mountains, or the fierce Zulu in the open South African downs, the Burmese in his forests, the Soudanese on the Egyptian desert—all requiring different methods of working, but their efficiency depending in every case on the same factor, the pluck and ability of the scout himself."[48]

Chapter headings such as "Pluck, Self-Reliance, and Discretion" resonated powerfully with youthful readers. "The pluck required of a scout is of a very high order," Baden-Powell declared. A soldier taking part in a charge is considered to be a hero, but he has "comrades all around him and officers directing," he observed. "How much higher, then, is the pluck of the single scout who goes on some risky enterprise, alone, on his own account, taking his life in his hand, when it is quite possible for him to go back without anybody being the wiser," he wrote. "Such pluck is very much the result of confidence in himself."[49] Confidence was "the secret ingredient" he had displayed to such great effect at Mafeking.[50]

Baden-Powell showed himself to be a capable field tactician in later military engagements, but managed to fall out of favor with his superiors. In late August 1900, he was detached from the command structure by Lord Roberts, who assigned him to establish a constabulary to keep the peace in the Transvaal, the Orange River Colony, and Swaziland. This duty squared with his conviction that effective pacification strategies were needed to bring the conflict to an end. The British command turned to more brutal measures including the establishment of concentration camps for Boer civilians. But Baden-Powell envisioned a more humane and effective approach.[51]

Setting up headquarters in Zuurfontein, Transvaal, in early 1901, Baden-Powell exhorted his officers and troops to behave as "men of honour," putting his personal stamp on the unit in everything from its tactics to its distinctive uniform, which included an American-made Stetson hat.[52] Some historians maintain that Baden-Powell's "peace army" facilitated the Treaty of Vereeniging that ended the war in May 1902. The Boers saw his troops as occupiers, but they also delivered mail and inoculated both children and livestock against disease.[53]

Baden-Powell had proven himself a thinking man's soldier with diplomatic skills. In 1902, he was named Inspector General of Cavalry, a prestigious post with broad strategic and planning powers. Not only British adolescents had found *Aids to Scouting* good reading; Roberts once remarked that it was "quite the best book I have ever read on scouting, and is undoubtedly clever."[54]

Ensconced at the War Office, Baden-Powell divided his time between inspecting cavalry units in the British Isles, South Africa, and Egypt and more mundane duties—pinning medals on veterans and inspecting youth groups.[55] One such engagement took him in April

1904 to Glasgow, Scotland, for a parade drill of the Boys' Brigade, a military-religious group whose founder, former soldier William Alexander Smith, sought to encourage "the advancement of . . . all that tends towards a true Christian Manliness."[56] By 1904, there were 54,000 Brigade boys in Britain alone. Some 11,000 Glaswegians applauded as the proto-soldiers bearing toy guns marched past the reviewing stand "carrying their heads erect, and maintaining a well-balanced line."[57] Baden-Powell ventured to Smith that his membership should have been much larger by then. Smith challenged Baden-Powell to develop his own program for boys based on *Aids to Scouting.*

Baden-Powell suggested the creation of Brigade patrols emphasizing fitness and the development of powers of observation.[58] "I believe that if some form of scout training could be devised in the Brigade it would be very popular and could do a great amount of good," he wrote. Practice "noting and remembering details of strangers, contents of shop windows, appearance of new streets" would sharpen a boy's wits and "make him quick to read character and feelings, and thus help him to be a better sympathizer with his fellow-man."[59]

Through 1904 he mulled over such ideas and in December published a letter in the *Eton College Chronicle* proposing an organization for boys based, somewhat oddly, on the model of the medieval knight, rather than a military scout. Boys would be called on to do a good turn for their country and cultivate patriotism. Still very much the soldier, Baden-Powell suggested that if two hundred volunteers agreed to train ten boys each, "we should have 2,000 retainers trained and ready to defend their country the moment that Government wanted them and put a rifle in their hands."[60]

World War I was a decade away, but even as the Boer War came to an end, fears arose that England was vulnerable to German attack. Military preparedness and conscription were hotly debated between the National Service League on the right and pacifists on the left. Baden-Powell fretted about a "bolt from the blue" invasion by the German army across the English Channel.

Yet even as a military man, Baden-Powell marched to a different drummer. Fellow officers in his constabulary alluded to his "happy talk"—notions of human potential and the betterment of society. Delivering a lecture in Johannesburg after the war ended, he told some teachers that "one ought to take as much pleasure as one possibly can [in life] because if one is happy, one has it in one's power to make all those around happy." The soldier and the idealist co-existed, but Baden-Powell was finding increasingly more satisfaction in training boys than grappling with the British general staff.[61] His buoyant philosophy of life found attentive listeners, among them publisher and philanthropist Cyril Arthur Pearson, owner of the *Daily Express* and *Evening Standard* newspapers. A self-made man, Pearson had risen from obscurity propelled by a genius for promotion. In July 1906, Baden-Powell spent a weekend at Pearson's estate in Surrey. The millionaire was receptive to Baden-Powell's proposal for a scout manual.

Around that same time that Baden-Powell received in the post an unsolicited copy of *The Birch-Bark Roll of the Woodcraft Indians.*

CHAPTER 4

SCOUTING FOR BOYS

Though the tremendous success of *Aids to Scouting* led Baden-Powell down the path to youth training, he had failed to recognize what in his manual appealed so strongly to youthful readers—his detailed tips on scouting—and gone off track adopting the medieval knight as the model for his envisioned organization. Seton's *Birch-Bark Roll* seems to have opened Baden-Powell's eyes to the opportunity he was close to missing, though his initial response to its author gave no indication of its influence on his thinking.

Both men voiced concern about the deleterious effect of modern life on the health and character of youth. In the *Birch-Bark Roll,* Seton declared that "the whole nation is turning toward the outdoor life, seeking in it the physical regeneration so needful for continued national existence."[1] But his manifesto differed from other works for boys in its abundance of information on nature, animals, camping and Indian lore, and games to hold their interest while instructing them on life and manhood. Most youth organizations of the day were long on regimentation and short on fun, and Baden-Powell like many others had failed to see the outdoors as a training ground for life.[2]

He responded to Seton on August 1, telling him he was "sincerely grateful to you for your kindness in forwarding me your interesting *Birch Bark*." He said he had himself been developing "a scheme with a handbook to it, for the education of boys as scouts—which essentially runs along the same lines of yours." He told Seton he would "very much like to meet you if you are at any time in England."[3] Baden-Powell wrote again that September to say that he was "delighted to hear that I may soon have the pleasure of meeting you over here."[4]

Seton and Baden-Powell met for the first time on October 30, 1906, at the Savoy Hotel in London, Seton's base in England. Baden-Powell, forty-nine, and Seton, forty-six, exchanged ideas and agreed to meet again. Seton lectured around England well into December, and although Baden-Powell proposed one date after another for a second meeting, none was arranged.[5] The day after their lunch at the Savoy, Baden-Powell sent Seton a note enclosing "preliminary notice which I sent out early this year regarding my scheme of 'Boy Scouts.' " This was the memo on "Scouting for Boys" he had sent Boys' Brigade founder William Smith. "You will see that our principles seem practically identical," he told Seton. "If we can work together in the same direction I [shall] be very glad indeed—for there are very great possibilities before us." He separately mailed Seton a copy of *Aids to Scouting*.[6] Seton was effusive and self-effacing in his response on November 3. "I am not at all surprised that [*Aids to Scouting*] has run through so many editions. It is exactly the sort of thing that I am trying to carry on in America, though of course my experience has been very trifling."

Seton enthused about the American Indian as a model for youth. "Among the Indians generally the Grey Wolf is considered the ideal scout, because he sees everything and no one sees him," he wrote. "The Wolf, then, is the badge of their Scouting Order." Indians camouflaged themselves with a wolf's pelt, he noted, so "when they have to peer over a hill . . . they pass for a wolf if detected."

As for Baden-Powell's prospectus, Seton declared that it was "admirable throughout as an idea, and cannot fail of wide acceptance throughout this country as well as America." He signed with his name and a sketched wolf paw.[7]

That November Baden-Powell repeatedly proposed further meetings, asking Seton for his schedule of lectures so he might attend one. "When? Where?" he inquired. "You must eat at some time I suppose—so possibly you might do so with me either before or after [a lecture]—at any convenient spot."[8] But their schedules did not coincide. Baden-Powell said he was studying the *Birch-Bark Roll* section on tracking "with great interest," indicating that he would "like very much to quote it in my remarks to boys on the subject," noting that he had made similar points in *Aids to Scouting,* though without Seton's illustrations.

Baden-Powell added that he would be in London November 12 to 14, but again the two failed to connect.[9] They agreed tentatively to meet in Acton, where Seton was to speak, but that did not happen. Baden-Powell meanwhile was promoting his own initiative. "Last night I had a splendid audience of 1500 boys, and tonight we expect 2000," he told Seton. "I have broken the ice with them on the subject of Scouting."[10] Baden-Powell kept trying to coordinate schedules. On December 10, he wrote that "some friends of mine are passing through . . . and specially want me to come and dine with them—the only chance I shall get to see them." But if there were no alternative date, he told Seton, "I will give up my friends!"[11]

Given Seton's enthusiasm at their first meeting, it is surprising he could not find the time for a follow-up. Seton's schedule may have been too tight, but it is also possible he wanted to see how far he could get on his own before throwing in with Baden-Powell. That he wished to proceed independently is suggested by a letter he sent to Lord Roberts on December 8, 1906, indicating he wanted to "bring to your notice a matter which I believe will prove of great interest to you." Seton said he had established "two thousand separate camps" in which boys learned to ride, swim, camp, and shoot. "Everything is done . . . to make them competent outdoor men in time of peace, and first-class available material for time of war."[12] He asked for a meeting to explain how this "might prove a powerful auxiliary to the work to which you yourself are devoting so much time."[13]

But Seton appears not to have secured such a meeting with Roberts, returning to the United States later that month. Seton and Baden-Powell were not to meet again until early 1908. By then what initially had seemed a promising collaboration would take on a competitive—even litigious—aspect.

In early 1907, Baden-Powell's inspection duties took him far afield to Egypt and South Africa. In February, on the border between Egypt and Sudan, Baden-Powell put the last touches on two documents in which he gave his envisioned organization the name of "Boy Scouts." Though he would later say the name had come to him of its own, it had been used in promotional materials for a 1900 serialization of *Aids to Scouting* in *Boys of the Empire,* a magazine for boys whose editor lifted it from a rival publication, *The True Blue War Library,* which in 1900 chronicled the adventures of cavalry officer Harry St. George, the "Boy Scout," whose path led him into the South African Constabulary.[14]

"I am now quietly working up my scheme for Boy Scouts with most flattering encouragement from various authorities," he told Seton later that year, describing Pearson's holdings and seeking Seton's advice as to letting himself be "taken in hand by a big newspaper actuated largely by patriotic motives." He was also "gathering more opinions" and writing a manual "much on the lines" of *Aids to Scouting.* Baden-Powell assured Seton he would acknowledge citations from the *Birch-Bark Roll* and be sure to "copyright any whole-sale extracts in your name."[15]

Reassured by Baden-Powell's seeming desire to collaborate fur-ther and by the pledge to acknowledge his contributions, Seton closely studied the Scouting proposals. One, called "Boy Scouts, A Suggestion," confirmed they were now on the same track. Quoting a British politician who declared that the same forces that caused the fall of Rome were undermining Britain, Baden-Powell offered his plan for "putting on a positive footing the development, moral and physical, of boys of all creeds and classes, by a means which should appeal to them while offending as little as possible the susceptibili-ties of their elders," promoting "observation and deduction, chivalry, patriotism, self-sacrifice, personal hygiene, saving life, self-reliance, etc., etc."[16] Seton would have been reassured by the statement that "A somewhat similar idea was started in America a short time back by Mr. Ernest Thompson Seton, and has already attained phenom-enal success."[17]

In May 1907, Baden-Powell was promoted to lieutenant general and placed on reserve at half pay of £850 a year, a comfortable though not lavish income. He now had ample time to devote to "that Scouting fad," which Pearson was eager to develop through a Scouting manual. He informed Baden-Powell that he wanted to bring it out in serial form starting in January 1908, which would help to gauge the demand for a book published in time for the summer camping season.[18]

The ever-methodical Baden-Powell wanted first, however, to test his scheme and had found just the place to do so. On a fishing trip to Ireland that spring he met stockbroker Charles van Raalte, owner of a castle on a 500-acre island in Poole Harbor, on England's west coast. Baden-Powell knew Brownsea Island from his younger days and readily accepted Van Raalte's offer to allow him to use it as the staging ground for an experimental Scouting camp.[19]

Under pressure from his impatient publishing sponsor Pearson, Baden-Powell threw himself into completing his Scouting manual in a cottage on Wimbledon Common, London, the property of yet another affluent connection, complete with cooks and servants. He stayed there for ten days writing and dictating the draft.[20] On July 18, Baden-Powell breakfasted with Pearson, who presented him with a sheaf of stationary headed: "Boy Scouts, Scout Camp, Brownsea Island, Poole." All Baden-Powell needed now were some experimental scouts: he recruited the sons of upper-class friends from Eton and Harrow and enlisted working-class Boys Brigade members from Poole and Bournemouth, adding his nine-year-old nephew Donald for a total of 22 campers. His entire staff consisted of a comrade from his military days and an editor Pearson sent to observe the experiment for one day.[21]

On July 29, 1907, Baden-Powell, his military associate and the older campers raised a cook tent and an open-sided ridge tent for foul weather.[22] Two days later, after an opening campfire, Baden-Powell divided the boys into four patrols—the Wolves, the Bulls, the Curlews, and the Ravens. Each boy pinned an eighteen-inch colored wool streamer on his left shoulder indicating his patrol and sported a brass fleur-de-lis pin. Each patrol received a triangular flag with an animal drawn by Baden-Powell in green ink.[23] On August 1, the first full day in camp, the Scouts underwent tests in knot tying, tracking, flag lore, and so on. Then Baden-Powell presented each with a scroll-shaped brass pin bearing the words, "Be Prepared."

Each morning at 6 a.m., Baden-Powell emerged from his tent to sound a blast on a kudu horn acquired in his 1896 Matabele Campaign. The boys ate a biscuit with milk, washed, then cleaned the campsite and settled down to a demonstration of skills such as signaling, first aid, and tracking. After the raising of the flag—the Union Jack that had flown over Mafeking attached to a cavalry lance stuck in the ground in front of Baden-Powell's tent—came a half hour of physical drills and a proper breakfast at 8 a.m. sharp. Scouting exercises, games, and bathing in the sea took the campers up to 12:30 p.m.[24] The Scouting pioneers rested after lunch for an hour and a quarter, then launched into patrol competitions and games based on the theme of the day. Following tea at 5 p.m. and supper at 8 p.m.

came the high point of the day: a one-hour campfire presided over by Baden-Powell.[25]

After presenting the Scouting topic for the next day, Baden-Powell held the boys in thrall with yarns from his past. "I can still see him, as he stands in the flickering light of the fire—an alert figure, full of the joy of life—answering all manner of questions, imitating the call of birds, showing how to stalk an animal, fleshing out a little story, dancing and singing around the fire," recalled Percy Everett, the editor Pearson had dispatched to the camp.

Following the campfire, were fifteen minutes of prayers followed by lights out at 9:30. Later in the week, he set the twenty-two Edwardian boys to a survival test, each patrol wandering off with uncooked rations to fend for itself for a day.[26]

The camp ended on August 8 with parents present. The Scouts displayed the skills they had learned, and staged a tug-of-war contest, earning much applause. After the demonstrations, van Raalte invited everyone to his castle for a filling tea, with a local brass band playing on the terrace.[27]

The next morning, Baden-Powell dashed off a last letter, declaring the camp "a great success but hardish work."[28] Then he returned to Wimbledon Common to finish his manual, called *Scouting for Boys.* He corrected proofs in early January and Pearson sent the first installment to British newsstands on January 15, 1908.[29]

The little publication was packed with adventure and intrigue. The cover featured a sketch of a boy with Scout hat and stave peering from behind a boulder at a mysterious ship in the distance. Inside were Campfire Yarns that described the feats of the Mafeking Cadet Corps, a condensed version of Rudyard Kipling's *Kim,* and a play about explorer American colonist Captain John Smith, a forbear of Baden-Powell's, and his Jamestown romance with Pocahontas. High adventure was brought to thousands of British youth at a mere four pence an issue.[30]

The first installment quickly sold out and the second, published January 29, was eagerly awaited by readers. By April, Pearson was urging Baden-Powell to produce a weekly paper called *The Scout* to capitalize on public interest. Pearson promoted the publication energetically, inserting coupons promising the reward of a summer camp outing with Baden-Powell for the thirty boys sending in the most subscription orders.[31] Soon Baden-Powell was receiving expressions of interest from the entire British Empire and beyond, including the United States.[32]

Nine days after *Scouting for Boys* went on sale, Baden-Powell sent word to Seton that "we are going on with my scheme like your 'Woodcraft Indians.' And it promises well."[33] He made no mention of *Scouting for Boys,* though his letter was on Boy Scouts stationery displaying a fleur-de-lis and the organization's slogan, "Be Prepared." Baden-Powell added, "I hope you will allow me to make frequent mention of yourself and your tribes as an example to the Scouts." He urged Seton to stop in "for a chat" the next time he visited England. "I should like to get you to come and dine and meet some of my friends."[34]

Seton arrived in England the following month and the two men traded notes as they traveled from one lecture engagement to another. "Do tell me your moves," Baden-Powell wrote. "I should so much like to meet you again and have a chat, and get you to meet some people who would interest you." Finally Baden-Powell invited Seton to dine March 1 at his home in Prince's Gate, Kensington, London. "No party, just my brother and sister, 8 o'clock," he told Seton. "I should be so glad if you will."[35] Seton accepted, and by all accounts it was an agreeable meal with Baden-Powell and his sister Agnes— none of his brothers appeared.[36] Yet even then, Baden-Powell made no mention of *Scouting for Boys,* preferring instead to post a copy of the work to Seton at his hotel the following day.

Upon inspecting it, Seton was "astounded," he later wrote, "to find all my ideas taken, all my games appropriated, disguised with new names, the essentials of my plan utilized, and not a word of acknowledgment to me, or explanation why I should be left out of a movement I began."[37] Seton dashed off "a friendly letter of protest"[38] to which Baden-Powell did not reply until March 14.

"I much regret that I should have omitted mentioning the source of several of the games," he told Seton. He had made a "general statement" acknowledging the source of the games, but had moved it to the end of the book, not considering that readers would only see this after they had absorbed the material. "I very much regret this oversight, and it is most kind of you to have taken it in the good natured way in which you have done."[39]

Seton was somewhat mollified, but did not remain so. Baden-Powell's acknowledgment in the final installment of *Scouting for Boys* consisted of a note stating that several games were "founded" on those Seton described in his *Birch-Bark Roll.* Nor was Seton satisfied with his credits in the book version of *Scouting for Boys,* consisting of brief allusions in ten chapters to his work.

"I have gone carefully over your 'Scouting for Boys,' and note that you grudgingly admit having got 'a few details' from me," he later wrote. "Therefore, I make this emphatic general statement: Omitting the actual stories . . . there is not an important idea in 'Scouting for Boys' that I did not publish years ago in 'Two Little Savages,' 'The Birch-Bark Roll' and my Woodcraft and Scouting articles of which I furnished you with copies. The only important change you make is to give things new names and assume their authorship for yourself."[40]

Seton perhaps overstated the case, but had a legitimate grievance. Many elements of Baden-Powell's book appeared to have been lifted from the *Birch-Bark Roll.* Whether this amounted to plagiarism would remain a controversial subject within Scouting, pitting "Setonites" against "Baden-Powellites."

Yet the similarities were extensive. Woodcraft Indians passed a series of tests to become "first class braves." Scouts similarly graduated from "second class" to "first class." Woodcraft included mastery of knots, fire making, first aid, hiking, and reading wilderness signs; so did *Scouting for Boys.* Seton listed proficiency tests by which Indians earned "honors," twenty-four of which qualified a member as a

"Sachem." In Scouting, the acquisition of twenty-four honor badges brought the status of "Silver Wolf." Seton's Woodcraft Indians took a Vow and obeyed ten laws; Baden-Powell's Scouts took an Oath and followed nine laws.

New Indians received a horsehair "scalp" signifying personal honor; it could be lost through failure in a competition or task, and later regained upon approval by the Tribe Council. The First Class badge of Scouting could similarly be lost, then regained by a good deed as certified by a Court of Honor.

Seton told the Woodcraft Indian: "Hold your word of honour sacred." The First Law of Scouting was, "A Scout's Honour is to be trusted." Seton's Indians were to "Be helpful," while a Scout's duty was "to be useful and to help others." Seton told his Indians: "Obedience is the first duty of the Woodcrafter." Baden-Powell wrote: "A Scout obeys orders of his patrol leader or Scoutmaster without question." The *Birch-Bark Roll* instructed Woodcraft Indians: "Be joyful. Seek the joy of being alive." Similarly, according to *Scouting for Boys,* "A scout goes about with a smile on him and whistling. It cheers him and cheers other people, especially in times of danger, for he keeps it up all the same."

Setonites also reproached Baden-Powell for lifting games from the novel *Two Little Savages,* which Seton had sent him along with the *Birch-Bark Roll.* Seton's "Quicksight" game helped Woodcrafters develop their powers of observation by counting the spots on a card flashed before their eyes; Scouts learned the game as "Spottyface." Other games seemed to have been adopted by Baden-Powell, and though some were common, others appeared to have come straight from the pages of the *Birch-Bark Roll* with, as Seton complained, mere changes in name.

Thus opened a dispute that was to embitter Seton's relations with Baden-Powell and in time poison his relationship with the Scouting movement. Baden-Powell would later admit to having "cribbed" some elements from *The Birch-Bark Roll of the Woodcraft Indians,* and would over time acknowledge some debt to Seton. But he would never concede that fundamental aspects of Scouting were based on the Woodcraft Indians foundation Seton had earlier laid down.[41]

Historians of Scouting and biographers of the two men would divide on this issue, and in more recent years, as hagiographies of Baden-Powell gave way to more critical accounts of his life and leadership of Scouting, Seton would be more widely recognized for his contribution to Scouting. But from 1908 onward, Seton was to experience enormous frustration not only at being eclipsed by the Hero of Mafeking as Scouting became an international phenomenon, but by the dilution and eventual marginalization of concepts that he considered integral to the experience of nature and the development of authentic character in boys.

Some of the borrowed elements might seem trivial—and to be sure Baden-Powell very skillfully blended life instruction, patriotic sentiments, military arts, suspenseful tales, and woodcraft tips in a mix that British youth could not resist. But Seton clearly had brought to Baden-Powell key ingredients that were lacking in the first iterations of his concept for a youth training program.

Above all, Seton helped Baden-Powell understand that the experience of nature, beyond its intrinsic value, could be a powerful catalyst in developing and shaping young minds. From that it was a short leap for Baden-Powell to see that packaging the moral, ethical, and patriotic exhortations of his Scouting concept in the outdoors experience would increase the effectiveness of such messages. And emphasizing wilderness skills over military drill helped Baden-Powell shift away from his earlier martial conception of the movement. The objective of ensuring Britain's youth could take up the defense of the nation remained a selling point in dealings with establishment figures. But once Baden-Powell had the prospect of sponsorship by a philanthropist like Pearson, more emphasis could be placed on the humanistic and social benefits, as Seton had done from the outset.

Had Baden-Powell merely absorbed Seton's underlying philosophy and from there crafted his own solutions to the challenges of shaping the Scouting movement to attract a mass membership while achieving his higher ends, there would have been little basis for controversy. Seton would have been an influence like any of the other thinkers Baden-Powell cited in rebutting Seton's accusations: Epictetus, Livy, and Rousseau disciple Johann Pestalozzi, a proponent of child learning through spontaneous, self-driven activity, among others.[42]

But Seton's thinking was embodied in the specificity of the activities he devised for his Indians, as Baden-Powell biographer Michael Rosenthal notes in following the progression in Baden-Powell's approach between June 1906—when the *Boys Brigade Gazette* published his thoughts on "Scouting for Boys"—and his 1907 "Summary of a Scheme," in effect the outline for *Scouting for Boys.*

Although Baden-Powell's *Boys Brigade Gazette* article showed "substantial progress" toward the eventual concept of Scouting, Rosenthal contends that the idea "still lacked, among other things, a practicable structure." The next key date in the evolution of Baden-Powell's thinking was February 1907, when he issued a paper on "Boy Patrols." This "marks the complete conceptualization of the Scout movement," Rosenthal contends, deducing that Seton's *Birch-Bark Roll* must have come as a startling revelation and a catalyst for Baden-Powell.

The *Birch-Bark Roll* offered "a coherent scheme for organizing boys into manageable self-governing units. Its detailed system of outdoor training, its rules, honors, games, noncompetitive standards of excellence, and even its philosophy that 'manhood, not scholarship, is the first aim of education,' could not have failed to kindle Baden-Powell's imagination about the possibilities for his own Scouting aspirations. However conscientious Baden-Powell may have been about acknowledging his sources (and in fact he was not overly scrupulous about it), the extraordinary appropriateness of Seton's Indians to what Baden-Powell was hoping to achieve could not have easily been resisted. Beneath the Indian trappings, for which Baden-Powell had no use, lurked an organizational model that provided solutions for almost every problem he faced and that . . . could be translated into the language of Scouting without difficulty."[43]

Seton shared some blame in the matter. He might have been justified in reproaching Baden-Powell, but was naive in his initial dealings with him, says Seton biographer Betty Keller. His vestigial British patriotism disposed him to confide in Baden-Powell, inadvisably so. "Always eager to rub shoulders with the rich and famous, always anxious to increase his own status by associating with the 'right' people, Seton had taken Baden-Powell at the value placed upon him by the press and the adoring British public during the Boer War." Seton saw in the hero of Mafeking what he yearned to be, an urbane upper-class Englishman. But, "if Seton had realized that beneath that urbane exterior lay a man with 'dedicated and almost frenzied ambition,' he would never have put a copy of *The Birch-Bark Roll* in his hands, or been surprised at his actions when he did get a hold of it."[44]

Even after Seton concluded Baden-Powell had plagiarized his work, he did not pursue the matter as a breach of copyright, instead obsessing over the perceived wrong and damaging his relations with associates who might have been more sympathetic had he been more reasonable. And there is more than a grain of truth to Baden-Powell biographer Tim Jeal's contention that while the founder of Scouting borrowed liberally and was "none too scrupulous" in his early dealings with his would-be partner, what vexed Seton most was to see his Indians become "an irrelevant curiosity" as Scouting's success later blossomed.

"In his heart Seton must have known that . . . Baden-Powell created a world entirely different from that of the Woodcraft Indians," says Jeal. "The world of the Red Indian was a restricted place in comparison with the vast region over which the Boy Scout's imagination was invited to wander."[45] Baden-Powell "did his utmost to conciliate," but the insecure, envious Seton would not be placated.

And it is also true that Baden-Powell came up with much that was innovative and even brilliant in *Scouting for Boys* beyond what he appropriated from Seton. The book's huge impact was as much due to Baden-Powell's ingenious packaging as to Seton's creative ideas. In retrospect, *Scouting for Boys* could be seen as a hugely successful collaboration—though one that came about without Seton's consent and for which he failed to receive proper credit in his lifetime.

Seton's resentment at the unauthorized incorporation of his concepts in *Scouting for Boys* would increase as sales of the book soared and Scouting took hold in England and internationally, swelling Baden-Powell's reputation. Seton seems to have given Baden-Powell the benefit of the doubt; their correspondence remained superficially friendly through 1908. "My Dear Thompson Seton," wrote Baden-Powell in June. "I am much obliged to you for your encouraging note. The [Scouts] are going splendidly in every part of the country without much help from myself since I have now assumed my other work in the Territorial Forces." The British secretary of state for war, Richard Haldane, had called on Baden-Powell to assume temporary command of the Territorial Forces in Northumbria.[46]

Scouting as an organization was starting to take off on the back of brisk sales of *Scouting for Boy,* which came out in book form in May 1908 and went through four printings in its first year.[47] Baden-Powell signed copies for the British royal family, and sent several to Theodore Roosevelt, who would "easily find worthy recipients" for them.[48] Baden-Powell was not entirely happy with Pearson's role in the venture.[49] But he was contractually bound and owed much of his success to Pearson's marketing genius. "We are having camps in a great many districts now which I hope will give them a real practical training in the work which they have taken up," Baden-Powell wrote Seton. "I hope we shall see you here again this year and that I may have the chance of a chat and a comparison of notes."[50]

Baden-Powell made another conciliatory move in early July, writing to Seton enclosing "a request which I have received from America regarding the publication of my book on 'Scouting for Boys' in your country." He assured him he was "unwilling to go on with it for fear of interfering with" Seton's Indians. "If however, you should like to take up the book, I should be very glad to co-operate with you and you could effect such alterations in it as you thought desirable for your country."[51] Seton apparently was not interested, but offered Baden-Powell 900 copies of the 1906 edition of *The Birch-Bark Roll* still in stock at Doubleday as the revised 1907 version went on sale. Baden-Powell had a book of his own to sell, but he put an ad for the book in his organizational publication, *The Scout*.[52]

Seton, meanwhile, was having trouble taking his Woodcraft Indians to the next level. His editor at Doubleday, Henry Wysham Lanier, son of the Southern poet Sidney Lanier, suggested Seton contribute a monthly page to *Country Life* magazine giving parents tips on "how to get boys out of doors and interest them when you have them there." Such a column would bolster circulation and yield "practical results for your idea." Lanier also raised an issue that was to become increasingly problematic for Seton, declaring himself "more than ever convinced that the first step would be to get a better name" for the Woodcraft Indians. Too many Americans "think of Indians either as dirty and loafing degenerates, or as savages to make the idea popular" as an educational scheme, Lanier maintained.[53]

The editor pursued his proposal later that month, proposing an "Out-of-Doors Club, or something of that kind, with a little intimate word right under the title each month" from Seton to parents. Seton could offer tips on outdoor activities, emphasizing that woodcraft "isn't something abstruse and separated from the daily life of ordinary people, but that it is simply the knowledge of how to take care of oneself in the most normal and healthy surroundings that man or woman can have." This could lead to a book in Doubleday's *Every Child Ought to Know* series. "The more I think about this, the more I am convinced that one could do a big thing." Lanier enthused. Such a book could become a text for summer camps, he added, urging him to consider it and "let me know if you see the opportunity."[54]

Meanwhile, Doubleday along with Seton was becoming increasingly impatient with Baden-Powell: its London agent wrote to him to express concern over what seemed to be breaches of copyright. The communication caught Baden-Powell's attention and he responded in September 1909, saying "I regret exceedingly" having failed to credit Seton's *Birch-Bark Roll* properly in the introduction to his book.

But Baden-Powell added in his defense that "so far from giving no credit whatever to that gentleman, I have in the beginning of the book stated which games were taken from his book, and also have mentioned him on pages 9, 18, 38, 70, 76, 117, 139, 140 and 171. I hope it will be seen from this that there was no intention on my part to pirate any of his excellent work, but that, on the contrary, I was anxious to advertise it and make it more widely known to those interested in boys; and I hope that in this I have not been unsuccessful."

He added in a postscript that, "I have had many offers from the United States to publish our movement there . . . but I have always declined in order to avoid clashing with Mr. Thompson Seton's organization at work."[55]

When he next communicated with to Baden-Powell, Seton was mildly apologetic about the missive from Doubleday—but remained reproachful. Had he been consulted, "the letter would have been modified, but not exactly stopped," Seton told Baden-Powell. "I must say I have felt aggrieved over this matter."

Then Seton laid out the case against Baden-Powell that he would repeat and embellish for years to come, arguing that he had been "first in the field [which] should have been made clear when you were utilizing so many of my ideas and so much of my experience." The *Birch-Bark Roll* "in no essential" differed from *Scouting for Boys,* and "must have contributed to help you." But "you gave no hint of this. Next you have taken my games, Spearing the Sturgeon, Quick-Sight, Spot-the-Rabbit, Bear-Hunt, Hostile-Spy, made unimportant alterations in them, changing their names in most cases and giving them as though they were yours, in spite of the fact that these were invented slowly, developed in course of practice, and copyrighted solely by myself. This, you must admit, is not right," Seton declared. "They should have been given exactly as I left them and credited wholly to me. The changes made cannot have been the result of your experiences with them—are not improvements and look as though they were made to give a semblance of originality. This is one of the things that has riled the Publisher. It is an infringement on both the letter and the spirit of the copyright law and principle. But, more important to me, is the fact that you do not anywhere come out frankly and make it clear that for nine years I have been carrying on in America precisely the same movement founding camps and teaching woodcraft and scouting to the boys as a means of developing manliness and character."

Baden-Powell had promised to acknowledge the source of the materials, "but so far as I know have never done so." Seton acknowledged that Baden-Powell had cited the *Birch-Bark Roll,* adding that he felt "certain that it is not through any ill intent that the situation has arisen." In a conciliatory vein, Seton proposed further collaboration, and a division of markets for their works, Baden-Powell sticking to Britain and Seton to the United States. "If you like I will consult my publishers on this point," he offered.[56] But more than two months later, Baden-Powell had not answered this proposal. Seton wrote again enclosing a copy of the September 30 letter, urging his correspondent to "kindly let me hear from you at your earliest convenience, and oblige." Seton repeated his grievances, demanding that Baden-Powell "admit that [*Scouting for Boys*] was founded in my

Birch Bark Roll in all essential features and a great many of its details are taken direct."[57]

Having only feebly protested the unauthorized use of his material in 1908, Seton was now advancing unrealistic and unsupportable claims. His state of mind is clear in a December 1909 letter to *Ladies Home Journal* editor Edward Bok.[58] "I wonder if you noticed what Baden-Powell has done to me in England. I went over there, asked him to help me in establishing the boy camps, he came in as my assistant and now he has dropped me entirely and takes all the credit of the movement to himself. I must give him the credit of having made it a 'go' over there, but it passes my comprehension how he could steal all my plans and ideas and not say a word about where they came from." This was widely known among journalists, Seton told Bok, but he had discouraged articles about the dispute as, "I mean to give him every chance to make honorable amends."[59]

Baden-Powell made concessions in early 1910, telling Seton that he would acknowledge "my indebtedness to you for several details" in *Scouting for Boys*.[60] He inserted a note in *The Scout* "expressing indebtedness to that great authority on woodcraft [Seton] for his very valuable assistance. I hope that the future may bring opportunities for the Boy Scouts and their American cousins, the Woodcraft Indians, to . . . establish the bond of comradeship which ought to exist between them." But he then effectively nullified that acknowledgment, asserting that *Scouting for Boys* "was founded upon scouting for soldiers, which we started in India in 1898." Seton's book had merely yielded "several useful hints."[61]

Seton was dissatisfied with this response. That April he laid out his charges of plagiarism in an "Open Letter to General Sir Robert Baden-Powell" (though the communication was sent only to his adversary). Seton again listed the passages in *Scouting for Boys* where he believed his work had been appropriated. "I find little in your book that was not in mine and supplied by me to you," he wrote, declaring that "the serious charge I make is that the whole scheme was mine, copyrighted and published by me years before yours appeared." He conceded Baden-Powell might have had "some idea" of Scouting before their introduction, "but it was all in the air apparently, even in 1906, and not begun for a year or more later."

"No matter how much you may have had the general idea in mind independently, when you found that I was already in the field with the whole thing realized, your proper course was to acknowledge the same and work for the cause, if that was what you had at heart. It certainly was not right for you to come in as my assistant; then, *two years* later, take my fundamental ideas, all my work and methods, republish the substance of my books over your own name, and drop me out as soon as you thought you could go it alone."[62]

Yet Seton declared himself "satisfied that the situation has arisen without evil intent." He proposed "forgetting all that passed between us" on condition that the Scouting founder published "an amended statement in harmony with" the various stated grievances. Subsequent editions of *Scouting for Boys* he urged, should state that *The Birch-Bark Roll* was "incorporated, by arrangement." Baden-Powell would "refrain from introducing the book into America, including Canada." Seton would in turn fold portions of *Scouting for Boys* into *The Birch-Bark Roll.*[63] Such a combined manual would in fact appear not long after that in the United States—though not under the circumstances Seton might have desired.

Though Baden-Powell had implied he would refrain from promoting Scouting in the U.S. market, the publishing success of *Scouting for Boys* and international interest took the matter out of his hands. His Scouting found natural channels for expansion throughout the Empire and word also reached America. Within months of the first serialization of *Scouting for Boys,* troops had sprung up in Kentucky, New Jersey, and Kansas.[64] In May 1909, Episcopalian John Mitchell established one in Pawhuska, Oklahoma, instructing boys in camping, boxing, and military drill.[65] By August 1909, an Englishman in Chicago by the name of O.W. Kneeves was instructing his Scouts in outdoor basics in Hamilton Park and taking them on hikes through farm country beyond the ends of the city's elevated rail lines.[66]

Even as Kneeves and his boys tramped the Illinois plains, Chicago publisher William Dickson Boyce was on a path that would lead him in February 1910 to register the Boy Scouts of America as a corporation in Washington, D.C. Ernest Seton was to assume a central role in the new organization. However, his resentment of Baden-Powell and frustration at the progressive marginalization of the Woodcraft Indians would only deepen and intensify as Scouting put down roots in America.

CHAPTER 5

THE BOY SCOUTS OF AMERICA

L ondon in the closing days of 1909 should have been an agreeable place for a traveler to spend a few weeks. The holidays were in full flush with all the Edwardian trimmings and the theatres had rolled out their seasonal pantomimes: "Pinkie and the Fairies" diverted children and parents at His Majesty's Theatre.[1] But London's seasonal charms were lost on William Boyce, who was in the city on his return trip to Chicago from a disastrous expedition to East Africa during which he had failed to achieve the stated objective of the safari: to obtain photographs of an assortment of wildlife from the unique vantage point of a hot air balloon.

W.D. Boyce's African Balloonographic Expedition had been touted as a more enlightened version of Teddy Roosevelt's safari to the region. From April 1909 to March 1910, Roosevelt and his son Kermit with 250 porters and guides proceeded across British East Africa into the Belgian Congo then headed north to Khartoum in

91

the Sudan, exacting a heavy toll among animal life along the way. But Boyce's claim to U.S. public attention was that "the killing of animals will be secondary to picture making from balloons by means of telephoto cameras operated by an expert photographer," reported the *Chicago Tribune* in June 1909 not long before Boyce's August departure for Europe and Africa. The publisher was "convinced that pictures of a kind never before secured in Africa because of the density of the jungle and topographical features of the hunting country will be brought back by the expedition," *Tribune* readers were informed.[2]

But nothing went right for Boyce, who organized such expeditions to generate promotional material for his group of newspapers, which included the *Saturday Blade,* a weekly for farming communities hawked by thousands of newsboys, and the *Chicago Ledger,* a city weekly. Tons of equipment were shipped to Nairobi, British East Africa, including two silk balloons and sulfuric acid, which would produce hydrogen when mixed with iron filings. The balloons worked, after a fashion. But chief photographer George Lawrence could not produce the aerial photographs on which the venture was premised, having for one thing neglected to bring a telephoto lens. The disgusted Boyce took ship to London, instructing expedition secretary Charles Hughes to buy what photos could be found locally and wiring his Chicago office to take his name off expedition stationary.

From London, Boyce continued to cable orders to Hughes and another safari member, finally instructing them to wrap things up and head home via London. Accustomed to success, Boyce had a huge flop on his hands. He could not have been cheered by the news that Roosevelt, according to *The Times* "still shooting in East Africa," had been elected a corresponding member of the French Academy of Moral and Political Sciences, reflecting, as *The Times* put it, "the widespread feeling in France that the ex-President is the personification of Anglo Saxon energy and the model of what a responsible public man should be."

Boyce was not one to accept failure—or go home empty-handed. Fortunately, as he would later relate it, fate intervened on a London thoroughfare. "I was trying to find my way across a London street in a fog. A little lad of twelve noticed my futile efforts, and led me with a lantern in the right direction. I thanked him and offered him a penny. But he said: 'Thank you, sir, but I am a Boy Scout, and we never take tips for doing kind acts.'

"'What are the Boy Scouts?' I asked him in surprise. Then he told me that all Boy Scouts were in honor bound to do one kind act every day."[3]

Boyce later maintained that until this encounter in the fog, he had never heard of the Boy Scouts.[4] The encounter between the disoriented traveler and a dutiful English Scout would eventually become enshrined in the annals of American Scouting, the youth memorialized as the Unknown Scout. However, the preponderance of evidence suggests Boyce conjured up the story as a public relations device to explain why he returned to the United States not with a collection of photographic trophies but a newfound social mission.

For one thing, it seems improbable that Boyce could have been totally unaware of the existence of Scouting, which was taking hold in Chicago and other American communities and had been making news even in the United States. Shortly before Boyce sailed for England on August 4, the *Chicago Tribune,* his hometown newspaper, carried a report on July 26 about a visit by King Edward and Queen Alexandra to Wrest Park, the country home of Whitelaw Reid, then U.S. ambassador to Britain. The royal couple and the envoy attended church services in nearby Silsoe village where, the *Tribune* reported, "A squad of honor, composed of several corps of boy scouts from neighboring villages, saluted the party when it entered." The *Tribune's* correspondent added that: "Before returning to Mr. Reid's residence, the King inspected the scouts."

Boyce's story, moreover, would continue to change in significant details from its first appearance in the *Washington Herald* on April 21, 1910. As Boyce would some years later describe the supposed encounter, it took place not in December 1909 but four months earlier that August when he was on his way to East Africa.

"All day long the city had been in the hard grip of dense fog," Boyce wrote in this subsequent version. "Traffic moved slowly and cautiously. Street lights had been ordered on by the police before noon and night was coming on." Emerging from the Savoy Hotel, Boyce stood perplexed by the side of the Strand, a major thoroughfare, wondering how he would ever find a "difficult address in old London."

"A boy approached and asked, 'May I be of service to you?' I told him where I wanted to go and the boy saluted and said, 'Come with me, sir.'" About twelve and equipped with a lantern, the youth "forthwith led me to the desired spot."

Boyce offered to tip his guide, "but the boy promptly refused it and replied, 'No sir, I am a Scout. Scouts do not accept tips for courtesies or good turns.'"

Boyce asked him to explain. "The boy repeated and then added, 'Don't you know about the Scouts?' I was interested and said, 'No, I don't, but I would like to.' Then the boy said, 'Follow me.' I pleaded for an opportunity to do my errand and then when I came back, there stood this boy still waiting for me. Said he, 'The Scout office is very near here sir, and I will be glad to take you there.'"

"This was how I first came to the Office of General Sir Robert Baden-Powell and secured whatever printed matter they had on the Boy Scout Organization, including the Manual," he later told a BSA executive in a memo.

During his African sojourn, Boyce said (in one version), he had ample time to pore over the materials provided by the London Scouting office. He also spotted articles in the British press about the movement, leading him to consider "what a wonderful thing it would be for our American boys," he later said.

In this account, Boyce said he had intended to return home via the Far East, crossing the Pacific to San Francisco. But instead he backtracked through London and again visited the Boy Scout office in Henrietta Street. There, said Boyce, he "took up with whoever was in charge the question of their organizing in the United States, the same as they had in Canada. The reply, as I remember it, was that they were busy on British territory and that it would be better for us to organize in the United States as the Boy Scouts of America."

He observed that their manual "necessarily would have to be infringed upon or consent given to copy from it as I didn't see where we could change their plan or their work. The offer was made that if we organized 'on the level' and not for some advertising purpose, the manual would be released to us," he said.[5]

So it was, Boyce said, that he learned about the Boy Scouts and conceived the notion to launch them in the United States. But his encounter with Scouting in the impenetrable London fog contained numerous contradictions.[6] Even the aspect of the fog raised questions. Fog is barely mentioned in the official weather reports of the period, whether December or August 1909 is examined. On August 6 and 9, fog was "only occasionally reported locally" along the Channel, and the second half of August was "almost entirely [fog] free on all coasts," according to reports from the British Meteorological Office.[7] Much the same was true in December 1909—fog was only reported in Central London on December 21 between 9 a.m. and noon, about one-half mile from the Savoy Hotel where Boyce was staying. He left England at midnight on December 23, leaving him just two days to find the Scouting office and conduct his discussions with its management.[8]

Moreover, it is difficult to believe anyone in English Scouting other than Baden-Powell himself would have been in a position to grant rights to Boyce to launch an American affiliate—or to do so in such a casual manner, at the same time offhandedly committing to extend the rights to republish *Scouting for Boys*.

Surely Boyce would have been obliged to conduct detailed mail or telegraph correspondence with Baden-Powell as to such rights.

And Baden-Powell, who had shown great attention to detail and can-niness in his dealings with Seton and who had come to regret aspects of his deal with the Pearson group, would probably have proceeded with caution—and he was already facing challenges from Doubleday over his alleged infringements on Seton's copyright.[9]

Given these discrepancies, the question arises as to whether Boyce's account of being assisted by an "Unknown Scout" was part of a public relations exercise. Boyce's interest was at least in part com-mercial—very much as the British press magnate Pearson's interest in Scouting was motivated in part by sales. Putting a gloss of sentimen-tality over the matter might have helped to soften this aspect.

Even among those most closely associated with American Scout-ing, there was skepticism about Boyce's account. For his part, Dan Beard considered the Boyce tale of assistance in the London fog by an anonymous Scout "a lot of bunk," and Baden-Powell biographer William Harcourt also questioned the episode.[10]

However it was that Scouting came to his attention, Boyce lost no time establishing a legal claim to the name of the Boy Scouts of America.[11] On reaching New York in the last days of 1910, Boyce, rather than heading home to Chicago after five months abroad, took the train to Washington, where he met with Joseph Cannon, the senior Republican congressman from Illinois and House Speaker. Not without influence, Boyce asked Cannon to sponsor legislation granting a federal charter to what he proposed to call the Boy Scouts of America. There was, Boyce assured him, "no politics, religion, or money involved; it was all for the good of the boys." Cannon promised to do what he could, but cautioned that the Rockefeller Foundation had already sought a similar charter, so it was doubtful Congress would entertain another such piece of legislation in the same session.

Outgunned for the moment by Rockefeller's philanthropic forces, Boyce turned to incorporating his new organization. Through his Washington contacts, he met Colin H. Livingstone, a vice president of the American National Bank and former private secretary to Senator Stephen Benton Elkins of West Virginia.[12] Descended from the storied African missionary-explorer David Livingstone,[13] the lawyer earlier in his career had been a newspaperman. Livingstone recommended a law firm to handle incorporation of the Boy Scouts of America and papers were filed in the District on February 8, 1910.[14] In Ottawa, Illinois, location of Boyce's country estate, the *Fair Dealer* paper informed readers of his new venture under the headline "W.D. Boyce Is Heard From." The newspaper quoted the publisher as saying, "We intend to take the British idea and Americanize it."[15]

The frenetic pace of Boyce's activity in early 1910 suggests that he saw more in the Boy Scouts than a chance to do a good deed. Whether Baden-Powell had in fact given him tacit permission to launch the Scouts in America, Boyce had stolen a march on William Randolph Hearst, whose New York-based news organization would by mid-1910 establish a rival organization called the American Boy Scouts.

But Boyce found that getting such an organization off the ground involved a lot more than setting it up on a legal basis. He had hoped that his weeklies, read in 30,000 homes across the Midwest, would provide a channel to drum up interest in the movement. His many paperboys would join the organization and form a grass roots marketing network. In theory this would fuel subscriptions—but the cost of launching the movement would strain even his considerable means.[16]

So it was probably much to Boyce's relief that he received a telegram in April 1910 from YMCA executive Edgar Robinson, who had been following the phenomenon of Scouting and was interested in aligning the YMCA with it in the United States.[17] YMCA Boys' Work Scout Troops had already been established around the country. Robinson was acquainted with Seton's Woodcraft Indians, but knew that the movement had not caught on nationally. So he was very much interested in Scouting, whose general orientation was more in line with that of the YMCA, and which seemed to be taking root around the United States with little or no encouragement.[18]

Robinson was in the Midwest in April 1910 on YMCA business, when one of his local counterparts pointed out an item in a Chicago paper saying that Boyce had incorporated the Boy Scouts of America. Robinson wired Boyce and with other YMCA officials met him at his Chicago offices on May 3.[19]

Robinson suggested that the YMCA was well positioned to roll out Scouting in the United States. It had the organizational structure and had already sponsored some troops. Boyce readily agreed and pledged to provide financial support to the tune of $1,000 a month, writing a check for that amount on the spot.[20]

Teaming up with the YMCA also strengthened Boyce's hand in Congress. His efforts to obtain a federal charter had bogged down in the House Committee on Education. Even as Boyce shook hands with Robinson on May 3, a first hearing on the bill was taking place. Boyce's Washington attorney, R. Woodland Gates, told the committee his client had been detained in Chicago. He summarized the Scouting idea, telling Rep. Joseph V. Graff, also of Illinois, that, "Mr. Boyce wants to get the boys thinking of healthy things, to go out into the forests and the woods, and all that sort of thing." Unimpressed, Graff told Gates "it would be well for us to hear" Boyce in person. The committee adjourned until Tuesday, May 10.

When Boyce appeared on Capitol Hill the following Tuesday, he had with him not only Robinson of the YMCA, but Ernest Seton and two representatives of the English Scouting movement. After meeting with Boyce in Chicago, Robinson had hurried back to New York to meet Charles Heald, the organization's national secretary, and W.B. Wakefield, an English YMCA official involved in the Scouts. Their ship was due in New York on May 5 and they were scheduled to give a lecture at the Brooklyn YMCA that evening. But their steamer arrived too late in the day for them to pass quarantine. Robinson, faced with the prospect of addressing the crowd himself, telephoned Seton and "begged him to come to my rescue without delay."[21] Robinson, on stage making apologies when Seton got there, introduced him "with enthusiasm and relief."

Having cleared quarantine, the English emissaries spoke the next evening at the YMCA on Twenty-Third Street, Manhattan, and the next day in Newark, New Jersey, returning to Manhattan to address the Union League Club.

Their presence resolved a major problem for Robinson. Up to that point, all of his information about Scouting had come from printed material. The two Britons could respond to a deluge of questions. "Newspaper publicity had opened the flood gates and the pent up desire for information seemed like a flood that would sweep us off our feet," Robinson later recalled. "Our two English friends served as life preservers to help us keep our heads above the tide."[22]

The Scouting experts might also strengthen Boyce's petition to Congress. On May 10, Robinson, Seton, Heald, and Wakefield took the train to Washington to give testimony before the House Education Committee, this time presided over by its Republican chairman, Rep. James Francis Burke of Pennsylvania.

Robinson told Burke, Graff, and the other committee members that Scouting was of the greatest interest to the YMCA, which had 800 boys' departments in North America and had welcomed 12,000 to 15,000 youths to its camps the previous summer. "I am satisfied that there is great advantage to be gained from the introducing of some systematic way of conducting our outings, using the principle that the Boy Scouts organization has worked out," he told them.

"We also feel that there is some need of a unifying headquarters so that the idea may not be debauched, if I may use that word, by men who would use it for other purposes than for the benefit of the boys, and also by men whose intentions might be good, but who would lack judgment and experience in the matter," he said. "The movement is too good a thing to suffer, as some other movements have in this country, from the lack of central leadership."

Committee members expressed perplexity as to why Congress should grant the Boy Scouts of America a federal charter when it could just as well organize in each of the forty-six states. One told Robinson bluntly that, "It is a very rare thing for Congress to authorize an incorporation." Seton told the congressmen that his own experience in the nine years since setting up his Indian camp in Cos Cob had been "better than I dreamed of." By 1903, there were 140 Woodcraft camps, and "they kept increasing until they spread all over the United States, and although I kept myself out of sight as far as I could . . . the newspapers took it up against my wish." Seton acknowledged that Scouting had overtaken his Indians, so it made sense to cooperate. "The principle is so sound that I want it started again in some national form, with a charter which will protect the name—I do not care what the name is, the name proposed now seems to be the most acceptable."

Testifying last, Boyce was the object of the most pointed questions as to the need for a federal charter. Skepticism was evident in committee questions. Boyce tackled the issue head-on. "We would not have applied to Congress if we had felt that it could have been accomplished in any other way. This is big enough to be a national affair and for the Congress of our country to recognize it, or I do not care to have anything to do with it," he declared.[23]

Boyce came perilously close to butting heads with chairman Burke in the following exchange:

THE CHAIRMAN: You will understand that the questions asked by the members of the committee, while they may in themselves indicate either favor or hostility to this measure, are put by gentlemen who are sitting here in a judicial capacity, and that we are simply endeavoring –

MR. BOYCE: It is not necessary for you to explain that to me.

THE CHAIRMAN: We are simply trying to ascertain the reason back of this application. There is not a gentleman on this committee who does not appreciate fully the generosity displayed by the projectors of this movement, and our inclination is to help . . . but we can not under any circumstances forget the great difficulty that we will encounter in both Houses, or at least in the House, in light of established precedent, if we report a bill of this character and do not fortify ourselves with the very best information and most unanswerable arguments in support of it.

MR. GRAFF: It would be injurious to your movement to a very great degree if this committee should report the bill to grant this charter and it should subsequently be defeated in either House . . . and the committee would not be wise if they reported the bill when it was not clear that they could get it through. So we are endeavoring to get all the information we can. I think every gentleman here appreciates the great work.

MR. BOYCE: If you gentlemen will ask any questions I will endeavor to answer them . . . I never thought for a minute that there might be any opposition when neither politics, nor religion, nor money is involved in a bill of this kind. I can not see where anyone should object, but I can see that such things do arise in your minds now.[24]

Indeed, Boyce's bill soon thereafter died a quiet death. The committee's members had indicated concern about setting a precedent. Were Congress to give the Boy Scouts a federal charter, countless other organizations would demand the same recognition. But there was some suspicion that the legislation might have fallen victim to lobbying by Hearst, whose influence by far exceeded Boyce's.

Hearst's shadow had already fallen over the Boy Scouts of America. Before leaving for Washington, Robinson saw a reference to the American Boy Scouts in Hearst's *New York American,* and on May 9 attended a meeting called by Hearst at the Waldorf-Astoria.[25] Hearst said he would launch the American equivalent of the English Boy Scouts of General Robert Baden-Powell, with a clear military orientation—no surprise from one known for hyperpatriotic fulminations.

Robinson took the floor that warm May evening and informed Hearst and the others present "that the Boy Scouts of America was already in existence and that it would not be well to have rivalry between the organizations." Noting that the name of the American Boy Scouts was likely to lead to confusion with the Boy Scouts of America, Robinson asked whether the name had been chosen because Hearst's *New York American* was sponsoring the new organization.

Hearst made no answer to this, but his aide, James McGrath, soon to become national secretary of the competing Scout organization, said the group would push on—adding condescendingly that "the other Boy Scout movements could come in under the banner of the American Boy Scouts."[26] Hearst set up headquarters for his American Boy Scouts at his flagship newspaper, the *New York Journal*. American Boy Scouts officers included Admiral George Dewey, commander of U.S. Naval forces at the Battle of Manila Bay in the Spanish-American War, who in April 1898 famously uttered the order, "You may fire when ready, Gridley."

Hearst also recruited Major General F. D. Grant, son of the Civil War general and U.S. president. The American Boy Scouts had an unquestionably military cast, purposing to instruct members in army drill and tactics.[27]

Hearst's initiative had at least one beneficial effect from the standpoint of the Boy Scouts of America. The emergence of the American Boy Scouts drove most of the other Scout-type organizations in existence into the arms of the Boy Scouts of America, including the United States Boy Scouts, founded by the retired Army Colonel Peter Bomus; the National Scouts of America, founded by Brigadier General William Verbeck,[28] principal of St. John's Military School in Manlius, New York; and a Scouting offshoot of the National Highway Protective Association. Scattered groups like the Leather Stocking Scouts and the Peace Scouts also entered the fold.[29]

On June 1, Robinson established the headquarters of the Boy Scouts of America in a room next to his own in the YMCA's offices on East Twenty-Eighth Street in Manhattan, engaging Philadelphia YMCA official John L. Alexander as managing secretary, and one stenographer. Inquiries poured in from around the country until "unopened letters at times were stacked like cordwood on the floor."[30] Within weeks the burden became crushing. On June 21, Robinson called together the representatives of twenty organizations involved in social work and education, seeking advice and aid. The meeting set up a committee on permanent organization with executive powers. The inclusion of social science experts and reform advocates lent the undertaking weight.

One of its members was Dr. Luther H. Gulick, who had directed physical education in New York City public schools and now headed the child hygiene department at the Russell Sage Foundation, established in 1907 to improve U.S. social conditions.[31] Others included the journalists Lincoln Steffens and Jacob Riis, whose *How the Other Half Lives* in 1890 documented New York tenement life in photos and text, stoking public outrage and prompting reforms.[32]

Ernest Seton was named chairman of the committee and "threw himself into" the work, Robinson observed. For Seton it seemed a golden opportunity to graft his Woodcraft Indian model onto Scouting as it took root in America.

"His zeal and energy were astounding," Robinson later wrote. "He wanted to contribute all of his Woodcraft Indian program to this new movement, to have it merge in the blood stream and lose its identity as a separate outside movement. He stood prepared to give freely all of his ideas and experience and ability."[33]

But Seton's hopes were to be dashed. "He was astounded at the reluctance of this new Committee to swallow at a gulp what he was so eager to give," wrote his YMCA sponsor. "With increasing bewilderment it dawned on him that this new movement in America, true to form, only wanted to pick and choose from the program that he had created. To him it seemed that the tendency was to choose the less important, and ignore the more important items in his program."[34]

Though Seton's expertise in naturalism, woodcraft, and Indian lore, and his reputation as a best-selling author, were valued by Robinson and the organizers working to set the Boy Scouts of America on its feet, their main point of reference was *Scouting for Boys* and Baden-Powell's organizational structure.

Seton found himself obliged to come to terms with his British competitor, though their literary dispute was unresolved. The matter had simmered along into early 1910. In addition to his complaint about the borrowing from his *Birch-Bark Roll,* Seton informed Baden-Powell that he had heard from New York publishing sources that the rights to *Scouting for Boys* had been offered to an American publisher. Frank Doubleday fired off a cable to Baden-Powell demanding clarification.[35]

"I am so very sorry to have left your note of March 3rd unanswered for such an unconscionable length of time," Baden-Powell wrote to Seton on May 31, "but I have been rather overdone with business and allowed it to get overlooked until a cable from Doubleday reminded me of it." He told Seton he could not "entirely confirm" the acknowledgment of Seton's contribution to *Scouting for Boys* that Seton had proposed. Baden-Powell assured Seton that he had no knowledge of any forthcoming American edition of *Scouting for Boys,* adding that "if it should be desirable and agreeable to you I would produce it in collaboration with you." Adapted to "suit the American boy," it would surely "have a great success." He added that he would be in Canada in August, and could stop in New York.[36]

Despite their differences, collaboration on an American edition was enticing to Seton and moreover suited his purposes as chairman of the BSA Committee of Organization. One priority for BSA was a manual along lines of *Scouting for Boys* to answer the many questions about Scouting arriving in the mail each day in the office on East Twenty-Eighth Street. Here was Seton's chance to shape Baden-Powell's vision of Scouting into something closer to his own.

With the Boy Scouts of America fast taking shape, Seton must have had second thoughts about publicly throwing down the gauntlet to Baden-Powell. On receiving Baden-Powell's letter of May 31, he extended an olive branch. "I do not think it is worth while discussing on paper some of the matters mentioned in my letter. You and I are agreed upon all the main principles that we wish to have the boys actively interested in, in this movement. While both of us have been in it for many years, I realize that yours is a better form of organization than mine, therefore I wish to use [it] in America."

Seton proposed "reproducing a portion" of *Scouting for Boys.* "Just how much, I am not yet clear, but in each subsequent issue I should expect to publish less of it." Seton could see that the starting point had to be the Baden-Powell model. But once a framework was set, he believed he could shape the substance of American Scouting on lines closer to his Woodcraft Indians.

He bluntly told Baden-Powell that "only the outline of organization . . . interests me," and "that, you know, is neither copyrighted here, nor copyrightable. Still, I wish to feel that we are working together," he said, proposing to pay $250 for exclusive U.S. rights. He proposed a large edition for sale at twenty-five cents a copy, though this would entail "considerable loss" for him personally.

"Of course," Seton added magnanimously, "I should give you complete credit for your splendid achievements in this field."[37]

Later that summer, the Scouting organization staged a critical test of Seton's Woodcraft Indians model. In the woods around a YMCA conference center on Silver Bay, an inlet of Lake George in upstate New York, Robinson and other YMCA officials for two weeks closely observed the Seton method with the aim of deciding whether to make an amalgam of Scouting and Woodcraft.[38]

Robinson had proposed the late-August camp at Silver Bay to Seton in the form of a challenge, to resolve questions as to whether

Woodcraft was right for the purposes of the YMCA. "Yes, your camp is fine, your ideas are fine, but just how far our Y.M.C.A. leaders will accept them is another matter," Robinson later recalled telling Seton. "Will your ideas work with the kind of older boys with whom we have to deal? Are you willing to demonstrate to a group that I will assemble at Silver Bay, New York, next August?" Seton agreed to the test.[39]

Meanwhile the naturalist was throwing together the first manual of the Boy Scouts of America, combining *Scouting for Boys* with his *Birch-Bark Roll*.[40] This was complicated by a clash with Beard, similarly recruited by the YMCA, who was exhibiting sensitivity as to his role in the emerging Scouting organization and what seemed to him to be a lack of recognition of his contribution in founding the Boy Pioneers.

Managing Secretary John Alexander spotted the potential for complications in a note from Beard accepting an invitation to Robinson's June meeting to muster the help of like-minded organizations. "I am glad that my move has been copied in England and flattered that you should think so well of it as to start a national army of boys here," said Beard.[41] His implied claim to originating the Scouting concept was only the first of many he would put forth, much to Seton's irritation. But Seton could not object to Beard's inclusion—his rival's work with boys in the outdoors was well known and he was a public figure. And Beard's reputation had been brought to the fore in the public mind in April 1910 upon the death of Mark Twain, then his close neighbor in Redding, Connecticut.[42]

The *New York Times* described the scene after Twain succumbed to a heart condition. "Although surrounded by flowers, there was nothing on the coffin except a wreath which Dan Beard had made of bay leaves gathered the night before, at the request of the family, on the hill behind the house where Mark Twain spent a good deal of his time."[43] Beard traveled with Twain's remains into Manhattan. After a funeral in the Brick Church on Fifth Avenue at Thirty-Seventh Street, Twain was buried in the Elmira, New York, cemetery where his wife, Olivia Langdon Clemens, had been interred six years earlier.

But Beard was unable to maintain the loftier and better-humored outlook that had characterized his relationship with Twain. He may have feared, too, that the recognition he had achieved through his association with America's most beloved writer was rapidly fading. He displayed eagerness to lay claim to originating the outdoor youth movement. Despite substantial interest in his Boy Pioneers, Beard had been scraping along on writing and illustration work including a monthly fee of $100 from the *Pictorial Review,* home since early 1909 to his Pioneers.

His editor and employer Arthur Vance was a good friend—but also a tough negotiator. "Now I want to pay you $75.00 a month for the first articles up to September," Vance told him in January 1909, promising a raise to $100 a month on relaunch of the Pioneers. Urging Beard not to "hem and haw," Vance promised to "boom Dan Beard for all he is worth and expect you to give us some blame good stuff, not too complicated for the average boy to make."[44]

Beard aligned his Boy Pioneers with the Boy Scouts in June 1910, though he continued to look out for his own interests. Beard assured his employer later that summer that the Pioneers had nothing to fear from the Scouts. "I am on the inside and know what moves they are making," he wrote. "If we play our cards right the Boy Scout movement will only be an advertisement for ours." Replied Vance, "All right sir, we will back you up and knock the power [*sic*] out of that bewhiskered imitator of yours named Seaton [*sic*]."[45]

Relations between Beard and Seton soured that June when Beard spotted a notice of a forthcoming Seton article in *The Outlook* on Scouting's origins. Beard made his displeasure known to mutual friends, among them William Hornaday, who told Seton, "There is serious work for you to do in retaining the friendship" of Beard, who was "much annoyed" at the magazine notice.[46] Hornaday assured

Beard that Seton did not claim to have originated Scouting by him-self, and told Seton that the two "need to make common cause against a common enemy [i.e. Baden-Powell], who will rob you *both* of your well-earned credit for what you have done for the boys of America." Hornaday counseled, "In your forthcoming article . . . be sure to put in something that will give a lot of credit to Beard for his Sons of Daniel Boone and Boy Pioneers. You two men *must* stand together."[47]

Beard's ire mounted after he saw the Boy Scout manual Seton compiled that summer. Beard had been asked to undertake this task, but declined, saying that he "could not undertake a 'Thank you' job of such dimensions."[48] It was decided that Seton and Alexander would collaborate. But little material was forthcoming from Alexander so it fell to Seton to cobble together the manual.[49]

From *Scouting for Boys,* Seton took Baden-Powell's system for recognizing achievement, speaking of "badges of merit" instead of "proficiency badges," the Kipling story "Kim's Game" as a test of ob-servation, the "Eengonyama Chorus" of the Matabele warrior, Baden-Powell's nine Scout laws, and many Baden-Powell drawings, as well as the essential structure of English Scouting. From the *Birch-Bark Roll,* Seton took his system of tramp signs, tent-raising instructions, tips on building a fire, shooting a bow and arrow, and identifying constel-lations, notes on the American dialects, and many of his cherished camp games.

Seton also poured in his Standard of Honorable Exploits: Red Honors for heroism or excellence in riding, athletics, mountain climbing, shooting, field observation, and so on; White Honors for accomplishment in camping, scouting, archery, fishing, and so forth; Blue Honors for mastery of subjects or activities like naturalism, ge-ology, and photography. High Red Honors were bestowed for killing a lion, elephant, tiger, or bison; less bold Scouts could earn simple Honors besting a black bear, deer, gray wolf, or crocodile at least fourteen feet long.[50]

Furiously cutting and pasting through early summer 1910, Se-ton and the BSA staff rushed the *Handbook* into print in July. At 192 pages, the manual externally resembled *Scouting for Boys.* The cover showed the same image of a Stetson-hatted young Scout standing on a rock with the sea in the background—though the fluttering Union Jack was replaced with the Stars and Stripes.

Baden-Powell was listed as co-author, but two-thirds of the *Handbook* came from Seton. He had wanted to give it an American flavor, excising an account of the Mafeking cadets and replacing it with a lesson on the American flag. Seton, anticipating criticism from those familiar with *Scouting for Boys,* wrote a preface to explain the changes, underscoring his contribution to the movement.

"The Woodcraft and Scouting movement that I aimed to foster began to take shape in America some ten years ago," he wrote. "In 1904 I went to England to carry on the work there," and "invited" Baden-Powell to "cooperate in making the movement popular. Accordingly, in 1908, he organized his Boy Scout movement, incorporating the principles of the Indians with other ethical features bearing on savings banks, fire drills, etc., as well as by giving it a partly military organization, and a carefully compiled and fascinating handbook."[51]

A first printing of 5,000 copies sold out in a month.[52] BSA managers commended Seton for his "unremitting zeal and effort" in delivering a book in less than final form to satisfy "insistent requests from the field."[53] But not all were pleased. Some felt Seton went too far in downplaying Baden-Powell's vision and style while importing wholesale from *The Birch-Bark Roll.* They considered a close alignment with Baden-Powell's version of Scouting to be indispensable to the success of the American organization.[54]

Beard was also far from pleased with Seton's production. Alexander sent him a copy in early August, asking his opinion.[55] "*Boy Scouts* received," Beard said, "and I see that Seton still claims to have originated them." He insisted Seton had acknowledged publicly in a YMCA meeting "that I am the originator and am still running the first Boy Scouts." The next edition, Beard insisted, should make this clear. "We are both professional men and this thing of being a tail to another man's kite is not in my line, especially when I invented the kite."[56]

Anxious to placate Beard, Alexander advised him to "not take much stock in" an edition brought out "so hurriedly that there were more mistakes than anything else in the entire book. We are now getting ready for the second edition and I am going to keep everything you have said strictly in mind." Alexander added that he was sending Seton a copy of Beard's letter because "such lifelong friends as you are ought not to be separated in any way whatever by a matter of this sort . . . it is more Thoughtlessness on Seton's part than anything else."[57]

To Seton, Alexander reported that Beard "is feeling very badly about this thing" and that the next edition needed to "make due allowance for his feelings." He also tried to paper over differences between Seton and Baden-Powell in light of the general's proposed visit to New York that September, telling Seton that "if he does come I hope that you may be able to entertain him at Cos Cob, in order to impress upon our American Scout friends the close alignment of yourself with the general." Alexander suggested that he and Seton discuss the matter further when they met later in the month at the Silver Bay demonstration camp.[58]

Beard continued to vent in periodical dispatches to Alexander. "Everybody knows and especially the boys, that I started and am still running the original Boy Scout Society and it will put me in a wrong light to allow the misstatement in the preface to go unchallenged."[59] Seton told Beard, "I think you are a big enough man to realize that you, Baden-Powell, and myself have all been trying to do the same thing," he wrote. "But there is no blinking the fact that Baden-Powell has done it better than any of us."[60] Seton proposed they settle the dispute by staking out the dates of publication of their first articles about their organizations, noting that his first Woodcraft articles appeared in the *Ladies' Home Journal* in May 1902. "I may be wrong but I believe you made no organized attempt at the Boy Scouting idea until September 1905."[61]

Beard conceded in a marginal notation on Seton's letter—though not, it seems, to Seton himself—that his rival had a point.[62] Beard had in fact launched his Sons of Daniel Boone in *Recreation* magazine in July 1905. Yet he believed that whatever the chronology, his contribution had been unique and decisive.

The two men came together at the experimental camp on Lake George—though Seton was not over-eager to have Beard present. Around the start of the camp, Seton heard from Robinson that "Dan Beard is feeling sore at not being invited. Wouldn't you like too send him a friendly word?" Seton sent a telegram to Beard: "Come and visit us in Silver Bay Camp. We need you."[63]

In the old days Beard had often visited Woodcraft camps bringing with him a keg of cider.[64] But such camaraderie had faded. Seton noted that the bewhiskered bantam gave the campers lessons in tomahawk-throwing, disfiguring "every big tree in camp," and leaving Seton to take the blame with their YMCA hosts. Adding insult to injury, Beard insisted that while the Indians were due credit for inventing the tomahawk, the American settlers had improved it, regaling the boys one night with grisly tales concerning how some "Kentucky scouts murdered certain Indians."[65]

At Silver Bay, groups of six boys, each led by an adult, raised shelters, cooked meals, and met each evening around campfires hosted by Seton.[66] There on behalf of the English Scouting organization was E.B. Wakefield, one of the two Baden-Powell emissaries who had arrived that May. Nominally he was there to offer tips on the function of scoutmaster. But in fact he was there to "curb the heresies of 'the red Tory,'" as Seton's British colleagues had by then labeled him.[67]

Camper William Edel of Baltimore recalled the not-so-subtle competition between the Seton and Baden-Powell systems. Campers constantly discussed the merits of the two approaches. But "the leaders of the camp were preaching Boy Scouts, and they convinced us, there's no question about that."[68]

Yet Seton made a deep impression on the youth, who after reading *Two Little Savages* had joined a Woodcraft tribe sponsored by his local YMCA. Seton "was a tremendous man, well-muscled, heavily built but active, and with a shock of gray hair and brilliant blue eyes—he was really a figure," he recalled. "He usually talked about woodcraft, forest life and trees . . . and those of us who had read his books about animals were thrilled to hear him tell some of the same stories."[69]

But the BSA organizers had made up their minds. On September 5, days after the Silver Bay experiment concluded, the BSA Executive Committee gathered to assess the camp and decide the direction the organization would take. It was resolved to comprehensively adopt the Baden-Powell's approach.[70]

Seton could hardly have been pleased, under these circumstances, to be asked by the organizers to serve as official host to Baden-Powell, who had sent word from Canada that he would stop for a day in New York before taking a ship for England. Alexander convened the Committee on Organization to "perfect arrangements" for the September 23 visit. That would be Baden-Powell's only day on U.S. soil, so it was "only a question of how best to use the opportunity," Alexander told Seton, urging him to invite Roosevelt. "I think you can do it and I think it would be the greatest stunt on earth to actually accomplish the thing."[71]

This was not to be. Despite letters and telegrams from Colin Livingstone in Washington and appeals from other BSA backers, Roosevelt sent his regrets. "I wish I could accept," he told Seton, "but to do so at this time is absolutely out of the question. Every minute of my time is taken up. I was never busier." Roosevelt added: "Pray present my regards to your distinguished guest. I regard the Boy Scout movement as of real importance, and I most earnestly wish it well."[72]

Preparations for the visit proceeded. On his day in New York, Baden-Powell would meet with a dozen major BSA backers at a 1 p.m. luncheon at the University Club, then with 200 scoutmasters at the Waldorf-Astoria Hotel. This would be followed at 6:30 p.m. by a reception in the Waldorf-Astoria with "representative business men," followed by dinner at 7 p.m.

There would be remarks by one or two "men of prominence," Robinson told Baden-Powell, but "the bulk of the evening [is] reserved for your address."[73] For Robinson and other BSA organizers, the objective of the visit was to secure the public blessing of Baden-Powell's on their enterprise, in particular in light of the still-formidable threat from Hearst's American Boy Scouts.

Seton wrote to Baden-Powell on September 17 to offer his assistance in New York. "If you will let me know I will meet you at the train and relieve your mind of all worries of how and where." Seton warned that "there is some danger of a trap being laid for you in New York" by Hearst, "the socialist, anarchist, etc., who is largely responsible for the assassination of President McKinley. As soon as he found that the Boy Scouts was likely to take up, he started the American Boy Scouts as an advertising scheme for his *American Journal*," Seton said. "It is quite likely he may have a deputation to meet you or call on you."[74]

Seton updated Baden-Powell on their proposed joint publishing venture, to which Baden-Powell had yet to assent, assuring him that "I do not think you will find there is anything wrong." Seton optimistically concluded in words he later on might have regretted: "All differences of opinion can easily be adjusted."[75]

On the morning of September 23, Seton, Beard and Robinson met Baden-Powell at the Hotel Seville on lower Madison Avenue where he had checked in after arriving from Canada the previous day. The group proceeded to the *Outlook* offices in the United Charities Building. Seton wanted to see that Baden-Powell met Roosevelt while in New York[76]—though the two had already met in England when Roosevelt was there to attend the funeral of King Edward VII.

The former Rough Rider lost no time bonding with his fellow advocate of the robust life and manly character, echoing the endorsement of Scouting contained in the note he gave Seton to be read that evening at the Waldorf-Astoria. "I should value the chance to meet General Baden-Powell," Roosevelt wrote, "and I should value even more the chance to identify myself with so admirable a movement as this. I believe in the movement with all my heart."[77]

Leaving the offices of the *Outlook,* the group returned to the Waldorf-Astoria where Baden-Powell had an 11 a.m. business meeting with Doubleday, then to the University Club luncheon. Next they visited the BSA offices on Twenty-eighth Street, where a photo session was organized on the building's flat roof. A banner with fleur-de-lis served as a backdrop. Baden-Powell, Seton and Beard took their places—Seton to the photographer's left, Baden-Powell at the center, Beard to the right. Moments before the shutter snapped, Baden-Powell decided to seat himself on a ventilator casement, resting his straw boater hat on his knee. Seton and Beard remained standing at his flanks, each holding his slouch hats by his side.[78]

Seton would later see this arrangement as subtle positioning by Baden-Powell to signal seniority. Certainly Baden-Powell's years in military service had tuned his hierarchical sensitivities; he no doubt assumed he was entitled to this status. "You and I had to stand," Seton later complained to Beard, "by which trick he made us his subordinates, although he was the latest to enter the field" of outdoor work with boys.[79] Whether Baden-Powell was as calculating as this, there could be no doubt later at the Waldorf-Astoria that he was the man of the hour.

According to an account provided the next day to readers of the *New York Sun,* the Astor Gallery was filled to capacity. "General Baden-Powell was greeted by a combination of Chautauqua salute and Waldorf war whoops, from the four hundred men interested in the Boy Scouts of America. The boys were absent, but their mothers and sisters filled the balconies."[80] Beard delivered opening remarks which he tartly noted had been vetted by BSA executives.[81] Following a lantern slide presentation, Seton took the podium, telling the room that Roosevelt had agreed to become Scouting vice president, thereupon reading Roosevelt's letter to the distinguished assemblage. As the *New York Times* reported, Seton added "parenthetically, as it were, that the Boy Scouts of America . . . was not at all the same as the American Boy Scouts run by William Randolph Hearst," and that Baden-Powell had declined to review a parade of the competitors.

Seton told the gathering that "not one boy in a thousand was bad, but that [boys] have badness thrust upon them." American youth did not need reforming, but "protection from deformation." The natural development of young men was "the chief reason for the existence" of the Boy Scouts of America, Seton said, putting his own philosophical spin on the undertaking.

Then Seton introduced Baden-Powell in words that in all likelihood did not come from his own pen, describing him as the "Father of Scouting." The ballroom burst into applause as Baden-Powell stood. By then an accomplished public speaker with fine diplomatic instincts, Baden-Powell without doubt appreciated the import of what he was about to tell the room, especially for Seton and Beard.

"You have made a little mistake, Mr. Seton, in your remarks to the effect that I am the Father of this idea of Scouting for Boys," Baden-Powell declared. "I may say that you are the Father of it, or that Dan Beard is the Father. There are many Fathers. I am only one of the Uncles, I might say."[82]

Perhaps moving to defuse Seton's resentment, Baden-Powell offered a capsule history that confirmed his own standing while applying a balm to the sensitivities of Seton and Beard. "The scheme became known at home," he said. "Then it was that I looked about to see what was being done in the United States, and I cribbed from them right and left, putting things as I found them" into Scouting.

This rendering would not satisfy Seton. But it served to paper over their differences in front of this audience full of potential sponsors.

In complimenting the BSA founders on their accomplishments, Baden-Powell drew somewhat awkwardly on the U.S. financial and industrial structures so familiar to many in the elite audience, suggesting that the U.S. organizers "had organized a combine, a trust," and recruited Roosevelt to its executive ranks. "Upon this trust you can depend," the general declared.[83]

For Colin Livingstone, John Alexander, and Edgar Robinson, the dinner could not have been more successful.[84] The New York press reports the next day—with the notable exception of the Hearst papers—made clear that the Boy Scouts of America had received Baden-Powell's wholehearted stamp of approval.[85]

On September 24, the day after the dinner, Baden-Powell boarded the *S.S. Arabic* for his return to England. On board, he dashed off a thank-you note to Seton for his hospitality in New York. "I cannot leave without telling you how very sincerely gratified I have been by the exceedingly generous reception which has been accorded to me by yourself and those connected with the organization of the Boy Scouts movement in the United States." He added, "I am, from the personal point of view, most deeply grateful—and from that of the movement I feel confident that it's in the hand of such capable workers."[86]

Seton's own feelings were more mixed. Baden-Powell had thrown him a sop in identifying him as a father of Scouting—but the distinction had to be shared with Beard, undercutting its value to Seton who still believed that Baden-Powell had purloined his best ideas. Yet he had little choice but to swallow his pride and resentment and work within the movement that Baden-Powell was universally regarded as having founded. Any remaining hopes Seton might have had of infusing the movement with Woodcraft were quickly dashed.

BSA Managing Secretary Alexander also sent Seton a letter September 24 about an article Seton had submitted for comment. "You will notice I have blue-penciled freely, taking it for granted that you really wanted me to do so," wrote Alexander. It would be "foolishness," he added, to make changes in Baden-Powell's version of the Scout law, as Seton was proposing to do.

While he found Seton's revised Scout law "a far better code than BP's," Alexander noted the continued Hearst threat in cautioning against any tinkering with Baden-Powell's formulations. "I feel that we will lose all the hold we have gotten, as recognized BP men, by attempting any change whatsoever in any of our literature, or in any official statement, or semi-official statement, from any of our leaders. For the same reason, I should advise an absolute use of the BP nomenclature for the time being, until we have absolutely overcome the enemy, not merely routed them," Alexander told Seton.

"In the same way, I should be very careful to make the American people feel that you are interested in the movement only because it is a movement, and not because of any desire to be recognized as the founder in priority."[87]

Alexander could not have written a letter more certain to vex Seton. Though chairman of the Committee on Organization, Seton was subordinate to Alexander at Scout headquarters. His frustration could be seen in a note scribbled at the bottom of a business note Alexander sent him September 29.

"My dear Mr. Seton," Alexander began. "There will be a meeting of the Committee on Organization of the Boy Scouts of America, Tuesday afternoon, October 4th."

Seton jotted a terse response. "Don't call meetings without consulting me," he peevishly told Alexander.[88] Seton's relationship with Scouting was already showing signs of strain—a pattern that would repeat itself over the next several years.

CHAPTER 6
WEST TAKES THE HELM

The men who had taken the Boy Scouts of America in hand during 1910 and made it the legitimate offshoot of Baden-Powell's English Scouting movement had much to be satisfied with as the year ended. Though BSA had not obtained a congressional charter, its excellent Washington connections helped it secure an even more valuable token of recognition from the executive branch. That October, President William Howard Taft's secretary informed board member Lee Hanmer that Taft "directs me to say that he will accept the honorary presidency of the national council of the Boy Scouts of America, and thus sustain a similar retention to the movement in the United States" as King George did to Britain's Scouts.[1]

Yet BSA managers faced mounting financial difficulties as a torrent of inquiries poured into their Twenty-Eighth Street offices, overwhelming the small staff and driving up expenses. The Committee on Organization heard a sobering report from managing secretary John Alexander on October 5.[2] The movement had recruited 2,500 scoutmasters in 44 states, but funds were short. Alexander described

BSA's condition as "somewhat critical."[3] Adding one more concern to these, he then asked to be relieved of his duties at the end of 1910.

The financial difficulties were partly due to Boyce's failure to make good on his pledge of $1,000 monthly from July through October 1910. Boyce made the first monthly payment after meeting with Robinson in Chicago that May, then the checks stopped coming. Facing insolvency, Robinson contacted Boyce's Chicago office only to be told the publisher was out of the country. He and other senior organizers made an appointment to see John D. Rockefeller, Jr., intending, as Robinson put it, "to get before him our whole financial situation." No doubt they hoped Rockefeller might helpfully write a check—as he eventually did. But for the time he advised Robinson to go to Chicago to "collect what I could."[4]

Before he could do so, Robinson was visited by Boyce's business manager, Col. William Hunter. Robinson was struck by his "expansive personality and girth, even to the excessively heavy watch chain and Masonic charm on his expansive vest." Hunter informed Robinson that he had stopped the payments because the organization had not, in its publicity, used photos of Boyce that he had supplied, and "pointedly intimated that we were willing to take Mr. Boyce's money, but unwilling to give him due credit."

Robinson sought advice from other YMCA and BSA managers and advisors, including Washington lawyer Colin Livingstone, who had represented Boyce in his initial BSA organizing steps. Livingstone agreed to contact Boyce, thought to be in London, firing off a telegram as well as a letter noting Hunter's complaint that Boyce's name was not "properly mentioned" in releases. To the contrary, on "every occasion at which I have been present you have been given full credit for the starting of the entire movement in this country." He intimated Boyce would be wise to maintain ties with the organization, noting that "I have been assured of the support of some very prominent national characters."

Livingstone heard shortly from Western Union that his telegram could not be delivered in London—Boyce had returned to Chicago. Nor, it appeared, had the publisher received Livingstone's letter by October 19 when he met Robinson in Chicago and assured him he would hold up his end of their agreement.[5] Perhaps Boyce had learned that Taft would be associating himself with BSA. He may have simply decided to do the right thing. In any event, Boyce traveled to Washington soon after that, meeting on October 25 with two of his partners in the incorporation of BSA. The three adopted bylaws and elected an executive board of eleven men that included Boyce, Livingstone, and Robinson. It was noted that BSA had received financial contributions from other sources, and more help was anticipated from Mrs. Russell Sage, a New York philanthropist, who had "without solicitation honestly signified her interest in the work." It was envisioned to ask her for $1,000 a month over three years to meet the cost of hiring an executive secretary and set up a headquarters "with the necessary equipment."[6]

Having lined up Taft's patronage and brought Boyce into line, Livingstone now helped recruit an executive secretary to take over from Alexander. A member of the board, Luther Gulick of the Russell Sage Foundation reached out to Ernest Bicknell, director of the American Red Cross and a member of the BSA National Council. Bicknell recommended two individuals, including James West of Washington, a lawyer with much experience in social endeavors.[7]

West, according to Bicknell, was "one of the most resourceful, energetic and indefatigable men whom I have ever seen in social work." He was "thoroughly businesslike in the matter of expenditures, accounting and all those . . . details which are so often burdensome and neglected" by social activists.[8]

West had been the motivating force behind a White House Conference on Dependent Children in January 1909 that led to the placement of orphans in foster homes instead of their consignment to orphanages.[9] West had been working with novelist and social reformer Theodore Dreiser, who after the failure of his first novel, *Sister Carrie,* took up the editorship of *The Delineator,* a women's magazine. Dreiser launched a "Child-Rescue Campaign" in the pages of the monthly, profiling homeless children and offering assistance to readers ready to take them in. He inveighed against the "machine charity" of orphanages that were often no more than warehouses for children. Dreiser hired West in 1908 to oversee the campaign, and together they founded the National Child Rescue League to build popular support for broader legislative reforms.[10]

Energetic and enterprising, West wrote to Roosevelt at his Oyster Bay, Long Island, home in August 1908, securing a meeting that autumn, following which West sent him a proposal on child welfare which in turn led to the White House conference in January 1909. The gathering, attended by 200 of the country's most eminent social reformers, considered the plight of "children who are destitute and neglected but not delinquent." The assemblage passed resolutions urging that the children of destitute parents "of worthy character" not be removed to orphanages, but that their parents be provided with financial assistance to care for them. It also greatly advanced the new practice of placing of children in foster homes.

The conference was a watershed leading to the contemporary U.S. welfare system, concludes one modern scholar. "The asylum had sought to develop good citizens through the management of an artificially created social environment. The reformers at the White House conference aimed at the management of the real thing. They abandoned the orphanage in order to take up social engineering."[11]

Roosevelt praised conference secretary West. "I have always thought well of you, but I now feel that you are one of those [noble] and patriotic citizens to whom this country stands under a particular debt of gratitude."[12]

West was not entirely a disinterested advocate of orphans—he had himself been placed in an orphanage at a tender age and, like Roosevelt, overcome childhood disabilities. West's father, a Tennessee businessman, died shortly after his birth on May 16, 1876, and his mother, Mary Tyree West of Virginia, succumbed to tuberculosis in July 1882 at the age of thirty-six. Her son, James Edward West, six years old, was entrusted to the Washington City Orphan Home.[13]

West's first years there were made more painful by a tubercular infection of the hip and accusations by orphanage officials that he was malingering. Only the fortunate appearance of a family friend, Mrs. Harrison Dingman, wife of the head of the Government Printing Office, spared him further neglect. Sent to the Washington Children's Hospital, the young West spent eighteen months strapped to a board. Discharged as a "hopeless case," he remained on crutches for thirteen years and even as an adult would require a cane. At the orphanage, he received three hours schooling a day, then was sent to work sewing or caning chairs.

Through this ordeal he developed an extraordinarily determined character. By age fourteen, he had sixty boys under his supervision, and by the time he was nineteen, he had taken on more substantial responsibilities. District of Columbia authorities in 1895 refused him permission to run the institution's steam heating plant. But he nonetheless oversaw building contractors for the orphanage board. He entered the Washington Business High School where in his first year a teacher observed that "he possesses the necessary tact and judgment to enable him to teach" others. West managed the school's football team and started a school paper. Graduating with honors in 1895, he stayed active in the alumni association and as president in 1901–1902 secured a $250,000 appropriation from Congress for a new building. James West was a natural-born executive.

West established credentials as a social worker with the YMCA, becoming the local branch's acting secretary general when the incumbent enlisted to serve in the Spanish-American War. He organized services to troops, among other duties, while working full time as a War Department clerk. He managed the renovation of the YMCA building in Washington after a fire at no cost thanks to in-kind contributions by merchants and tradesmen. West impressed those around him, one YMCA official noting his "remarkable aptitude for holding and influencing boys, especially those whose management was regarded by others as particularly difficult."[14]

He took a law degree from National University Law School, receiving his diploma in 1900 from the hands of President William McKinley. The next year he received a Master's in law while working days in a law office. In October 1902, he was appointed a judge of the Federal Board of Pension Appeals, and made an assistant attorney general at the Department of the Interior in 1904. He kept up his interest in child welfare, leading to his contacts with Roosevelt and the White House conference. But he was shouldered out of his job by a Taft appointee once Roosevelt left the White House, and he resigned his position on June 10, 1909.

"The regrettable part," West told Dreiser, "is that I should personally suffer because I have been making such a heroic effort to help others without regard to personal advantage or advancement." Dreiser agreed that "the least that Roosevelt could have done would have been to arrange with his successors for the proper adjustment of your affairs." But, "You are just the kind of man who rises under difficulties . . . and I will wager anything that within six months you will be asserting that that is the best thing that ever happened to you."[15]

Dreiser was correct, though off on the timing. Meanwhile, West had a family to support, having in 1907 married fellow Business High School graduate Marion Speaks. He was trying to establish a private law practice when approached by Livingstone about the BSA executive position. The glowing recommendation from Bicknell held up under Livingstone's inquiries in Washington and Robinson offered West the position during an interview on November 22.

West responded in mid-December, having meanwhile visited the BSA office in New York and met its staff.[16] He said he would accept the offer, but initially for just six months. "Not having full confidence as to my qualifications and ability to bring to the Movement all that it requires at this time," a trial period seemed in order. "Notwithstanding the attractiveness of the work to me at this time, it may develop that I will feel unsuited to make of myself a professional philanthropist."[17] West agreed to start in January 1911.

West settled into the BSA offices at Fifth Avenue and Twenty-Third Street on January 2, and with the help of a staff of seven set to work. Various issues pressed: Hearst's troublesome American Boy Scouts, BSA's financial condition, institution-building. But West soon found that none of these would consume quite so much of his attention as the rivalry between Seton and Beard.[18] "It is literally a fact," he would later write, "that the first few years of my effort to promote Scouting here were handicapped by both Ernest Thompson Seton and Daniel Carter Beard and their everlasting controversy, which actually took about one-third of my time and a great deal of the time of the members of the Board and the various committees that were appointed to meet with them" in efforts to settle such disputes.[19]

On January 3, his second day on the job, he responded to an irate letter from Beard complaining about the "English invasion," referring to a planned U.S. visit by Baden-Powell.[20] Like Seton, Beard was increasingly frustrated with what he considered a BSA bureaucracy too heavy with non-Americans. In October 1910, he vented irritation when his name was left off some new BSA stationery, firing off a letter to Alexander, who promised to amend the offending letterhead. But this did not mollify Beard, who ticked off the nationalities of board members, singling out Seton as an "English man" and noting Robinson's Canadian nationality.

Seton was critical of the new stationery for different reasons. "It is contrary to law to put Mr. Taft's name in the form in which it is presented," he sternly told Robinson that November. "Theodore Roosevelt has especially asked that he be called Colonel, etc. I hope we shall have to print more paper before long. Please let me proof it. Kindly send me a stock of the present for use."[21]

Alexander penned a tactful response. "I am the guilty party," he confessed. "I arranged all the names, and as you noticed, they are alphabetically arranged in order that no one may feel favored. I understand that I have made at least one mistake in not putting Honorable before the President's name."[22]

Beard took umbrage in December at being referred to in one of Alexander's dispatches as "another founder," complaining to Robinson of "the discourtesy of our secretary, Mr. Alexander." He acknowledged his "undoubted usefulness," but, "our acquaintance has been short and we are not on intimate enough terms to admit our familiarity so akin to rudeness as were his remarks."

A few days later Alexander wrote to Beard to say that he was "somewhat chagrined and disturbed" by his letter. "I do not think that you are exactly fair to me on the different points you make in your letter. I had no intention of hurting your feelings, and in fact I have been more of a friend and champion for you than you might imagine. I should be very glad to talk the matter over with you if you can arrange to see me sometime, or barring this, I shall write you more clearly."[23]

Beard in response was conciliatory. "Do not think that the whole contents of my letter is intended for you personally. It has been my pleasant duty to champion you on occasion and even had you expressed no chagrin I should still continue to champion your work. But at this season of the year I have no heart for discussing any real or fancied discourtesy, and will close the incident by most cordially wishing you a happy Christmas and a prosperous New Year."[24]

Despite such flaps, BSA officials knew Beard had a following and they could not afford to alienate him. He was greatly in demand as a speaker among Scout groups around the country, so much so that by late 1910 he found himself obliged to impose a fee for engagements, asking $150 for a speech in Kennebunk, Maine, noting, "I gave one address the night before last and two last night and I am down for another for tomorrow night," he wrote. "The thing is absorbing so much of my time that I have been compelled to put a charge upon what at the start I did for nothing."[25] Beard was also becoming disgruntled that he was performing such duties for scant compensation while BSA professional managers in the New York head office drew full salaries—something that would increasingly bother him and fuel his resentment toward West in particular in years to come.

Whatever their differences—and there would be many—Beard recognized that West was a "masterful organizer." For his part, West sought Beard's level-headed though often cantankerous advice on a range of matters—though at times he would also seem to use Beard as a convenient foil to the less biddable Seton. West urged Beard to attend the BSA National Council's first annual meeting in Washington in mid-February, and asked him to assess English scouting laws carried over from Baden-Powell's organization, also soliciting his suggestions for an envisioned new manual. "It is our desire to thoroughly Americanize the Boy Scout Movement,"[26] West told him. He asked Beard early in February to prepare brief remarks to be delivered at a dinner after the council meeting in Washington, requesting an advance draft "so that it may be printed for the press."[27] Roosevelt declined an invitation to attend, but added a further endorsement. "You stand for true patriotism, true citizenship, true Americanism. I wish all success to a movement fraught with such good purposes."[28]

On the afternoon of Tuesday, February 14, an expanded National Council shaped up at the Willard Hotel to "march in a body to the White House" where President Taft received its members in the East Room.[29] Lee Hanmer read some prepared remarks, telling the president that, "We men who have come here, come from all walks of life . . . and we are all working for this one aim in order to make our American boys more resourceful and more manful men. I think that is a platform upon which we may stand."[30] Taft made a suitable response and the council members repaired to the Willard to elect a chairman, hear reports from West and other managers, and plan BSA's "organization and extension."[31]

Beard was recruited to a committee on "Standardization of the Scout Oath, Scout Law [and] Tenderfoot, Second Class and First Class Requirements," Seton was named to a panel for "Badges, Awards and Equipment."[32] Both men took these seemingly small matters very seriously, and minor differences of opinion would generate heated disagreement in the months and years to come.

Seton was particularly concerned with the contents of the new Scout manual, reflecting his desire to infuse the American scouting movement with as much as possible of his Woodcraft knowledge and ethos. The handbook that Seton had cobbled together the year before had sold 40,000 copies by the end of 1910 and went through two more printings totaling 20,000 in early 1911.[33] But production of the new manual was entrusted to an editorial committee headed by Alexander, who had agreed to stay on at West's request. Differences between Seton and the committee arose almost immediately. Apparently convinced he would remain the principal author of the Scout manual, Seton presented the panel with a draft of the second edition which the committee however declined to adopt in its entirety. Having gone to England in early 1911, Seton called upon social worker Luther Gulick to meet with the committee on his behalf. At the end of January, Gulick wrote to Seton in London in an effort to smooth over what he saw as a misunderstanding. "The reason why they are not willing to have the manual written by you is not that they want to take credit from you or use your material without giving you due and full recognition for your work, but that they do not believe that your material is written in such a way as to make sufficiently prominent the spirit of service which is the soul of the whole movement," Gulick told Seton after meeting with the committee.

"The reason why Baden-Powell succeeded was not because he took your material, but because he put the spark of life into it by making everything turn upon some concrete service every day, instead of making the object the securing of credit by personal achievement.

One emphasizes service, the other emphasizes personal achievement. One is of service to others, the other emphasizes self-aggrandizement. I wish they had frankly told you this as they did to me today, right out flat-footed," Gulick declared, hastening to assure Seton that the committee needed and wanted his help on portions of the manual, and would make sure he received full credit for his contributions. Once the new Scouting manual was out, he could publish his own book "containing such additional material as will aid in the development of the movement," though the committee had emphasized that Seton should make clear it was not an official Scouting manual.[34]

Work on the official manual picked up after Seton returned from England at the end of March. Yet although Seton eventually took a prominent role in preparing the manual, he did not sit on the editorial board and soon began to chafe under its decisions on content and style. He made clear that he did not intend to be treated as a mere contributor, writing on April 12 to editorial board chairman William Murray that as Chief Scout and editor of the original manual, he understood himself to be a member *ex officio* of the editorial board.[35] That same day he wrote to the full editorial board to suggest institution of an Eagle Scout badge to replace the English movement's Royal or King's Scout badge. And instead of referring to a patrol "sign," BSA should adopt the term "totem," arguing that "the word 'sign' means twenty things and is already overworked in the present connection."[36]

A third communication sent that same day was unlikely to have endeared him to editorial board members. Referring to some "curious sentences" in a chapter on patriotism, he derided its "schoolboy" prose. "Why should we 'defend' American patriotism?" he asked. "Nobody is attacking it." A paragraph on "Our Country" was "still more unfortunate," Seton continued. "In 1783 America was doubtless the 'freest' country on earth, but since then other countries have advanced and America has suffered in many ways . . . Every American politician and public man will tell you that there is less political liberty in America than in several European countries, and much more political corruption."

The United States, he continued, was "far from leading the world in army, navy, arts, sciences, literature or contributions to the development of mankind." He assailed the writer's historical analysis. "America was right in both her wars with England, but not her war with Mexico . . . and if it is desired to know what the world thinks about America's Indian wars for the last hundred years, get an American's account of them called 'A Century of Dishonor.'"

He also objected to including Baden-Powell's injunction, "Be Prepared," suggesting, instead, "Be Ready." He further took issue with Baden-Powell's advice to Scouts to whistle in the face of adversity. "I . . . have suffered tortures on every railway journey I take through some ill-bred, stupid, discourteous fool shrilly whistling in the car, a torment to everybody else."[37]

After haranguing the editorial board at length, Seton in May proceeded to reveal serious deficiencies of editorial judgment in an overwrought "Message From the Chief" which he proposed as a preface to the manual. He inveighed against "arrogant, ignorant and . . . degenerate" Americans, deploring "money grubbing, machine politics, degrading sports, cigarettes, town life of the worst kind, false ideals, moral laxity and lessoning church power." Scouts should "get back to the good old ways and thoughts [of] the Revolution . . . to the outdoor life; the healthful training of eye and of hand, of lung and limb, of heart and thought."

Seton did himself no service in the passage that followed on the perceived threat from Chinese immigration. Seton proposed to tell every Scout reading the manual that "John Chinaman" had "a sound body, a respect for his parents and [a respect for] the simple life," which, "added to his numbers, his brains and his fortitude should warn us that the 'yellow peril' is no empty scare." He continued: "What are we to do to hold and be worthy of this the fairest land that ever saw the sun-rise. *Certainly not down the Chinaman.* It is a poor plan to down a fellow who is excelling us. Men tried to down the Jew when they came to fear him; it only hardened the Jew, No, our plan is to *raise ourselves.*"[38]

Beard, reviewing the draft, spotted trouble. "Better let Mortimer Schiff go over this,"[39] he noted in the margin. Schiff was a member of the executive board, chaired the committee on permanent organization, and, more to the point in this instance, was prominent in New York City's Jewish community.

Beard was gleeful at Seton's uncharacteristic jingoism. "Ain't it funny?" he wrote to West. Seton "has, as usual, jumped aboard the band wagon, 'painted it green' and claimed it has his own. But it's all right, I don't care, for he is doing just what we have been working to have him do; he has turned *American* and, in using my very words and phrases, he is paying me the highest compliment in his power. But Lordy, Lordy, how can he suddenly turn flip-flops and go back on all he held so dear and so vigorously defended? I wish he was a sincere convert."

But, "I am doubtful about the propriety of the wording in the 'Yellow Peril' part and 'hardening the Jews.' Think that can be [re] written to advantage."

West responded to Beard: "Your letter of the 15th inst. is certainly a clever production. I appreciate keenly how you feel. The Editorial Board has requested Mr. Seton to rewrite his letter. We all agree that it is too military and that the reference to the Jews and the Yellow Peril is unfortunate."[40]

By early May, the *Handbook for Boys* was nearly complete with chapters circulated to experts for comment. Some of the criticism received was valuable, but some "has been very sweeping or destructive in its scope," Alexander said regretfully. "In hardly a single case among these has there been any attempt to constructively aid the writers of the various chapters." Some had gone so far as to opine that the prose was "very bad." Alexander attributed this to the multiplicity of authors, hinting at tension in the writing team. "Two of the authors consider the English of each other very bad, the one writing with a free, easy expression, and the other with an academic desire for precision." But he considered the writing of both to be "good English," so any disagreement was simply a matter of style.

In any case, speed was of the essence, so editorial board members should "go carefully through the entire material, straighten out a sentence here and there if necessary," keeping in mind that the manual "is to encourage boys to do Scouting and that the motive in its production is not the sending of a literary masterpiece." Doubleday had promised to supply galley proofs three days after receiving the manuscript, and page proofs one day after the return of corrected galleys.[41] On June 20, 1911, the Boy Scouts of America shipped 5,000 "Proof Edition" copies of the *Handbook for Boys* to Scoutmasters across the United States. The manual went to press two weeks later with an initial run of 100,000 copies.[42]

Seton's message as Chief Scout was much changed from the "Yellow Peril" version that had raised eyebrows at headquarters. "In the Manual we have kept in mind the evils that chiefly threatened our Country and its boys; and have struck at them not by open attack, but by fostering in each case the better things that are opposed to them," making it "binding on our Scouts that they learn courage, loyalty, patriotism, brotherliness, self-control, courtesy, kindness to animals, usefulness, cheerfulness, cleanliness, thrift, purity, honor."[43]

Compliments on the manual came from Ernest Bicknell at the Red Cross in Washington, who added in a note to West: "I take it for granted that you have decided to continue with the Boy Scouts . . . I feel strongly that you have not only made good in your present position but that you have accomplished a very great deal of valuable progress under difficult circumstances."

West would have "unusual opportunities to perform a highly useful work and to achieve an honorable reputation such as any man may properly strive for." He added that West should be better paid and "freed from hampering details which will prevent you from rising above the days' work where you can get a broad view of the entire field."[44] The BSA board agreed, extending West's contract for a year with a retroactive raise of $1,000 as of the previous February and increasing his salary to $6,000 a year as of the following month.

The BSA directors were clearly anxious to retain his services. West took the offer under advisement, asking that it be understood that "the question of compensation would not be" a determining factor in his eventual decision.[45] Meanwhile Baden-Powell wrote from England to congratulate West on the new *American Scouting* handbook which would surely "do an immense deal to develop the movement on sound lines and to spread the right spirit all through it."[46]

Anything but the right spirit, however, was reflected in communications between Beard, Seton, and West in the late summer of 1911. Once again the two American founders were quarreling, this time over an article published by Beard in *The Columbian* and soon to be republished in the *Review of Reviews*. It was in most aspects an innocuous description of the Boy Scout movement—but Beard could not resist depicting himself as the originator of the scouting impulse that by his account later inspired Baden-Powell. Beard took credit for the term "scout," which had not figured prominently in his Sons of Daniel Boone or Boy Pioneers though he used the term in its literal sense in references to the American frontier experience. Beard accorded Seton a subsidiary role, implying that as a non-American he had made a relatively unimportant contribution.

"Scouting is typically and intensely American," wrote Beard. "It is safe to say that no full-grown man can appreciate the real meaning to the youth of the United States of the word Scout, unless that person is in full sympathy with American institutions, tradition and history, and familiar with the potential power, manly self-respect, personal integrity and personal dignity only to be realized under a

Republican form of government, the only form of government that has no tendency to make menials of its citizens."

The success of the movement hinged on the word "scout," Beard said. "The mystic charm, the magic talisman, which caused the President of the United States in 1907 to keep busy statesmen waiting in the cabinet chamber while he carefully read the prospectus of the Boy Scouts, lies in its name." Beard was taking liberties with history in this embellishment of his 1907 meeting with Roosevelt seeking a presidential endorsement for his Sons of Daniel Boone.

The name "caught the attention of the famous English gentleman, Baden-Powell," who "cribbed" it, Beard said, alluding to Baden-Powell's speech a year earlier at the Waldorf-Astoria. But, Beard assured his readers, "I do not wish in the least to detract from the great and very important work done in developing and popularizing the movement by Baden-Powell [nor] do I wish in the least to detract from, or minimize, the work done by that other loyal and talented recruit, Mr. Ernest Thompson-Seton, who with his band of youthful Indians joined our forces in 1910 and is one of the founders of the present National Organization, which is an up-to-date amplification and evolution of the original idea, and is indebted to many people and many minds for its present recognized excellence."[47]

Beard's generosity was not appreciated by Seton, who "bombarded" his associate's mailbox that September demanding changes in the article before its reprinting. Seton turned to West seeking redress. It was "utterly unnecessary and unprofitable to keep up this discussion of priority in the Boy Scout work"—but if the subject were to be raised, "nothing but the truth should be printed."

He informed West that his Woodcraft Indians had been founded in July 1902, whereas Beard's Sons of Daniel Boone had started in 1905, yet in the offending article, "I am made to appear as a follower of Dan Beard."[48] Through West, Beard fired back that he had "never claimed" that the Sons of Daniel Boone "antedated his Indians, or the Y.M.C.A., or the Roman Catholic Church, or the New Testament." His only claim was that "mine was and is a boy

scout society—the first one organized." Seton's movement took for
its models "a lot of bloody savages," whereas the Sons of Daniel
Boone took for its models "a splendid lot of manly white men of the
best type of American manhood."[49]

More important concerns preoccupied West, though, as he attempted to soothe Beard and placate Seton. Baden-Powell had mentioned that a lecture tour would bring him to the United States in
1912. "If I can be any use to your association when I am so engaged
you will let me know—for though my lectures will not necessarily be
directed on Boy Scouts, I can easily put in anything that might be
helpful."[50] West spotted a promotional opportunity. Baden-Powell's
last visit had generated immense good will for the fledgling BSA and
it would be of great benefit now to have Baden-Powell crisscrossing
America on behalf of the organization. West's first aim was to expand
membership, but it was also important to stamp BSA in the public
mind as the one and only legitimate Scouting organization, although
the threat from the American Boy Scouts was much diminished.

Just as West was coming on board in late 1910, Hearst and a
number of highly influential ABS sponsors had disassociated themselves from the organization in a highly public manner. Hearst ran
his letter of resignation on the front page of his *Journal-American*
on December 9, charging that funds had been raised "through false
representation and in other manners that I heartily disapprove of."
The press baron was particularly outraged that ABS managers had
granted commissions of 40 percent to third-party fundraisers. "I consider these methods outrageous and disgraceful," he said, stating his
intention to refer the matter to the law.[51]

BSA officials were highly pleased with this development.[52] Much
confusion had resulted from the similarity of the names and funds
intended for the Boy Scouts of America had gone to its competitor.

ABS members and supporters migrated to the Boy Scouts of America, but ABS managers continued to raise funds, West noted, suggesting that BSA board members approach men listed as ABS honorary vice presidents to make sure that they "fully understand all the facts."[53]

An American tour by Baden-Powell was just the thing to vanquish the American Boy Scouts, but West soon learned of a major complication: Baden-Powell had signed a contract with a New York promoter who thereby controlled his schedule. "The Baden-Powell deal is possibly off," West jotted at the bottom of a letter to a Washington correspondent. Lecture promoter Lee Keedick wanted $35,000 to release Baden-Powell. He eventually settled for $15,000, retaining the right to organize lectures in Boston, Washington, Chicago, Pittsburgh, and a few other cities excluding New York and Philadelphia.[54]

The price was steep but the investment was worthwhile. The new Scouting handbook was scheduled to come off the press in a print run of 100,000 copies in August 1911, in time for the back-to-school season and Christmas several months later. Baden-Powell's tour in February 1912 would help BSA crank up national publicity during a normally slack period, laying the groundwork for further expansion in the 1912 summer camping season.[55]

Yet not everyone was enthusiastic. "Do you know I am very much afraid that a trip through the country by Gen. Baden-Powell is going to hurt rather than help the . . . movement," a Denver juvenile court judge wrote West, expressing concern that his appearances might nurture suspicions Scouting was militaristic in nature. "These suspicions of the proletariat are just now being finally allayed, and his visit . . . is almost sure to start the whole thing in motion again."[56]

But West told Beard said he was not concerned because Baden-Powell "is himself so emphatic on this subject, and will, I believe, help us in having the Scout movement better understood." Yet the letter from Denver "is suggestive of the many problems we have before us in connection with this trip."[57]

Baden-Powell set out from England in mid-January aboard the British liner *S.S. Arcadian*. West sent a letter he hoped would reach him at Cristobal, in the Panama Canal Zone, confiding concerns about Keedick, who had distressed local BSA officials in some cities by proposing military sponsorship of Baden-Powell's lectures and was "not leaving unturned any opportunity of making the most" out of the Boy Scout connection. But, West wrote, "We have told him plainly what we think you stand for [and] he will see that it is absolutely necessary for him to conduct himself in a way which will meet with your approval as well as ours."[58]

Preparations for the visit moved apace. A dinner in Baden-Powell's honor was to be held February 10 at the Hotel Astor. Former U.S. Bureau of Forestry chief Gifford Pinchot, lined up as Chief Scout Woodsman, had agreed to "cooperate in securing a more personal interest on the part of ex-President Roosevelt as toast master or one of the principal speakers at the dinner," West noted.

A menu was prepared suitable to the occasion and guests:

Grapefruit aux Cérises de la Marasquin
Consommé aux Quenelles de Volaille
Filet of Kingfish, Nantua, Potatoes Lorette
Mignons de Boeuf Princesse
Asparagus tips, Haricots verts
Suprème de Volaille George V
Timbale de Riz
Sorbet à la Romaine
Roast Philadelphia Squab au Cresson
Salade de Saison
Glace de Fantaisie
Petits Fours
Fruits Assortis
Café Noir[59]

Hardly Scout fare—but West understood that a well-dined philanthropist is an open-handed philanthropist. He was candid about this in a communication telling the board that invitations would be sent to "men and women of influence, and wealth, not only in New

York City but all adjacent territory within convenient railroad distance" in the aim of securing BSA's finances for three years.[60]

BSA's fiscal situation was not all it should be, West noted, telling the board that "for the first time since I have been connected with the movement we have a deficit," run up commissioning new badges and promotional materials. At least $10,000 needed to be raised by year's end "to care for our obligations."

Field secretaries were required to support the movement's expansion. He was confident Baden-Powell's visit would generate funds for this purpose, "it would be unwise in my judgment to postpone the employment of these men until that time." Seton was arranging a meeting with the philanthropist Andrew Carnegie, and West would reach out to other "men of means" for assistance.[61]

Baden-Powell stepped off the *S.S. Arcadian* in the port of New York on January 31, 1912. It had been a fateful voyage for him in personal terms. During the crossing, Baden-Powell, then fifty-four, met and courted the twenty-two-year-old Olive Soames. The military legend and English maiden shared the same birth date and many interests. They were to marry within the year.[62]

At the pier in New York, Baden-Powell was greeted by fourteen-year-old Scout William Waller of Brooklyn, who had earned a Lifesaving medal by saving a drowning boy. The youth handed Baden-Powell a letter from President Taft in which Roosevelt's successor extended his best wishes for the success of Scouting worldwide.[63] A photographer captured Baden-Powell in Derby hat, high starched collar, tie and overcoat, the young Scout for all of BSA's disclaimers in military tunic, jodhpurs, puttees and boots, and flat-brimmed Stetson service hat.

Baden-Powell did not tarry in New York after his official welcome, heading first for Boston, returning to New York for a tea hosted by the Andrew Carnegies, then traveling to Washington for a reception at the White House. With President Taft and the British ambassador, he reviewed a parade of five hundred Scouts who then demonstrated signaling, first-aid, wireless telegraphing, and fire-lighting.[64]

Baden-Powell swung back to New York on February 9 to visit Roosevelt at Oyster Bay and dine on *Suprème de Volaille* with prospective donors at the Hotel Astor on Broadway at Forty-Fourth Street. Scouts "lined the corridors, and when the international chief showed his face in the doorway they cheered as only Boy Scouts can cheer," the *Times* reported. Toastmaster Gifford Pinchot introduced Baden-Powell as "the man who is able to lead boys as no man can."

According to the *Times* account, "Sir Robert, his coat glistening with medals of honor" informed the room that "under his dress shirt he wore a combination flag of two nations, the United States and the British Empire. Then there were cheers and the evening from that moment on was entirely Sir Robert's."

Baden-Powell told his audience that his mission and that of all those in the movement was to "teach boys character in the way that they like to be taught." He emphasized that despite the military garb of the Scouts, the movement is "not one of war. As far as I am concerned, I hope the world will never, ever have any more war. The movement is not one of religion, either. All that we want is to have the boys put the principles of their various religions into practice."

The lights then went down and a montage of photographs was projected on a screen showing images from London slums to the American plains with Buffalo Bill "chasing buffaloes for dear life," reported the *Times*. Cheers went up from the crowd in response to a photograph of Roosevelt, "seated on a white charger." The former president, Baden-Powell declared, was "the best type of a war-and-peace scout that the boys of America can follow."[65]

Baden-Powell continued his speaking tour with stops in Albany, Buffalo, and Pittsburgh, writing to Livingstone February 19 from Niagara Falls to say he had received West's "modified scheme" for the tour and to apologize for being in less than good health. "You know I have the movement very much at heart and that anything I can do I will do to promote it. I am only so sorry and ashamed that my physical condition is so low—and it's got much worse since I started on tour. I only hope that I can hold out till the end of it." West joined him in Cleveland and they proceeded through Detroit, Chicago, Louisville, St. Paul/Minneapolis, Denver, Salt Lake City, San Francisco, Portland, and Seattle. The only untoward incident came in Portland, where Baden-Powell was heckled by members of the Independent Workers of the World, also known as the Wobblies, who denounced Scouting as a militaristic movement led by a general.[66]

From Seattle on March 11 Baden-Powell took ship for Australia. Offering his host the parting observation that the American boy was ahead of his British counterpart in "individual intelligence," Baden-Powell added diplomatically that, "according to some authorities he lacks discipline."[67] Aside from the jeering by Oregon trade unionists, the tour had been highly successful. It reinforced Scouting in the consciousness of the American public and stimulated donations from sponsors.[68]

Yet the solid footing on which BSA stood as 1912 began was very much the accomplishment of James West in his first year as manager, which Livingstone acknowledged in a letter to the executive in late 1911. "All our reputations are made safe when in the hands of so competent an executive as yourself, and I am sure we all have reason to congratulate ourselves on having you at the helm."[69]

CHAPTER 7
THE FORK IN THE TRAIL

Though James West in his first year as BSA executive secretary had earned the confidence of the organization's board, he was less successful in establishing a bond with Ernest Seton. At best their relationship was uncomfortable, and over time feelings between them approached antipathy. Though Seton had contributed significantly to BSA's development editorially and by his readiness to lend the organization his name as naturalist, author, and pioneer in training boys in outdoor skills, he presented West with serious management challenges.

Seton had reluctantly accepted Baden-Powell's primacy as the founder of Scouting as an organization, but he still considered himself its intellectual founder and wanted to influence its development in the United States. Thus he attached an inordinate significance to seemingly small issues that arose as West and the other professional managers he gathered around him tried to give shape to Scouting in terms of standards, uniforms, icons, awards, and other appurtenances, and to market it to the U.S. public.

Such matters had already created bad feeling within BSA. Seton's insistent, impatient style made itself felt around the issue of pennants BSA was selecting for Scout patrols. Each bore the image of an animal—a fox, a buffalo, and so forth. Seton as a naturalist and artist might rightfully have considered himself to have particular expertise on the subject of wildlife iconography. But these sharp discussions foreshadowed deeper and more damaging disagreements.

Writing to West in October 1911 about pennant designs provided by a contact in England, he declared them to be "samples of how far wrong a man can go who doesn't understand the subject."[1] A month later Seton further belabored the topic in a letter to the editorial board that was unlikely to reduce tensions. His comments were sensible, but the tenor of his letter was condescending. Noting a "lack of understanding of the pennant idea," Seton gave forth at length. "I know something about heraldry and I know a great deal about patrol emblems," he told the editorial board.[2] West consulted Beard. "Mr. Seton is so earnest about the matter that I am appealing to you for advice and help."[3]

Beard dismissed Seton's objections. "I think he is making a mountain out of a molehill." But Beard also was resistant to adopting British conventions. "The fact that I am constantly accused of lending my aid to foisting an English institution upon American boys, is disquieting enough in itself and personally I think if we can't run this on American ground with American emblems we had better quit, and acknowledge ourselves to be incompetent mollycoddles."[4]

Responding, West said he had written to England seeking more information, concluding: "I think Mr. Seton is all wrong in this matter."[5]

Beard would often serve West as a convenient foil to Seton, but he could be every bit as exasperating in pressing his claim as Scouting's American founder. The vexed question arose again that May when Seton wrote to Beard asking him to review and approve a statement he had drafted in response to questions from the public on this point. Some time before this—no doubt at the urging of West—Seton and

Beard had agreed not to advance competing claims. But Seton could not resist proposing a correction to Beard's own history, taking exception to a recent article in which Beard credited Baden-Powell with introducing first aid to the Scouts. "Baden-Powell got that from me," Seton complained, "just as he got the 'shilling in the savings bank' from the Government and Post Office Savings Banks and from Booker T. Washington's address to the negroes. But his daily kind act was taken from the Sunshine Society and many others. In a word, he originated nothing but happily combined materials from all quarters."[6]

"My dear Seton," Beard wrote. "There are several important errors in your account. I also am continually receiving requests for a history of my own personal connection with the Boy Scout movement, but since our agreement I have cut the personal part out of all articles and to make it certain that I lived up to the spirit of the agreement I have submitted everything I have written to headquarters before it was published." He "most decidedly" objected to Seton's version.

"Why not stick to the agreement and cut it out—forget it?" Beard said. "Lord knows I am tired of it and so are all of our friends."[7]

West and other BSA officials were again drawn in. "There is no way of preventing Seton from making any statements he pleases about himself," attorney and board member William Murray told West. "I wonder if we could get him . . . to state the facts and let the public form their own conclusions as to who was the founder of the Boy Scout movement." Seton might simply state that he had started the Woodcraft Indians, took the idea to England, and collaborated with Baden-Powell. "He has not been called upon to make any statements as to what Dan Beard did nor did not do. It seems as if he is bound to make some statement and I feel that this might be a way out of the trouble."[8]

From his vantage point at the Russell Sage Foundation, an exasperated Lee Hanmer told West that "the only way to deal with this ever present controversy is to have a good straight talk with the fellow who starts it every time he makes a start." If West were to speak with

Seton about it "he would be reasonable enough to see the necessity of letting this matter rest. Mr. Beard has certainly shown the proper spirit in refusing to reopen the controversy."[9]

But Beard remained agitated, drafting a heated letter to Murray that he filed instead of posting. Seton seemed determined to "trap me into some statement or admission which he can use to my disadvantage," he wrote. "I am tired and sick of the whole business, and wish some of you men would sit on him hard."[10]

In two letters to Seton that May, Beard accused him of anti-Americanism, a charge he would fling repeatedly at his rival, to his face and in communications with others.[11] Such accusations would stick over time, damaging Seton's position, though in this as in other matters he was his own worst enemy. He rejected the charge by Beard, but acknowledged he had "condemned the U.S. war against Mexico, as he had criticized Britain's Opium War against China. As to the references to the flag, I never in my life said or thought such things as you ascribe to me."

He reminded Beard that the subject of the U.S. flag had come up at a meeting of the Camp Fire Club, to which they both belonged. The conversation had touched on ideas for a new club flag. "I said, 'Do let's have something artistic. The only national flag that has any art merit is the Japanese.' Someone said, 'What's the matter with the stars and stripes.' I replied, 'It's as bad as the British flag, and that's pretty bad.' Any more than this has been added by others."

"As to the subject in general, you seem to forget that my wife, my child, most of my best friends and interests are American. America is my home," Seton told Beard. "I am very sorry you have so long entertained such eroneous [sic] views about me, but I am glad to have them out. I appreciate the sensible concluding part of your letter and will do my part for harmony. I think it would be a good idea for you to meet me sometime and tell me frankly if you have any other misunderstandings of me. Things can be settled in a moment of friendly conversation, but on paper they are apt to look awfully serious."[12]

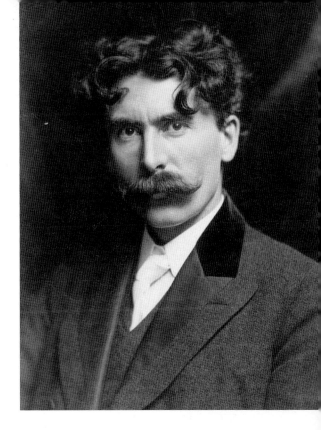

Ernest Thompson Seton in his prime (above),
"the most picturesque guest at the table."
(Clockwise) Daniel Carter Beard in 1904; Seton
promotional portrait, 1902; Grace Gallatin Seton
around 1900; Lobo the King of the Currumpaw,
rendered by Seton.

Well done, Gallant little Mafeking The Empire is proud of you.

INVESTED OCT. 11th 1899.
RELIEVED MAY 17th 1900.

BADEN-POWELL.

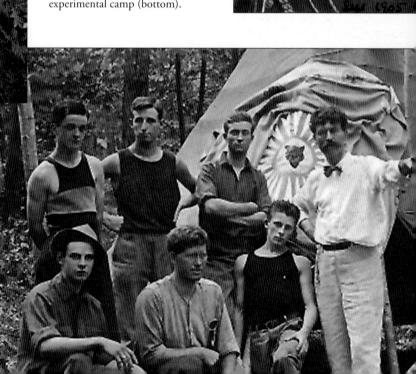

Mafeking commemorative post-card; Robert S.S. Robert Baden-Powell, "the very model of a modern major-general" (right); Dan Beard in his trademark white buckskins (left); Seton and some of his Wood-craft Indians at the 1910 Silver Bay experimental camp (bottom).

Ernest Seton with his Woodcraft Indians (above). Charles Fletcher Lummis visited the Cos Cob estate where Seton taught boys "not only to be hunters, fishers, swimmers, and wrestlers, but to be Men." (left); Hamlin Garland, author, poet, friend of Seton and Beard, and an advocate of Native Americans (below).

President Theodore Roosevelt at Union Station, Washington, D.C., in 1904; famed scouts Buffalo Bill, Pawnee Bill and Buffalo Jones in 1910, armed with "self-reliance (in their) ability to meet and overcome any unlooked-for difficulties" (left); Seton, Baden-Powell and Beard at BSA headquarters in 1912 (below); the Waldorf-Astoria Hotel, where "everybody in the world that is worth knowing would … happen along" (below left).

James West as a young Washington lawyer (left). He earned praise from Theodore Roosevelt for his organization of a 1909 White House conference on child welfare before his 1910 recruitment as BSA executive secretary; (clockwise from top) Seton friend and advocate Edgar Robinson; advertising executive Frank Presbrey; lawyer and BSA historian William Murray; BSA President Colin Livingstone; Dr. Luther Gulick of the Russell Sage Foundation; and BSA incorporator William Boyce.

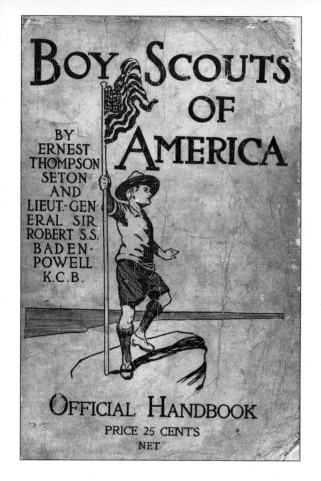

The first *Handbook* of the Boy Scouts of America (left), which Seton drafted combining Baden-Powell's *Scouting for Boys* and his own *Birch-Bark Roll of the Woodcraft Indians;* a young Scout at Arlington National Cemetery in the 1930s (above); a group of Boy Scouts in 1912 (below).

During World War I the Boy Scouts of America raised more than $200 million in Liberty Loan bonds and stamp sales (top); James West as chief scout executive in the 1930s (left); Stanford University President David Starr Jordan, a BSA vice president and advocate of pacifism (below left); conservationist William Hornaday, who drew public attention to the looming extinction of the American bison in the late 1800s (below right).

A Scouting icon serving "th
sacred thing we call boyhood
Uncle Dan Beard offered tips o
camping, preached patriotis
and dispensed wisdom in th
pages of *Boys' Life* magazine (left
National Scout Commission
Beard in a later portrait.

Ernest Seton pursued the Buffal
Wind to New Mexico where h
established the College of India
Wisdom and preached the Gos
pel of the Redman (above); Juli
Buttree experienced "an electri
thrill" at a Seton lecture in 1918
eventually becoming his secre
tary, wife and College of India
Wisdom dean (left).

Beard signaled his readiness to make peace. "If it is deemed absolutely necessary to make a history of this Movement, at some future time I will meet with you and I think by cutting out all disputed points we can make a history which will satisfy the public, and also the people at Headquarters."[13]

Seton by this point was not well looked upon at headquarters. His public reputation was seen as an asset for the organization, but he continually tried the patience of West and other managers. He believed boys should be encouraged to develop in tune with nature, outside the constraints of modern life. But West and other Scouting managers and backers were intently focused for the time being on building institutional structures. They were conservative, looking to Wall Street and Main Street for funding and values. Seton, though highly conscious of social standing, was at the same time a nonconformist. His literary success had given him the means to re-create the wilds in miniature on his Connecticut estate, he could hold audiences in thrall with his highly animated lectures on the natural world and its inhabitants, and he could exert an almost charismatic influence when he chose to make himself agreeable. But Seton lacked experience in public life and the weight of personality necessary to convince men of the world to embrace his vision and follow the path he traced—and he had a knack for alienating people.

Moreover, Seton and West were at opposite poles in their personalities. Both had struggled in earlier life to overcome obstacles establish themselves, but the similarities ended there. By temperament artistic and inward-looking, Seton sought self-fulfillment and recognition through his art and his ideas; West made his place in society by assuming ever greater responsibilities and seeking opportunities for service—though he, too, over time, would exhibit a yearning for prestige and a taste for power. Seton considered the Woodcraft Indians—and wanted Scouting to become—a means of escape for boys from the trammels of modern life, a path to individual authenticity and fulfillment. West was sold on Baden-Powell's vision of Scouting as a method or discipline that could produce capable men and dutiful citizens. This disparity of vision ensured collisions.

One observant witness of this developing conflict was Julian Salomon, who gravitated to the Boy Scouts of America after joining the Woodcraft Indians and the Sons of Daniel Boone. Seton "ran up against a Rock of Gibraltar" in West, the "the hard-boiled executive, very practical in everything he did. He had very little imagination and very little appeal to kids." At the same time, Salomon could see that West "wanted to be a Seton . . . wanted to be a Dan Beard." But he "just didn't have it in him . . . tried hard, but never, never could do it." Scheduled to visit a troop in Brooklyn, West called Salomon in to instruct him in tying Scout knots so he could then demonstrate them to the Scouts across the East River. "So you put a fellow like that, a hard-boiled executive, up against a guy like Seton, and neither one could see what the other one was trying to do."[14]

Seton had admirers among the early founders of American Scouting, like Edgar Robinson, who had provided an early impetus and organizational support from his senior position in the YMCA, John Alexander, and others. But Seton's often-abrasive style and unconscious egotism irritated the businessmen who, with West, established firm control over the organization, not only through their financial backing, but in their hardheaded approach to building and managing the institution. These were men who could obtain a meeting with Rockefeller or Roosevelt with a note or a phone call. Seton had his own relationship with some highly placed figures, including Roosevelt, but these were less substantial and turned out to be of little use when his standing within the Boy Scouts came under serious attack.

Other aspects of Seton's persona diminished him in the eyes of those running Scouting. "Seton's corporeal presence was preceded through life by his smell," writes biographer John Wadland. "He seldom shaved or bathed. His wild and shaggy locks, like untended sails, luffed madly in the breeze."[15] This was not a person to inspire confidence in pin-stripe-suited businessmen. Some of them might appreciate him around a campfire—but not at the board table.

No doubt West was relieved to hear that Seton and Beard had— at least for the moment—agreed to forswear further discussion of their rivalry. He had other business on his mind in the spring and early summer of 1912. Having put BSA on a financially sound basis, his next objective was to acquire or launch a magazine to disseminate Scouting information, strengthen the link with Scouts nationwide, and promote interest in the movement. Such a publication might not only pay for itself, but could generate revenues.

West had been exploring this idea since late 1911 with the help of publishing executives in the BSA network. "I think we should have a magazine of our own at an early date," West told Seton that October. A Scouting magazine "would tend to promote efficiency better than any other agency" and "give you and other men who are such tremendous assets . . . an opportunity to be of greater service in carrying forward the scout program because we could assign to each of you a certain space [for] a definite program of instruction."[16]

A number of magazines for boys were already in print. One in particular followed BSA so closely it styled itself the "unofficial Boy Scout magazine."[17] Ironically, *Boys' Life* was a byproduct of the American Boy Scouts. ABS official George S. Barton of Somerville, Massachusetts, launched it in 1910. When Hearst disavowed ABS, Barton also decamped. With two associates he helped to convert his local ABS branch into the New England Boy Scouts. In January 1911, Barton brought out the first eight-page issue of *Boys' Life*.[18] The second issue came out in March 1911, by which time Barton had hired Joseph Lane[19] as assistant editor and advertising manager. The publication was relaunched as a forty-eight page semi-weekly magazine selling for five cents a copy or $1.20 a year in advance.[20] In June 1911, it settled into a monthly publishing schedule, and Barton brought on a new treasurer, Jack Glenister of Winthrop, Massachusetts, who had won fame as the first man to swim the Niagara rapids. More importantly, Glenister had acumen in building magazine circulation, and by January of 1912 the subscription list of *Boys' Life* was estimated by Barton at around 65,000 names.[21]

West was in touch with Glenister in October 1911 (it appears Glenister had parted company with *Boys' Life* by that date), seeking his opinion as to the advisedness of BSA launching its own magazine. Glenister offered an optimistic opinion: with BSA's membership ready to subscribe, the magazine could generate $1,000 a month in profits on sales of 40,000 copies.[22] Others were more skeptical. Griffith Ogden Ellis, publisher of *The American Boy*, to whom West had passed on Glenister's memo, dismissed its conclusions. "As a prospectus I find only one defect in it; namely that it isn't true," he said, warning that reaching profitability or breakeven would take "a very large sum of money and a very considerable period of time, if my own experience and the experiences of all the other men who have gone into that business afford any criterion for judgment."

Ellis suggested BSA would be better off agreeing with an existing magazine to carry Scouting material. It was not his intention to propose *The American Boy* as such a vehicle, Ellis said, but if the Boy Scouts of America decided upon such a course, "we shall be glad to hear from you as to what you . . . would want us to do." He added that "*The American Boy* can do the movement more good than any publication now in the field or any other that might be started."[23]

Publishing professional Morton Radhner agreed with Ellis that Glenister was overly optimistic, but found "real merit" in the notion that BSA should have its own publication. He agreed most new magazines had to spend heavily to draw readers, and many failed. But, "Not one magazine in five hundred . . . has an army of several hundred thousand readers waiting for it, ready to call it their own." And major advertisers like Colgate and Eastman Kodak would be disposed to advertise in a publication with a relatively small, but very loyal, readership. In short, "a Scout magazine for the Scouts should be able to pay its way."[24]

Boyce got wind of the project and sent a telegram to Livingstone proposing to finance a Scout magazine for three years on condition it be published in Chicago. Livingstone diplomatically declined—the BSA board had concluded that to support Scouting "in the fullest sense," the magazine had to be brought out under the "closest touch and supervision" of Scouting managers. But Livingstone said he would welcome Boyce's "expert advice as to how to proceed" to bring out a magazine quickly and he had named a committee to work with him. But Boyce demurred.[25] "I am awfully busy," he wrote. "I'm glad that you have decided to proceed along the lines which you believe will best advance the interests of the Boy Scouts," he said. But, "I do not believe . . . that at this time I will be of any special use to you. You have your own ideas—I have mine, not as to what should be published in the paper . . . but possibly as to the matter which will sell the paper and the way to sell it." Boyce offered, however, to respond "promptly and to the best of my knowledge and ability" to queries.[26]

West opened negotiations to purchase *Boys' Life*. After meeting Joseph Lane in New York, West made an offer in April 1912 to purchase *Boys' Life* for $3,000 cash, or for $5,000 out of magazine revenues over five years.[27] Barton did not accept the offer, saying he wanted $8,000, $5,000 paid on closing the deal, the balance of $3,000 to be paid over three years. He and his partners had put more than $10,000 into the magazine, "to say nothing of the hard and consistent work required to bring it to its present position." He would consider a "small reduction" of $500 for a cash deal, for a price of $7,500, if West kept Lane on board.[28]

West sought advice from William McGuire of the *St. Paul Dispatch* who told him it "probably would be advantageous to take over a going publication," though he had reservations about *Boys' Life* as a magazine that was "not making its tone jibe with the tone of your organization." But McGuire acknowledged that BSA could "elevate its standard, purify its influence, print nothing (even in the line of fiction) that is not in strictest accord with the *ideals* of Scouting."[29]

Responding, West enumerated the advantages of buying a going concern, in particular that it could take months to get approval to send a new magazine by second-class mail. But the main attraction of *Boys' Life* was that "we immediately get possession of an official organ without investing one cent, because under the latest purchase proposal the magazine would be paid for out of its own cash flow over a three-year period."[30] In the end, BSA reached agreement with Barton to purchase *Boys' Life* for $6,000[31], a third to be paid by November 1, 1912, a third to be paid in a year, the final $2,000 to be paid in eighteen months. West urged Beard to ask friends to subscribe. "Under the rules of the Post Office Department, the number of complimentary copies which can be sent out is very much restricted [so] it is essential . . . to secure a number of bona fide subscriptions at 50 cents a year."

Beard, soon to become identified with the magazine as the author and illustrator of countless articles on outdoor life and do-it-yourself projects, gave West some advice, "Don't let well-meaning good-souled but misguided men dissuade our editors from securing the interest of the boys. Get their *interest* and you have *got* the *boys,* and when you've *got* them you can teach them anything—and they'll *learn*. *Lose* the interest and you LOSE THE BOY!"[32]

West informed the wider Scouting movement in June. "At last—it is an actual fact," he wrote telling members of the *Boys' Life* acquisition. "Needless to say it will be greatly improved, in fact, almost entirely changed as rapidly as possible." It would publish stories "of interest to all boys," and "first-hand information" on the Scouting movement. *Boys' Life* would "stimulate and vitalize" interest in Scouting, West said, as "no unofficial publication could possibly do."[33]

The purchase and relaunch of *Boys' Life* expanded Dan Beard's role in the Scouting organization. But for Seton the summer of 1912 marked a turning point in his relationship with BSA. Since the outset, questions had remained as to his role in Scouting and position as Woodcraft Indians founder. Nowhere was this more evident than in editorial matters, especially his primary authorship of the first Scouting handbook. Copyright to the work was held by his publisher, and Seton commissioned a private printing as an edition of the *Birch-Bark Roll.* His prominence as author was diluted in the revised 1911 manual. But his work permeated it, and Seton drafted the introduction.

This was not lost on BSA's managers and board members, among them lawyers like William Murray and publishing professionals such as advertising executive Frank Presbrey. This became a more serious issue in June 1912 when Seton submitted the manuscript of his latest *Birch-Bark Roll* to BSA's editorial board, on which Murray sat with West, Robinson, Pratt, Hanmer of the Russell Sage Foundation, and others. Seton, aware of the potential sensitivities, noted he had been working for fifteen years on various versions of the book, and he couched the matter in a loose proposal to merge the Woodcraft Indians with the Boy Scouts as a junior branch of the movement. Noting that the manuscript was in the hands of his publisher, Seton declared his "hopes that it will be acceptable to you as a guide in forming the junior organization, although it must be clearly understood that I am to publish this with Doubleday Page & Co., and retain full control of it myself in every form, sense and in all applications." Were BSA to desire to use it in launching the

"Indian Scouts," he added, "you would have to make arrangements direct with Doubleday" for copies.[34]

"I should, of course, be glad to consider any suggestions from the Board," Seton ended, little anticipating what sweeping "suggestions" he would receive.

BSA managers were alarmed by Seton's proposed title page, which in a number of ways conflated Scouting and the Woodcraft Indians:

THE BOOK OF WOODCRAFT

A Manual of
SCOUTING AND LIFECRAFT

Containing the Standards, Games, Constitution,
Laws and Ideals of the
WOODCRAFT INDIAN SCOUTS

Founded July 1st, 1902
By
ERNEST THOMPSON SETON

Head Chief of the Indian Scouts and the Seton Indians,
Chief of the Boy Scouts of America

Meeting in late July, the BSA editorial board adopted five resolutions laying out its concerns with Seton's manuscript. The fear was that it "would be injurious to the Boy Scout movement to . . . print a book so evidently modeled on the Boy Scout manual because it will lead to great confusion." The board further resolved that under no circumstances should Seton publish a book "relating to Scouting or outdoor life" without its approval, and that he should "not . . . make use of the word 'Scouts' in connection with 'Indians.'"[35]

BSA staff member A.S. Moffat, who sat on the editorial board, drafted two memos for the panel. He compared the proposed *Book of Woodcraft* with the BSA *Handbook for Boys*. Another memo compared Seton's proposed schema with an earlier *Birch-Bark Roll* edition, and concluded that it was "vastly different" from the one outlined in that

1908 edition. "In fact, the *Book of Woodcraft* may easily be compared to the *Handbook for Boys*. There is practically no comparison in its methods of work with the scheme of the *Birch-Bark Roll*." Chapter IV on Scouting Outdoors "may be compared with Chapter II in the *Handbook for Boys*." As to the chapter on camping, "Much of this material was used in the chapter on camping in the first manual." Material on tracking, Moffatt added, was "identically the same" as in the *Boy Scout Handbook*.[36]

Based on this analysis and the board's deliberations, a letter was sent to Seton on August 15 signed by Murray, philanthropist George Pratt, and YMCA official Albert A. Jameson. The manuscript "indicates much labor on your part and contains much valuable material [that] would be of great value to the Scout Masters and in fact to all people generally," they said. But the board desired that "a plan may be devised for the publication of the material in a way which will not confuse it with the Boy Scouts of America." Publication in its present form would confuse the public "and in the end partly destroy the usefulness of the Boy Scout scheme in its fullest sense." Nor should he use the word "Scouts" in connection with the Woodcraft Indians. Seton received copies of the memos comparing the *Book of Woodcraft,* the *Boy Scout Handbook,* and his earlier *Birch-Bark Roll,* which he would find "self-explanatory." The board concluded: "It was voted that your attention should be respectfully invited to an error on the title page of your manuscript to the effect that the 'Woodcraft Indian Scouts' were organized on July 1st, 1902." He "evidently" meant the "Woodcraft Indians," as the board had not found any prior use by Seton of the term "Woodcraft Indian Scouts."[37]

Seton was nonplussed when he found the letter on his return from a trip out West. On August 25 he hammered out a three-page response. "First," he stated, "I have always used the word 'scout.'" He provided five citations in the 1906 *Birch-Bark Roll*. Second, "I decidedly object to being told that I modeled this book on the Boy Scout Hand Book. That hand book was modeled *on my work*." Third, "you seem to think that the *Birch-Bark Roll* was my only publication . . . or you would not have made so many extraordinary misstatements," Seton fumed.

He exhaustively rebutted the board's points. "I have always had Tribes divided into Bands which you justly claim to be the exact parallel of Troops and Patrols. Thus the Flying Eagle Band consisting of the Arrow Band, the Setting Sun Band and the Flying Eagle Band proper," he said. "I have always had merit badges, fifteen in number, as follows," detailing for half a page his honors scheme from the "Red Sub-Sachem with twelve honors in Personal Prowess" to the "Blue Grand Sagamore with forty-eight grand honors in Nature Study."

Seton acknowledged he had not originated the term "Boy Scout," and he disclaimed any association with the terms "Troops" and "Patrols," which he considered "most unfortunate" in their military aspects. "They are causing us a great deal of trouble. The Military Drill, and the staves which are really dummy muskets are not mine, and I always disapproved of them. After watching their effect I am convinced that they have cost us thousands of dollars already, and will continue to cost us dear until we drop them. I respectfully urge that they be eliminated as soon as possible. So much for detailed criticism."

Seton then vented his frustration with the editorial board. "Two years ago I offered you this book freely as a gift. You refused it. I told you I would publish it myself. Last January I placed it before you for critical reading, stating that it was to be published soon. For months you gave no signs of life, notwithstanding several requests from me that you consider the matter," he wrote.

"I have revised and corrected the last galley . . . The whole thing is in the hands of the printer and will be published in October. Now when too late you write and ask me to revise it." He added, on a more conciliatory note, that he had already, "for some reasons of my own," made some of the requested changes. "I had eliminated the word 'scout' as far as possible. It does not appear in the title page nor in the official name." His ties to Scouting were not mentioned.

"I have ever been ready to make concessions in the interests of harmony," he concluded. But he disagreed that his *Book of Woodcraft* presented any conflict with the *Handbook for Boys.* "Its price, $1.75, alone should prevent that," he added. "As I see it, and I hope that you will also see it, this is merely another book" that might supplement the *Handbook* for young readers.[38]

Further disagreements were ahead. In late 1912, Doubleday brought out the first in a series of topical handbooks, called *The Forester's Manual.* Beard was critical of the profits he imagined Doubleday and Seton were deriving from sales of the 1910 *Manual* and subsequent books. "You must have had some inkling of the immense commercial value" in the Scouting brand, he chided West, insisting that "the Boy Scout Movement should receive a royalty on everyone [sic] of these books that have been sold under these conditions."[39]

Beard had divided allegiances of his own, though. In 1911, West asked him to set aside his Boy Pioneers, but he refused. The Pioneers had served the movement by "ploughing the ground," Beard maintained, and there were personal financial considerations. Giving up the Pioneers would put an end to his job at the *Pictorial Review* and sales of his *Boy Pioneers* book. "You are asking me to give up a life's work, after . . . making possible the great revival and moral uplift embodied in the movement I started." The Boy Pioneers was "a friendly organization," and "it would be as if I was acting as a traitor to them to abandon them now."[40]

But Beard's outlook changed by late 1912—the acquisition of *Boys' Life* raised the prospect of more plentiful writing assignments. He informed the BSA executive in October that he envisioned a "scheme by which I can gradually turn the Boy Pioneers into members of the Boy Scouts of America," with the consent of *Pictorial Review* editor Arthur Vance. But, "it is a delicate situation, and I must handle it with great care." He did not want the Boy Pioneers to feel "deserted," and hoping that they might find familiar references in the Scouting *Handbook* gave BSA the right to adopt whatever might be of use from his *Buckskin Book,* "of course, giving credit, as is the custom in all such cases." Beard hinted that he felt under-appreciated, observing to West that "it is always difficult for the theoretical men to understand or appreciate the value of the work of the practical men who are face to face with the personal problems of dealing personally with the boys. In the latter line, I have probably had more experience than anyone."[41]

Despite such outbursts, Beard was adjusting better to the new Scouting order than Seton. Seton was increasingly at odds with head-quarters. Chafing at the restrictions imposed by the editorial board, he devoted more time to his Indians, justifying this in a letter to Alexander, by then at the International Sunday School Association. "A great many of the Boy Scout Organizations . . . are using the Woodcraft Indians as a higher circle of their group and in some cases as a junior circle, but I have not yet got it worked out as to the best method."[42]

Seton raised his tone in a November 1912 missive to the executive board criticizing aspects of Scouting that seemed militaristic. In the early days, he had "protested vigorously against all the military features that had been introduced by foreign contributors," a clear reference to Baden-Powell. Again he denounced the use of staves by Scouts. "They may have use for staves in England," he said, "but in this country all legitimate purposes can be served by a stick or pole picked up as occasion may require." Staves, he repeated, were "dummy muskets," and drills made scoutmasters into "sergeants." He urged the board to "eliminate as many of these" features as soon as possible, "and all military drill and maneuvers."[43]

His position was undercut a few months later when staves held by Scouts serving as parade marshals in the streets of Washington helped them to separate abusive crowd members from marching suffragettes. It was with evident satisfaction that West sent Beard a clipping from the Washington *Evening Star* about the episode. "The work done by Boy Scouts Monday in their effort to hold the crowd in check in or-der that the suffragettes might march unmolested shows that the staff is the most important part of their equipment," the paper reported. "Without them the boys would have been powerless to hold back the thousands of people who were closing in on the marchers on both sides." The *Star* expanded on noted versatility of the staves, which

"have a score or more of uses in the camps of the Scouts. They serve
as tent poles, as cranes for cooking, as poles for their signal flags and
as levers for moving logs, rocks, etc."[44] This implicit rebuttal of Seton's position on staves also contained an irony that he could hardly
have missed: his wife, Grace Seton, was an active suffragette.

Soon after, Beard took another jingoistic swipe at Seton. "Inas-
much as we have, for our Chief Scout a very distinguished subject of
Great Britain, an alien who has stated in unequivocal language his
disapproval of the principles upon which this Country is founded,"
he wrote to West, "I should long ago have pointed out to the Board
the danger of appointing an alien and an enemy of our institutions to
that high position in our organization."[45]

Beard clearly viewed Seton as a rival not only for the distinction
of being the foremost American Scouting founder, but as a possible
competitor for editorial assignments from the BSA organization. He
would continue to play the cards of nativism and patriotism against
the British-Canadian naturalist.

A far more serious breach, meanwhile, was widening between
Seton and BSA management. By early 1914, Seton was deeply dissatisfied, eliciting consternation and exasperation from West, Beard,
and others. Seton and Beard had once shared grievances as to their
place in Scouting, especially relative to Baden-Powell. But Seton's relationship with BSA was ever more complicated and adversarial. The
smallest irritants led him to vent his displeasure. In January 1914, he
stirred up a small tempest in an overwrought letter to West urging
him to ban chewing gum advertisements from the pages of *Boys' Life*.
"I find it hard to use temperate language in referring to the vulgar,
disgusting American habit of gum-chewing," Seton told West. This
"degrading practice," he expostulated, had been "fastened upon our
youth as a dope habit by the unscrupulous gum trust."[46]

Beard was incensed at Seton's somewhat gratuitous aside to West that, "abroad, the common name for Americans is 'Swine,' on account of their manners and habits."[47] England, Beard said, "would be ready to welcome the prodigal on his return from doing the 'swineherd' act here in America." Beard added that he was "totally unable to understand the characteristics of a man who believes in the monarchical form of government who owes his allegiance to such a country, who looks with contempt upon republicanism and democracy and who, in spite of all this, lives among us, makes his money out of us, insults us and then expects us to support him."[48] He sent a copy of this communication to West to executive board member Frank Presbrey, charging that Seton's "ill-advised" letter "thinly veils a rabid and intense hatred of America."[49]

Beard was finding his place in American Scouting, declaring at BSA's fourth annual meeting: "The Scout Movement is no longer an experiment. It is a success and has been proven that it is needed by our schools, our churches and our civic bodies." Beard reaffirmed Scouting as a way to transmit American values. "The wilderness is gone, the Buckskin Man is gone, the painted Indian has hit the trail over the Great Divide, the hardships and privations of pioneer life which did so much to develop sterling manhood are now but a legend in history, and we must depend upon the Boy Scout Movement to produce the MEN of the future."[50]

Despite his dalliance earlier in life with the American left, Beard was in tune with Scouting's values. Though his father came from humble origins, Dan Beard was a son of the American establishment and was already shaping his own role as a font of authenticity for the movement as it expanded its membership and influence.

Yet Beard could be every bit as self-centered as Seton. Never one to suffer a slight in silence, he chastised West at one point for listing Seton's name before his own in a *Boys' Life* press release. Though the Chief Scout outranked the National Scout Commissioner, where *Boys' Life* was concerned, Beard "declined to appear in the second place" with Seton, his junior in years and, he maintained, experience with youth. It was "humiliating" to see a BSA release published in a newspaper in Flushing "with an alien's name ahead of the advocate of Americanism."[51]

As Seton grew increasingly estranged from Scouting management, his ire with the editorial board intensified. He resented not being appointed to the panel when he felt he should have been made its chairman. In May 1914, he catalogued his grievances in a meeting with West and Murray, giving Murray the draft of a five-page letter of complaint addressed to the executive board.[52]

"It seems impossible for myself and this Board to continue together unless we arrive at a clearer understanding about certain matters of policy," he opened. Then he developed the case that his Indians laid the foundation for Scouting—"this was the Boy Scouts," in its essentials, maintained Seton, a point of view "admitted by all of the fair-minded persons in touch with the subject." Baden-Powell had only "rechristened" his Woodcraft Indians as Boy Scouts, Seton insisted.

Turning to editorial matters, he charged that once BSA had been launched, "an effort was made to take the *Manual* out of my hands," and ceded control of the *Manual* to the editorial board on condition he be its chairman. "Imagine my surprise on returning from England to find that I was not even a member of the Board; but the control of my work [was] given to a group of men without literary positions or editorial experience in a professional sense. I let this pass, believing that possibly it would be better for the movement even if I had to sacrifice myself and lose control of my own life work." But, "[a]fter close observation I found that in the main contention also I was right and the Board was wrong," because it was making the *Manual* "more and more of an impersonal cyclopedia."

Seton continued his philippic, "I have to complain further of an utter lack of candor on the part of the Board in their dealings with me. Never once have they come to me frankly and asked me to do thus and so, for the good of the cause, but have always tried to trick me into it." He had heard the board was embarrassed by his defense of Scouting activities on Sunday. "Why does not the Board tell me about their embarrassment, instead of everyone but me?" he demanded.

"Not so long ago Mr. West notified one of my boys in charge of a camp that no Indian activities were to be tolerated.[53] When I spoke to Mr. West about it he said that he was acting for the Board. How is it I never heard about it? Why can't I also know the wishes of the Board where it concerns me."

Seton then went to the heart of the matter: his lack of any substantial role in BSA. He was not a member of the executive or editorial boards. Instead, "I am put on the Finance Committee for which I am not fitted and on which I decline to serve again." He had volunteered to lecture thirty days a year for BSA, but "No notice was taken." He offered to spend one day a week at headquarters handling Scout business at his own expense—this too was ignored. His offer of a traveling crafts exhibition brought the response from West that he would approve or reject the exhibits. "As I do not propose to take orders from Mr. West I dropped the subject," Seton informed Murray.

"And above all I have objected to the continual and unceasing militarism you are injecting into this movement," he wrote, "inculcating under the specious name of patriotism the arrogant, unfair and monstrously selfish spirit that has caused most of the shameful wars of modern times." Management, he said, had eliminated "all beautiful, picturesque and spiritual thought" from Scouting.

Seton closed by declaring that "I cannot work with a Board that does not take me into its confidence" and "will not continue with any organization that is working towards militarism and secretly building up an army."[54]

Seton voiced his frustration in a note to Edgar Robinson, addressing him by the Indian name of "Gitchee Saka," or "Big Stick," which he had given him. "I suppose it is hardly necessary to tell you that we have reached the fork in the trail. I cannot longer continue with those people on the present basis. They may be actuated by honorable motives but they have the most cowardly ways of putting them in practice. They have never yet come to me with a statement of what they think ought to be done, but have laid traps for me, or waited till I have been abroad before taking action which they know I should not approve."[55]

Seton apparently received no satisfaction from Murray, for on June 21 he wrote directly to the executive board demanding to be named chairman of the editorial board, failing which he would re-claim all the material he had contributed to the *Handbook* and pub-lish it independently. By July he seemed ready to follow through on this threat. BSA had "violated every condition on which I gave them the use" of his editorial contributions. So he served notice that "I withdraw that *Manual* absolutely and will henceforth attend to its publication myself." Lawyer West was not impressed. "There is . . . comparatively little material in our present *Handbook* of which Mr. Seton can claim control," he told Beard.

Seton's aggravation mounted. Later that summer Frank Double-day at his instigation met with BSA Treasurer George Pratt seeking to elucidate matters, noting in a letter to Seton on August 19 that he had waited for twenty-four hours after his talk with Pratt before responding. "Confidentially, I was not impressed with Mr. Pratt's attitude," Doubleday told Seton. "Apparently he and I don't look upon the values and proprieties connected with literary property in the same way, and I understand now for the first time the difficul-ties . . . you have encountered and the cause for the irritation which has been such a constant source of difficulty." He suggested Seton take more definitive action.

"My advice," wrote Doubleday, "is to write a pleasant letter to the President of the Boy Scouts, whom I understand to be Mr. Liv-ingstone, and to say to him that you have had so many disagreements with the organization, and in so many particulars your ideas do not coincide, that you think it better to resign from all association with the organization" as chief Scout and as a writer, requesting that his name and material be removed from the next edition of the *Manual*.

Such a move might be welcomed by BSA, Doubleday said, for Pratt "did not hesitate to say to me that he thought your resignation would straighten out many complications." He added that "it would be unfortunate for everybody if it got around that there was a row; it would do neither you nor the Boy Scouts any good; for, after all, you are anxious not to do anything which will prevent boys from getting all the good that can be secured from this Boy Scout organization." This, Doubleday told Seton was his best advice. "I see no way of your getting any happiness or satisfaction in being associated with the present organization, and I have no doubt that the present organization have put money into the plan and will stay in command. I am sorry to write you in this way, as it is exactly the opposite of what I expected to write, but facts are facts."[56]

But for months Seton was unable to act.

CHAPTER 8

SETON TAKES LEAVE

The collapse of relations between Ernest Thompson Seton and Scouting gathered momentum with the outbreak of war in Europe in August 1914. Seton found himself in an ambiguous position as a Briton immersed in American isolationism in the conflict's initial stage. Dan Beard could not resist a jibe. "There is a splendid opening abroad for him now where he can gain Laurels, decorations and the name of a hero," he crowed in a note to West, declaring himself "delighted . . . at the great opportunity which England offers him as an English patriot for a chance to win everlasting Glory or lay down his life for the land he loves so well."[1] Seton's alienation deepened even as U.S. nationalism swelled with the likelihood that America would enter the war.

Increasingly marginalized within the Scouting organization, Seton turned to John Alexander for a sympathetic ear. The Scots-born Canadian had left BSA for the International Sunday School Association in Chicago, but the two remained good friends. They talked over Seton's plight late that summer at a YMCA camp, and

Alexander wrote to West in September informing him that Seton was "very much disturbed and perturbed over the whole business." Seton had told Alexander that West and other BSA managers "will not accept his resignation and are very much disappointed that he even offers it." Yet "you will not allow him to take any definite part in the moulding of the policies of the organization. He even says that you do not wish anything else but the use of his name in an official, ornamental way. I think this pretty nearly sums up the way he put the matter to me, and I have an idea . . . that this pretty much sums up the whole matter from your end as well." He told West that it was "purely selfishness" on the part of BSA to bind Seton, concluding that "it seems to me that this is the time for you to release Mr. Seton from any further obligation to the Scouts and at the same time relieve yourself and [BSA] of all embarrassment coming from his attitude toward you."[2]

Even Beard, never one to back Seton, concurred, telling West that "we have no excuse for not accepting Mr. Seton's resignation, it would show a lamentable weakness upon our part to decline to do so." BSA should free Seton to go back to his Woodcraft movement "and run it to suit himself." Any other course of action would be "unjust," un-American, and unbefitting of Scouting ideals.[3]

West responded to Alexander that "we have realized for some time that Mr. Seton has been disturbed, but many of the facts which you present are new to us." Seton "is laboring under a grave misapprehension of the real facts," having been re-elected chief Scout in February 1913 in line with an amended BSA constitution specifying that he was "honorary head of the organization" with a staff of experts on various aspects of Scoutcraft. He was an honorary member of all committees, including the editorial board, so "he has a right to object to his not having been invited to meet with the Committee if he so desired," though as a practical matter, "honorary members are never invited to take part in such meetings."

West dismissed Seton's contention that his contribution of material to the Scout *Handbook* had been on the condition that he chair the editorial board. The records showed "precisely the contrary," he insisted. Seton had sought the chair of the editorial committee, "but it was thought . . . that it would be better not to have either Mr. Seton, or Mr. Beard serve actively" on the panel. The editorial board had solicited Seton's advice and took some of it, but "it could not adopt all of Mr. Seton's suggestions," West explained.

The Scouting executive told Alexander he had "patiently listened" to Seton's grievances on the eve of his re-election as chief Scout at the organization's 1914 annual meeting in Washington, and underscored the opportunity for Seton to develop his nominal staff, including Chief Scout Citizen Theodore Roosevelt. Seton could have played an active and practical role "along lines which would be of immense value to the movement and to the propagation of outdoor life." But, "I fear that he has not keenly appreciated just what this opportunity presents."

West then turned to what he considered the source of the dispute: Seton's British citizenship, which had come to public attention through Grace Seton's suffragist activities. She was vice president of the Connecticut Woman Suffrage Association, which won the vote for women in school board elections in 1914.[4] But when she attempted to exercise this franchise, "her right to register was challenged on the ground that Mr. Seton was not a citizen of the United States," West said. "The New York papers could not resist the opportunity of making a great deal of this matter and it became quite generally known," he continued, and the controversy was "brought to my attention in such as way as to require action." West was "loathe to believe" the reports, "but upon inquiry it was ascertained that Mr. Seton was not a citizen of the United States." He cited communications from Scouting officials "strongly objecting to continuing in an organization with a Chief Scout who, it was alleged, maintained his citizenship abroad."

Taking up the matter, a special board committee concluded that "the only fair and least offensive thing to do" was to bring the matter to Seton's attention through a friend who might "advise him of the embarrassment he was causing" the Boy Scouts, and ask that he either become a citizen or resign. The committee eventually settled on Frank Doubleday as the man best placed for the job. At West's request, Doubleday sent Seton a note "of the most personal character bringing the matter to his attention in a kindly way."

Individual board members met with Seton, but these conversations did little to resolve the situation. Seton repeated his demand that he be appointed editorial board chairman, threatening otherwise to pull his material from the handbook and publish a manual of his own. The board wrote Seton telling him a review of BSA records found no evidence of a commitment to name him head of the committee, adding that it was thought "unwise" for any author to hold that position.

Following these deliberations in June 1915, Frank Doubleday met with board member George Pratt at Glen Cove, Long Island, where "the matter was discussed most frankly," West told Alexander. Pratt laid out the board's position on Seton's citizenship. Doubleday responded that Seton objected to becoming a citizen under duress, whereupon Pratt "frankly told him that the only course open for Mr. Seton then was for him to resign." West assured Alexander that he had done all he could to avoid such an outcome, "knowing full well . . . that it would injure him immeasurably with the American people who have been so good to him."

There was little sympathy for Seton among BSA managers, West confided to Alexander. Seton's attacks on editorial and executive board members, his "threats to go to the newspapers with his story, with the charge of militarism and the failure of the Scout movement to be really spiritual, etc. etc. have, I believe, been provoked by anger and are not truly representative of Mr. Seton himself, but these threats and comments have none the less provoked some of our people to a point where they are not inclined to be patient with him."

But, West continued in what would seem a rather disingenuous statement, "Very fortunately, in this whole matter, the relationship between Mr. Seton and myself has been most cordial and happy. I have a great deal of regard for him and, fortunately, have been able to see the question from both sides, but I believe that the best evidence of my friendship, is the effort I have been making to have Mr. Seton brought to the point where he will do the right thing for himself and for the movement. It seems to me that all of his friends should work in the same direction and I sincerely hope that you can see your way clear to take this matter up with him in a most frank manner and point out the course of action he should follow."[5]

A copy of this letter went to Beard, who told West that he was exercising undue forbearance. "I think in your effort to stand straight, you are leaning backwards and have overrated the services of a certain party."[6] West also shared Alexander's letter with Doubleday, who was still trying to patch things up, with a copy of his response. The board had tried to keep the question of citizenship from becoming a matter of record. Attorney William Murray, "a most estimable, fair-minded gentleman," had talked it over with Seton in a one-to-one meeting at his law offices, whereupon Seton "promised, without reservation, to take steps to take out citizenship papers upon Mr. Murray's assurance that we had suffered some embarrassment because of the situation."[7]

But West's explanation did not sit well with Alexander. "I do not think that the American citizenship business figures very largely in the matter at all. In fact you will excuse me if I think it is a rather flimsy position." Alexander had seen a newspaper article about Grace Seton's disqualification from voting,[8] but the tenor of it was that "it was considered sort of a joke on her after all her work for equal suffrage." In his extensive travels, Alexander added, "I have never, in any place, heard a single word against Mr. Seton because of the fact that he was a British subject, [and] I do not think that any right-thinking man who wants to be at all fair would hold this against Mr. Seton for a moment."

Alexander went further in defense of his "dear old friend" Seton. "If I was in his place and someone was to club me into becoming an American citizen, by threatening to withdraw from me an honorary or honorable position, I should not hesitate to let the position go just as fast as it could. I do not think that is the track to take, if you will allow me to express my honest opinion."

Nonetheless, Alexander could see where matters were headed. "I do not think that Mr. Seton and the men who direct the Boy Scout movement are ever going to work together; and I really believe it is to the best advantage of all concerned to have a peaceful parting. For this reason I have advised Mr. Seton to insist upon the acceptance of his resignation, but to avoid all newspaper publicity in the matter, and to simply say that he withdrew from the Chief Scoutship in order that he might better develop his own Woodcraft Indian plans."[9]

Not long after, Alexander dropped Seton a note. "My dear Black Wolf," he wrote. "I hope you will get the Boy Scout matter settled as quickly as possible," he told Seton, advising him to take his earlier advice and "sever . . . connections without publicity and give [your] attention wholly to the Indian work."[10]

What West failed to mention to Alexander was the specific source of the pressure for Seton to acquire U.S. citizenship. Legislation was pending in the U.S. Congress to grant the Boy Scouts of America a federal charter enshrining BSA's exclusive right to make use of the terms "Scout" and "Scouting," among other considerations. Boyce, Livingstone, and the other initial BSA incorporators had not been successful in gaining such recognition since 1910. But BSA by this date had established itself as a national institution and had powerful friends. A federal charter would provide ironclad protection against competition. Hearst's American Boy Scouts were much diminished but were a potential source of trouble though the publisher had severed his ties with it over alleged financial irregularities and deceptive fund-raising practices, taking with him most other supporters.

The American Boy Scouts had changed its name to the United States Boy Scouts in mid-1913 following a decision by the New York

Supreme Court that was intended to relieve public confusion.[11] But another case loomed that was not to be resolved for years. The U.S. Boy Scouts made a half-hearted effort in April 1914 to settle matters, proposing a merger. A certain Major Physioc told West a donor was ready to back the deal with $5,000 in funding. The new organization would be called the U.S. Boy Scouts of America and although it was to be non-military in character, would have a division called the U.S. Boy Scout Army and Navy with a hierarchy based on the federal structure. Roosevelt would be chief scout, West would be chief executive, and Physioc would be chief of staff and adjunct general of the Boy Scout Army and Navy, commanded by General E.A. McAlpin. BSA's leadership had little interest in such an arrangement.

But the U.S. Boy Scouts no longer offered real competition, and the proposal that Scouting should have a military wing was guaranteed to raise the hackles of purists who believed that Scouting should have no military aspect whatsoever. West in any case was by this time intent on securing the BSA franchise, and in August 1913 sought a federal charter. House Resolution 755 was introduced by Rep. Charles C. Carlin of Virginia, and the measure would become law eighteen months later. It reserved the phrases "Boy Scout" and "Scouting" for the exclusive use of BSA.[12] Yet passing the special legislation presented a number of difficulties, not least the residual suspicions of the Catholic Church and the trade union movement.

Some issues were more easily resolved than others. Reviewing the legislation, Beard fretted, telling West that, "If I am not mistaken I use the words Boy Scouts both in my Book *The Boy Pioneers: Sons of Daniel Boone* and in my *Buckskin Book* both of which were written before we organized the Boy Scouts of America. Of course I cannot agree to have either of those publications deemed illegal or so considered by anyone." He complained that the movement "has thoughtlessly already injured me financially and subjected me to great injustice, but this was due to their lack of knowledge of conditions and facts and I know that they will not knowingly make an effort to further penalize me for being the pioneer in a movement of which all of us are justly proud."[13] West assured Beard that the new status "will not in any way affect your rights or raise any question which could by any possible interpretation harm the distribution of your books." To make certain of this, West inserted a phrase in the resolution stating that it was "distinctly and definitely understood that nothing in this Act shall interfere of conflict with established or vested rights."[14] Relieved, Beard signed off on the draft.

For Seton this process had far more troubling implications. The bill was six months away from passage when the European war began in August 1914, and in the ensuing months BSA's political sensitivities focused on Seton. One provision of the legislation required all BSA board members to be U.S. citizens. Seton over the years had considered acquiring U.S. citizenship, but never followed through. As West noted, his nationality came under scrutiny in part because of his wife's suffragist connections. But Seton had never been shy about expressing his anti-militarist sentiments, and these were not out of step with the conviction among many Americans that the United States should stay out of the war in Europe. But such isolationist attitudes were often accompanied by nativism and more than a touch of xenophobia. And as U.S. opinion shifted in the other direction, it was not a good time for Seton to take up the banner of anti-militarism, but with many in BSA taking a pacifist stance, he readily expressed his opposition to the current in the country favoring military preparedness. As it happened, this comforted his old entrenched resentment of General Sir Robert S.S. Baden-Powell.

Yet the self-described "advocate of Americanism," also objected to what he saw as a drift toward militarism. Beard blamed Baden-Powell for what he considered militaristic strains in Scouting, citing the motto "Be Prepared" as "a war phrase, originated by a warrior and intended for the very war that is now devastating Europe." It was "weak and snobbish of us" to adopt it, he told West. "Those of you who make a study of psychology, must recognize the seriousness of our tendency to be weak-kneed and to have a lack of confidence in our own ability and our own sense, and our own Americanism."[15]

Such questions weighed ever more heavily on the Scouting organization, complicating Seton's relations with its top ranks. In late
December 1914, Seton went over West's head to Colin Livingstone,
BSA's Washington-based president. "Some time ago a friend asked
me whether I had adjusted my differences with the Executive Board,"
Seton's letter began. "I replied, 'No, and it seems almost hopeless. If
these were low-minded men with a selfish purpose in view it would
be easy to defeat them, but there is not a man on the board with an
axe to grind, or any selfish or unworthy end in view. They are united
in wishing to advance the Boy Scout movement as a national benefit
and are freely giving their time and money to it. Their motives are
above suspicion. But alas, they are utterly blinded by a wrong ideal
and imperfect knowledge of the means."

In over nine typewritten pages Seton outlined his grievances
with BSA, mingling his resentment at Baden-Powell's appropriation
of his ideas with a denunciation of the militarism which, due to
Baden-Powell's influence, seemed to him to permeate the *Scouting
Manual.* "Of course it does not appear openly as such, but the idea
is clearly instilled by its teachings" and the instruction of Scouts in
"drill, rifle shooting, army signaling" and inculcating "blind obedience to his country's leaders." America had been in twelve wars
from the Revolutionary War to the Spanish-American War of 1898,
Seton said. "In both her wars with Great Britain, America was absolutely right, and in all the other wars she was shamefully and wick-
edly wrong . . . a murderous treacherous bully, ignoring all treaties
and solemn obligations for the sake of territorial gain."[16] Scouting,
he warned Livingstone, was "carefully nurturing" militarism and
jingoism "by adroit choice of books and stories in glorification of
these criminal wars, setting up as heroes the very man who were
responsible for them."

"In my work I attach great importance to the symbolical, the po-
etical, the beautiful, the appeal to the imagination," Seton declared.
"In Baden-Powell's work these are carefully eliminated and here our
Board has followed Baden-Powell. Of course. Why not? Are not such

things unnecessary to a soldier? Yes, even detrimental to the perfect mankiller." Scouting's leadership had failed to grasp "the bigness of the Woodcraft Idea," and had marginalized its originator. Coming to his differences with the editorial board, Seton refreshed his complaints and accused its members of "making the Manual less and less of a Boys' book for *character-building,* and more and more of an impersonal cyclopedia for *army-building.*"

Concluding, Seton set three conditions for his continued participation in Scouting. First, the executive board must state what it wished Seton to do in his capacity of chief Scout. Second, his contributions to the *Manual* "must either be accepted on my conditions or not at all." Third, he would have to be "absolutely free" to pursue the development of his Woodcraft Indians. Otherwise, he would tender his resignation. "I am My Dear Sir," he closed, "Yours Sincerely, Ernest Thompson Seton." Underneath was his trademark paw print.[17]

Livingstone didn't respond to Seton until late January, after meeting over lunch with relatively neutral board members to discuss Seton's points. The matter was put to the board, whose members met January 29 and "reaffirmed their broad view that the Boy Scout Movement was greater than any individual connected with it," Livingstone informed Seton, a position with which "we all felt sure you would heartily concur." From this, Livingstone proceeded to the issue of Seton's citizenship—to which Seton's long letter had not made any reference.

"The Board has been made aware of difficulties in some quarters on account of the criticisms made of the Movement for the reason that its Chief Scout is not a citizen of the United States. In the teaching of higher ideals of patriotism which are fundamental in the scout program, it is difficult to explain how it happens that the Chief Scout who should be an exemplar and inspiration, has not become a citizen of the country of his adoption. The Board is aware of the delicacy of your present position in this connection and was informed that it was your intention to become naturalized, but for the reason as stated to me as Chairman of the Board in a recent interview that you might be criticized for taking this step, when Great Britain, the nation of which you are a subject is at war."

"While sympathizing with you in the embarrassment which this step might cause, nevertheless the Board felt that it should receive some definite assurance from you that you would become a citizen of the United States in the near future." Pending Seton's return from a trip to Britain on which he was shortly to depart, and resolution of the citizenship question, BSA would leave the office of chief Scout vacant at its annual meeting in February, coming up in a fortnight.[18]

Seton left for England on January 30 aboard the Cunard Line's Royal Mail Ship Lusitania. Before the ship sailed, he sent Grace a note on ship's stationery to tell her that "I've written to the Boy Scouts to say it is my intention to take out my [citizenship] papers as soon as the European situation justifies it."[19] He wrote to her again on January 31, reporting calm seas and clear, cold weather, though "it gave us a sensation to pass between" two British battleships ten miles out of New York Harbor like "two bulldogs on guard." Running lights were covered up and portholes curtained against the risk of German attack. From ship he sent a wireless to the Boy Scouts, reiterating that he would adopt U.S. citizenship "as soon as the European situation cleared."[20]

Before leaving, though, Seton had drafted a letter of resignation, though he was not yet ready to send it.[21] It was addressed to Livingstone and the executive board and stated, in its entirety; "I regretfully recognize that our ideas on methods and ideals are hopelessly diverse therefore I hereby tender my resignation of all association with the Boy Scouts of America."[22]

Seton reached England safely, but the Lusitania's days were numbered. A U-boat torpedo sent the liner to the bottom on May 7,

1915, with the loss of 128 American lives out of a total of 1,195 victims. U.S. isolationism gave way to outrage and deepened anti-German feeling. The United States would not enter the war for another two years, when Congress passed a joint resolution on April 6, 1917, declaring war on Germany. But Americanism surged and the tense climate heightened sensitivities to questions of nationality. Despite the largely pro-British feeling among the American public, Seton's nationality became an urgent issue at the top of American Scouting, even as the movement itself struggled internally to define its position on issues of war and peace.

Such questions were not entirely new. BSA had been grappling for years with public perceptions that Scouting's purpose was to ready youth for military service. Baden-Powell's image as a war hero could not help but convey this impression no matter how much he downplayed the military aspects of the Boy Scouts—its organization into troops and patrols, the uniform which in America featured tunic, jodhpurs, and puttees. In Britain such accoutrements, and Baden-Powell's injunction to Scouts to be obedient to employers, fostered resistance among a working class embracing socialism as the substratum of trade unionism. U.S. trade unionists who had faced national guard gunfire in labor confrontations raised similar objections. West confided in Baden-Powell in September 1911 that "the labor people and socialists are opposing us bitterly."[23] An internal BSA memorandum that October listed thirteen labor federations in Colorado, Wisconsin, Indiana, Michigan, and Missouri that declared opposition to the Scout movement.[24] Determined to overcome such distrust, West opened a correspondence with Samuel Gompers, president of the American Federation of Labor, who informed him in December that the AFL executive council would soon examine the "influences, economic or otherwise," of Scouting.[25] West sent Beard a copy of the letter from Gompers, assuring him: "There can certainly be no doubt as to the outcome of this matter." But as one scholar would later note, BSA for a long time earned only the AFL's "grudging tolerance."[26]

BSA's defensiveness on the point of militarism predisposed it to develop ties with pacifist groups. In March 1911, for instance, West informed Beard that he and John Alexander, still with BSA at that time, had held meetings with William Short, executive secretary of the New York Peace Society, "with a view to securing the active co-operation of that and similar organizations." This interest may not have been motivated solely by pacifist conviction—the New York Peace Society's president was industrialist-philanthropist Andrew Carnegie, a potential sponsor who would be welcome as BSA sought to expand. Peace Society leader Short was "at first inclined to be skeptical" but was eventually "convinced of our sincerity in trying to avoid militarism in the Boy Scout movement," West told Beard. So much did West desire the good opinion of the Peace Society that at Short's behest he entertained suggestions from New York sculptor Kenyon Cox on how Scouting's fleur-de-lis emblem might be modified to minimize military connotations, including the addition of a pole star to reinforce the compass motif, clasped hands within the device, and an olive branch inserted below.[27]

Queried on the matter, Baden-Powell remarked that "it would truly be an ingenious boy who could discover a warlike meaning" to the fleur-de-lis, and that "such meaning never entered my head in devising it." He informed West that "the origin of the trefoil, lily or Shamrock, as a badge is practically identical with that of the Cross. The fleur-de-lis or lily being practically used as the sign for purity." This badge had been adopted by Scouts in "almost every civilized country," so "it would be a great pity for the American Scouts to change the Badge which is now universally recognized [as] that of our brotherhood." He dismissed the notion that his soldiering career must impart a military color to Scouting. This was "an advantage rather than otherwise because one who has seen something of the horrors and brutality of war must naturally be in earnest about peace-making [more] than the man who merely theorizes upon it."[28] The Peace Society's recommendations were filed away.

In the first year of the war, BSA strengthened its ties with organizations seeking to end the killing in Europe. Most influential in this regard was Stanford University President David Starr Jordan, a leading figure in the U.S. peace movement.[29] An accomplished naturalist, Jordan had conducted the Pacific portion of an 1880 survey of U.S. fisheries and maintained ongoing ties with the ichthyologists of the Smithsonian Institution. Jordan joined the BSA National Council in 1911 and by 1913 was a BSA vice president. He also contributed to *Boys' Life* at the urging of West, who declared that "anything from your pen, written especially for boys, would be avidly consumed by them."[30]

But with the outbreak of war, Jordan's reputation as an advocate of peace most interested West. "You know how all of us are shuddering with horror at the great calamity which has come upon Europe and is affecting the entire world," West told Jordan in September 1914 in a letter mailed to him at the London offices of War and Peace. "Familiar with your great devotion to the work for peace, I have thought often of the sorrow which this tremendous breach has caused you, and how much more clearly the horror of it must be revealed to you than to us in a neutral nation so far away." The war had delivered a blow to "the Scouting method which strives to instill a spirit of brotherhood and peace," West said. Jordan knew how hard BSA officials "have worked to keep militarism out of the minds of boys and therefore you can realize with what concern we have watched the activities of the Boy Scouts in the warring nations."

In England, Baden-Powell's Scouts were "doing their patriotic duty in a time of national trial by performing chiefly humanitarian tasks . . . consistent with the principles of the movement which have won the commendation of the world," he continued, asking his assistance in a BSA peace project. It was thought that the U.S. movement "should take advantage of the existence of the horrible war to strike its strongest blow in behalf of peace; that while America is shuddering and the boys are all excitement over the tales of bloody battles, we should emphasize . . . how needless and how terrible are such brutal conflicts."

Discussions with the New York Peace Society gave rise to a plan to publish an anti-war article in *Boys' Life* which Jordan was "preeminently qualified" to draft. This might be placed "in the hands of every school teacher in the United States, to be read in every school room; possibly in the hands of every boy in America." It could be published in leading periodicals and might, in its simplicity "differ from many of the peace arguments I have read which have been so phrased and so freighted with involved historic and diplomatic data and philosophical arguments as to be beyond the ready comprehension of all except the well-educated."[31]

West's letter did not catch up with Jordan for several weeks as he proceeded from London to Montreal to Boston, where at last a copy reached him around the end of September at the World Peace Foundation.[32] Jordan readily turned out the desired piece, which was published in the November 1914 issue of *Boys' Life.*

"I have just come back from Europe, where every nation has made a soldier out of every man fit to bear arms. And now the whole continent is impoverished and starving while its rivers run with blood of young men who have been killed by other young men, who had no quarrel with them at all," Jordan began. "It is a soldier's business to fight and kill or to stand up against other soldiers who are forced to fight and kill. It is a Boy Scout's business to help and to save, to make this world a better place for good men and women to live in." When the war was over, Scouting's true purpose would be realized: "to help each man and each other to realize that men are men . . . whatever language they may speak."[33]

West was delighted. "After many delays and difficulties we received the first copies from the printer last Saturday," he told Jordan in late October. Even as the proofs arrived, so did a peace statement from Carnegie.[34] The presses stopped to allow its insertion. West thanked Jordan profusely for providing the means to "remove from American boyhood whatever false impression may exist as to the character and significance of the battles now raging in Europe."[35]

That issue of *Boys' Life* was the high-water mark of pacifism at the Boy Scouts of America, however. American sentiment was already swinging away from the neutral position President Woodrow Wilson enunciated when the war started, urging all to be "impartial in thought as well as in action."[36] In doing so he was adhering to a policy of non-involvement in European conflicts dating to the first administration of President George Washington, later formalized in the Monroe Doctrine. But the position also reflected lingering Progressive distrust of military adventures and capitalist motivations. Yet the U.S. economy benefited mightily, pulling out of recession into boom as exports of steel, arms, grain and other goods surged four thousand percent from 1914 to 1916.[37] The sinking of the *Lusitania* galvanized U.S. opinion. But Wilson struggled to keep the country at peace, seeking re-election in 1916 on the slogan, "He kept us out of war," even as "preparedness" was becoming the national watchword.

Few were more insistent on the need for get ready for war than Theodore Roosevelt, as ever a powerful influence on American opinion despite his loss in the 1912 presidential election heading the Progressive or "Bull Moose" Party. He had polled 4.1 million votes to Wilson's 6.3 million, in the process helping defeat Republican incumbent Taft. In January 1915 Roosevelt published *America and the World War*, characterizing U.S. neutrality amid reports of German atrocities in Belgium as "unworthy of an honorable and powerful people," adding that "Dante reserved a special place of infamy in the Inferno for those base angels who dared side neither with evil or with good." Peace, said Roosevelt was "ardently to be desired, but only as the handmaiden of righteousness."[38]

The ex-president's blood boiled when a German diplomat warned U.S. citizens against traveling to Europe on the Lusitania, describing it as "liable to destruction . . . in the war zone." Had he not exercised utmost restraint, he wrote, such a statement "would make me favor instant war with Germany."[39] When the liner was torpedoed days later, Roosevelt railed at Wilson's "abject cowardice and weakness in failing to take energetic action" in response to the earlier sinking of the American steamer *Gulflight* off the Britain's Scilly Islands.[40] Wilson was "not carrying out a genuine American policy," he told another.[41]

Roosevelt had nothing but contempt for Jordan, Carnegie, and others who sought a European truce. He told one confidant that such men promoted "hideous wrongdoing at the expense of the helpless and the innocent. Our position should be the position of the just man armed, the man who scorns to wrong others and is fearless in the face of the wrongdoer, a position which men of the unworthy stamp of Andrew Carnegie, David Starr Jordan and [Colombia University President] Nicholas Murray Butler seem unable even to understand."[42]

Yet there were many in Scouting who did not share his views. Even the ultra-American Dan Beard worried that the movement would feel increased pressure to militarize. In June 1915, West forwarded a copy of a letter from Baden-Powell describing a trip to the war front where he received "wonderful reports" from officers who commanded former Scouts. "We have, as you know, some 18,000 of them in the Army and they are reported as not only being excellent 'ready-made soldiers', but of giving out good influence to others around them."[43] Beard was unimpressed. Though "very interesting," the letter would be "dangerous material for us to publish" given popular opposition to the war, and as a "military man through and through," Baden-Powell's "idea of civic work, while honest, straightforward and sincere, would be my idea of military work."

Beard continued: "At the present unsettled time, it behooves us to be more careful than ever with regard to anything pertaining" to the military. "We are not opposed to the army or the militia, but as Boy Scouts, it is absolutely essential to our success that we remain purely civic, and do not take sides . . . any more than we do on the question of religious denominations. Both of these have the red flag of danger, a warning which we must heed, without putting our foot in it as did David Starr Jordan on one side and as has Gen. Baden-Powell on the other side of the question, although the latter is perfectly unconscious of it."[44]

Soon after, Beard warned West that it would be "exceedingly unwise . . . to take any step which may be interpreted as a preparation on our part for warlike activities of our boys." Offering his opinion on a proposed nautical version of the Scouts, he saw no harm in Scouts acting as "Coast Guards, looking for Wrecks or vessels in distress, noting what vessels pass and what description of vessels they are, whether the vessels in the offing are freighters or passenger boats, steamers, gasoline launches, catboats, sloops, schooners, brigs, barkentines or full rigged ships. This would be 'fun and educational' " he conceded, "but it will be suicide for us to put the mark of militarism even very indistinctly on our organization."[45]

Yet West was under intense pressure from Roosevelt, still one of American Scouting's most influential sponsors though he never assumed more than a nominal official role in the organization. Roosevelt laid out his position in a voluminous article in August 1915 in *The Metropolitan,* of which he was a contributing editor, urging America to prepare for war. "The deification of peace without regard to whether it is either wise or righteous does not represent virtue. It represents a peculiarly base and ignoble form of evil. For this reason it is a positive detriment to international morality for any man to take part in any of these universal peace-at-any-price or all-inclusive arbitration movements." More pressing duties called. "First and foremost, the United States must prepare itself against war, and show itself able to maintain its rights and make its weight felt in the world."[46]

The former president soon after turned his glare of disapproval on the Boy Scouts of America. He had received distressing reports from Major General Leonard Wood, a former U.S. Army chief of staff whose career extended from the last campaign against Geronimo to the Spanish-American War. Roosevelt served under Wood as second-in-command of the 1st Volunteer Cavalry, or the Rough Riders. In the Taft administration, Wood overhauled the army, cutting red tape and increasing the mobility and versatility of the American forces.[47] He was a leading proponent of preparedness: even before Europe erupted in war he established voluntary citizen training camps intended as much to push the idea of preparedness as to turn out soldiers. From his redoubt on Governors Island in New York Harbor, he "talked preparedness day and night to whomever would listen."[48] His associates founded the National Security League to press for preparedness, and the American Legion, which created a voluntary reserve; Roosevelt and his four sons joined that force along with Baden-Powell's favorite scout, Frederick Russell Burnham.[49]

Though the tide of public opinion was shifting, BSA management was loath to make an about-face on an issue that resonated so strongly with its members, if on conflicting notes. In early October 1915, eleven members of the BSA Executive Board met at the Lawyer's Club on Lower Broadway in New York City. Livingstone came up from Washington and the discussion involved founders such as Robinson and Beard and the professionals who joined later: Murray, Presbrey, Schiff, others. The board took up a letter from its Brooklyn Council asking for "definitive action" on the question of preparedness. It concluded "it would be inappropriate for the Boy Scouts of America to take any official action with reference to any question of policy for the United States government in matters capable of differences of opinion of a political character. Each official and member should be given full opportunity for freedom of thought and action as an individual but not as a representative of the Scout Movement."

But the resolution also noted that while "the Boy Scout Movement is not anti-military [and] neither promotes nor discourages military training, the logical result of the program which the Boy Scout

Movement is promoting is in reality as strong a factor as any other one agency which the country now has for preparedness." Finally, "boys who have been Scouts will, because of their training under the motto 'Be Prepared,' prove themselves more virile and efficient in any emergency which calls for their services as citizens of the country."[50]

Yet Roosevelt continued to chafe. "I have been in communication with General Wood over the matter of the Boy Scouts," he told West in November 1915. "It is my understanding that as part of the wicked and degrading pacifist agitation of the last few years certain leaders therein, including Messrs. Carnegie, Jordan and others, have used the Boy Scouts organization as a medium for the dissemination of pacifist literature and have done everything they could to use the organization as a propaganda for interfering with the training of our boys to a standard of military efficiency." Repeating a favored formulation, he told West that "professional pacifists" of their ilk had "done more damage to this country and humanity than all the political and business crooks combined." Gathering his outrage into a massive Rooseveltian formulation, he declared that "The effort to prevent the boys of this country, of the kind who naturally should be gathered into the Boy Scouts, from being trained to arms so that they could serve the country in time of need, and the effort to prevent their acquiring the spirit of self respect which will make them eager and ready to fight for the right both as individuals and as members of the nation—these efforts from my point of view represent treason to the country and treason to the cause of humanity."[51]

Carnegie and Jordan were more or less impervious to such broadsides, though the tide of opinion and policy was turning against them. Even Wilson embraced preparedness in counterpoint to isolationism as he looked to the 1916 presidential election. But Seton was vulnerable given his tenuous relationship with BSA and his ill-considered remarks critical of American culture, politics, and foreign policy. The implication that he was a coward was unfair. Despite mixed feelings on the war, he tried to enlist in the Canadian and British military but was turned down for service because of his age.[52] But such a letter

from Roosevelt was guaranteed to stir West to action on the issue of
Seton's nationality and may have convinced him that Seton had to
be eased out of the movement entirely—though in such a way as to
minimize the public relations impact of his departure.

There is evidence to suggest that this course had already been
contemplated. Well before this, in March 1915, BSA efforts to obtain
a congressional charter had again come up short, this time on objections by a Catholic member of the House, James Gallivan, a Massachusetts Democrat, which, though eventually withdrawn, fatally
stalled the bill. Washington attorney and lobbyist Paul Sleman detailed to West his efforts to secure passage of the legislation, including
lining up prominent Catholics at the last minute to convince Gallivan "his fears were entirely without foundation." Sleman concluded,
ominously for Seton: "I think we can get the bill through allright [*sic*]
without any trouble next time, and as you say, we can eliminate the
objectionable names, and that will be worth something."[53]

BSA had already moved in this direction, declining at its annual
meeting that February to re-elect Seton as chief Scout on the flimsy
grounds that he was absent in Europe. Seton himself was about ready
to sever relations. Following his return from England that April, relations with the BSA leadership deteriorated further, such that on May
10 Seton wrote to Livingstone enclosing the letter of resignation he
had drafted before leaving for England at the start of the year. "In
view of all that has happened," Seton said, "it seems to me that there
is only one thing for me to do, and that is to resign all connection
with the Boy Scouts of America." His only desire was to resign "in the
quietest way, without reflecting on anyone, without hurting anyone's
feelings" or the Boy Scout movement. "I will see no reporters, make
no statements and write no newspaper articles, unless compelled to
do so in self defense by the actions of the Boy Scout Officials," Seton assured Livingstone, adding in what could only be a reference to
West: "I wish simply to drop quietly out of it. I think however it is
only fair to add that any doubts I had some time ago have been ended
by the behavior of a certain official."[54]

Informed of Seton's resignation, Murray had little interest in conciliating him. "I can see nothing for us to do but to accept" his resignation, he wrote West three days later. "His letter of resignation putting it on the ground that his ideas and ideals are hopelessly diverse from ours is a good reason why the resignation should be accepted."[55] Frank Presbrey told West that the board should "consider the incident closed."[56] But Livingstone, hoping to mend the breach, proposed that several members of the board should meet with Seton to seek a solution.[57] Schiff agreed to host such a meeting at his mansion in Oyster Bay, Long Island, in early June. Seton, Livingstone, and West came out on the train to join Schiff and Pratt for lunch. But it could not have been a particularly agreeable meal. West would note that Seton's position on patriotism and citizenship was "so out of harmony with our ideas as to what leadership in the Boy Scout movement should be that it was agreed by all that his usefulness as an official [of BSA] was ended."[58]

Yet the matter remained in suspense until Sunday, December 5, when Seton summoned reporters from the *New York Times* and other New York papers, as well as the Associated Press, to announce that he was resigning from the Boy Scouts of America. Whether he had gotten wind of Roosevelt's letter, or simply out of unbearable frustration, Seton leaped before he could be pushed. He told the reporters that BSA, in failing to accept his resignation in May, "had treated him and the public unfairly, especially in continuing to use his name."[59] He fired a parting shot at his longtime antagonist West, declaring of the Scouting movement that "Seton started it; Baden-Powell boomed it; West killed it."[60]

Seton told the reporters that he had submitted his resignation to BSA months earlier, but "the organization has not acted upon it. I don't know why nothing has been done, but I do feel that the organization is not acting fairly either to me or the public in allowing the public to suppose that they are still deriving their inspiration from me. It should be clearly stated, and I want it understood, that I esteem the Executive Board of the Boy Scouts to be a splendid lot of men, giving freely of their time and money to the work. My only criticism is that they have allowed all direction and power to centre in the hands of James E. West, a lawyer, who is a man of great executive ability but without knowledge of the activities of boys; who has no point of contact with boys, and who, I might almost say, has never seen the blue sky in his life," Seton declared.

"I wanted good-naturedly to resign from the Boy Scouts, but they still have my name on their papers, and I hear from people all over the country who still think that I am connected with the Boy Scouts. I bought yesterday a copy of the handbook of the organization and in it is printed an introduction signed by me as Chief Scout. I was the Chief Scout up to last February, but after that I resigned.

"I intend to resign from many things in order to concentrate my activities on the Woodcraft League, which best gives my message to the world."[61]

Seton had chosen the worst possible time for this announcement—the *Times* report hit the streets on the very eve of the launch of a BSA fund-raising drive that aimed to bring in $200,000 in the short period of December 7 to 10. On December 3, the *Times* had published an endorsement of the drive by President Wilson who as BSA honorary president issued a statement saying, "It is fine to have the boys of the country organized for the purposes the Boy Scouts represent, and whenever I see a group of them I am proud of their manliness and I feel cheered by the knowledge of what their organization represents."

For West Seton's statement was a betrayal, a declaration of war, and he responded in kind. The Scouting executive had received a telephone call at home around 6:30 p.m. that Sunday from a *Times* reporter who read him Seton's statement. West immediately conferred by phone with three New York board members, and placed a long-distance call to Livingstone in Washington. It was decided that a response would be prepared and issued under Livingstone's name. "This was accomplished under a great many handicaps," West told Beard in a letter written the following day. The statement was released to the press at 10:30 p.m.

"Mr. Seton's motive is as apparent as it is unfriendly and selfish," the official statement began. Listing the names of BSA's board members, the statement said the board unanimously approved the "action which has been taken with reference to Mr. Seton." This alluded to the February decision by national council not to re-elect Seton "because he had failed to satisfactorily respond as to what his intentions were about becoming a citizen of the United States."

The indictment continued. "In view of the position he had taken in a letter to the Executive Board and his derogatory criticism of American history, American institutions and the American people, the members of the Executive Board unanimously agreed that the only way they would be justified in continuing him in a place of official leadership in the Boy Scouts of America would be to require him to remove all doubt as to his loyalty to our country by becoming a citizen of the United States or expressing definitively his intentions to do so."

Seton had failed to do so before leaving for Europe earlier in the year, and on his return the question remained open following the conference at Schiff's home in Oyster Bay that June. "The position again taken at that time by Mr. Seton on the policy of the Boy Scouts of America in developing patriotism and good citizenship was so out of harmony with our ideas as to what leadership in the Boy Scout movement should be that it was agreed by all that his usefulness as an official of the Boy Scouts of America was ended." The board made this official in June, and on July 8, Livingstone continued, "I personally addressed a letter to Mr. Seton stating that in view of the fact that he had not been re-elected to any office in the Boy Scouts of America no further action was necessary with reference to any of the communications received from him." The letter, Livingstone added, "was duly acknowledged by Mr. Seton on July 9th."[62]

West's own comments to the press were even more damaging to Seton. "When it was discovered that Mr. Seton was in harmony with anarchist and radical socialist elements . . . as to whether the Boy Scouts of America should stand for patriotism and good citizenship, no time was lost in developing the issue," West told the *Times*.

"Mr. Seton was given a reasonable, fair opportunity to make himself clear on this subject, but he hedged and stated that he could not make a definite promise that he would ever become a citizen of the United States," West said. "Indeed, he went further and repeated his objections to the *Boy Scout Handbook* including a chapter on 'Patriotism,' and contended that the Boy Scouts . . . should not undertake to have boys pledge allegiance to their country, but should leave them free to support our country when they thought our country was right and to damn it when they thought it was wrong." This, West said, was the only reason Seton was no longer chief scout of the Boy Scouts of America. The comments ran December 7 under the headline: "West Says Seton Is Not a Patriot."[63]

Seton rejected West's broadside, telling a *Times* reporter that it was "quite the first time in my life that any one has taken such a view of me." He declared that West had "robbed the movement of its spirituality and introduced purely material meanings to it." Seton concluded that first, he disagreed with the "present trend of the Boy Scout movement; second, I think I have a national message to deliver; and third, I can deliver that message best through the Woodcraft League.

"Henceforth," he said, "I shall focus my activities on that work."[64]

Once more, Ernest Seton had been his own worst enemy. He gained nothing by publicly denouncing James West and the BSA board but a flurry of headlines and the opprobrium of colleagues and even some friends. His longtime associate William Hornaday expressed no

sympathy—quite the contrary, he wrote to West days after the controversy broke to say West's version of events squared "exactly with sentiments expressed to me by Mr. Seton about three years ago."

Over lunch with Seton at a downtown Manhattan restaurant,
Hornaday had expressed surprise that Seton had not acquired U.S.
citizenship. "He replied with the utmost scorn, about as follows:
'What! Become a citizen of this rotten republic? I would not think of
such a thing for a moment.'" Hornaday was taken aback but "for the
sake of an old friendship I let the matter pass," he told West. "I must
say I regret the fact that Mr. Seton is again seeking to be the leader of
an organization of American boys and girls. Any man who entertains
toward this country the sentiments that he entertains is not fit to lead
our boys and girls in anything," the naturalist wrote. "Seton's place is
on the firing line in France, with the British contingent."[65]

From the University of Wisconsin came a letter from J.C. Elsom, the director of physical education, dismissing Seton's arguments
against Scouting and West, adding the trenchant comment that the
naturalist "should sign his name with a little print of a jackass' hoof
instead of this little fox track, or whatever it is" and opining that
BSA would weather the "loud braying" of its critic.[66] The director of
physical education of the San Francisco Board of Education hailed
the removal of a "noisy Prima Donna always clamoring for the center
of the stage."[67]

So it was that West could inform David Starr Jordan later that
month that "the unfortunate Seton matter has done but little damage
to our movement, so far as we are able to judge from present reports.
It has greatly hurt Mr. Seton, and for this we are very sorry, although
he has no one to blame but himself."[68]

Somewhat ironically in light of Seton's complaints about mili-
tarization of the Boy Scouts, West assured Jordan that despite heavy
pressure from Roosevelt and Lt. Gen. Wood, "We are taking the position that, educationally, as well as from a practical point of view,
it would be unwise to introduce any military training whatsoever . . . into the daily life and program of the adolescent boy."[69]

West had indications that Roosevelt was not pleased with Seton's outburst. The former president was "particularly sarcastic in his references to Mr. Seton and stated that if Seton thought the Movement was getting too military, that was a good reason why he (Colonel Roosevelt) was the more interested in our work," wrote BSA staff member A.O. Olson, relating a conversation with Roosevelt's personal secretary.[70] Still, Roosevelt in a letter urged West to let the matter rest. "I think the aim of your organization and the aim of Seton's [Woodcraft] people are both excellent and not in the least inconsistent. I earnestly hope that there won't be another round of public controversy about the matter. Only damage can come from it. Let things rest as they are and have no further discussion."[71]

Seton was not without defenders. Publisher Doubleday took Livingstone to task over "cruel and unjust" statements from West containing "the innuendo that Mr. Seton is a coward, apropos of his citizenship papers and the Boer War. I hope you will feel like instructing your people in New York not to send out any more statements, as it only makes my task to keep Seton quiet more difficult."[72] He invited Livingstone to find another publisher for the Scout *Handbook.*

John Alexander and Edgar Robinson also expressed disapproval of the low blow West had inflicted on Seton in the press. Alexander sent West a note to express regret "that you ever felt it necessary to send out this material [which] does not honestly tell the animus back of this matter." BSA should simply have declined to respond and the tempest would have blown over.[73] Robinson told West: "I want to say to you privately that I am not at all in sympathy with the statement regarding Mr. Seton. I think you, and possibly some other members of the board, misunderstand him and consequently misjudge him."[74]

Livingstone met with Seton in Washington and defended BSA's position on his British citizenship. Having received "a number of very serious criticisms from the field" on the issue, "we had acted accordingly, without wishing to cause him any embarrassment or creating a distressing situation for himself or ourselves. I fully explained that we had no desire to belittle anything that he had done for the Movement while in it, or intended to do and that his life's work was respected by all of us, that he was perfectly free, so far as we were concerned, to go out and build any other organization," Livingstone told West. Seton was plainly suspicious of BSA's intentions, demanding a "cessation" of what he saw as newspaper attacks on him. "I told him that was . . . the attitude of every one connected with our Movement."

Seton "seemed particularly grieved that you should have, in your conversation with two gentlemen, members of his board, made an effort to poison their minds against him and to insinuate certain dangers they were running into by associating with him. I, of course, discredited this statement as much as possible and added that I was sure that you were not correctly represented and would be glad to have the opportunity to explain such statements. He requested that I agree, on behalf of the organization, to see that criticisms no longer emanated from headquarters if he should stop similar emanations from his side." Livingstone told Seton that the best thing would be to discuss the situation directly with West, and that BSA could not assume responsibility "for what the press dug up on its own account" or for statements originating from BSA branches around the country.

Seton, Livingstone related, remained bitter about his discussions with the board before his departure, charging that West "had gone out of [his] way to stir up trouble for him . . . and has sort of kept after his Movement with a hostile attitude."

Livingstone remained concerned about the potential for more trouble. "I am not satisfied, after my conference with him, here this morning, which was sought by him and not by me at all, that Mr. Seton will stay put in any of his attitudes toward us in any specific situation. He is an author and an artist and not amenable, apparently, to the same exacting interpretations I would feel, myself, bound by." But, "it is a situation that must be dealt with and I feel sure that any conference you and he may have, not at headquarters, but at some mutually agreed upon neutral place, perhaps the Aldine Club, you can work out a program for the near future that will be tenable for both."[75] In a postscript he urged West to wire Seton at the New Willard Hotel to arrange such a meeting. It does not appear that any such reconciliatory conversation between Seton and West took place.

So ended the turbulent relationship between Ernest Thompson Seton and the leadership of the Boy Scouts of America. Their wrangling had been prolonged by both sides much longer, perhaps, than it should have, given the ever-widening gulf between them on fundamental issues and the political climate of the time which exaggerated the importance of Seton's nationality. But as Alexander told West, the insinuations of subversion or cowardice served only to obscure "the real reason why Seton wasn't satisfactory to the Scouts."[76]

CHAPTER 9

INTO THE SUNSET

Seton lost no time in re-launching his Woodcraft League, as he now styled it. Two weeks after announcing his resignation from BSA, Seton held a meeting on Sunday, December 19, at the Congress Hall Hotel in Washington, at which there were "quite a number of members of Congress and Senators present," Livingstone informed West. "He unfolded his Woodcraft Indian proposition and, I understand, lined up with himself quite a number of people." Seton's program was so "closely imitative" of the Scouts as to constitute plagiarism, he added, though neither Livingstone nor West appeared to have raised any legal objections.[1]

In any case, the BSA leadership was more intently focused on the Boy Scout bill being resubmitted to Congress by its political allies on the Hill. That February the House Judiciary Committee recommended passage of House Resolution 755, noting that the Scouting movement "tends to conserve the moral, intellectual, and physical life of the coming generation, and in its immediate results does much to reduce the problem of juvenile delinquency in the cities." BSA was organized in "practically every community of 4,000 inhabitants and over, and in many smaller communities of the United States." The Boy Scouts had demonstrated the value of their training "as an auxiliary force in the maintenance of public order," providing "first-aid and practical assistance in times of great public emergencies," such as in the aftermath of floods in Ohio, and rendering service on public occasions like a Gettysburg reunion of Civil War combatants and President Wilson's inauguration "to general commendation." The committee concluded that the "importance and magnitude of [BSA's] work is such as to entitle it to recognition and its work and insignia to protection by Federal incorporation."[2]

West kept Beard up to date as matters progressed. "You will be delighted to learn that I have just received word from Mr. Livingstone by long distance wire later confirmed by telegram by Mr. Paul Sleman, our Washington attorney, that the Senate today passed our bill providing for Federal incorporation," he told him on May 31. Two minor amendments needed House approval.[3] Two weeks later, on June 15, 1916, the Senate and House enacted H.R. 755 incorporating the Boy Scouts of America "to promote, through organization, and cooperation with other agencies, the ability of boys to do things for themselves and others, to train them in scoutcraft, and to teach them patriotism, courage, self-reliance, and kindred virtues, using the methods which are now in common use by boy scouts."

Significantly, in light of the still-recent Seton controversy, the bill specified that "the governing board of the said Boy Scouts of America shall consist of an executive board composed of citizens of the United States." It also gave BSA "the sole and exclusive right to have and to use . . . all emblems and badges, descriptive or designating marks, and words or phrases now or heretofore used by the Boy Scouts of America in carrying out its program."[4] Whatever difficulties the Boy Scouts had encountered in the past with rivals such as the American Boy Scouts could now be more readily resolved. As the bill awaited Wilson's signature, there came further evidence of BSA's recognition as an American institution. Language in a new army bill being finalized by a House and Senate conference committee was, as the *New York Times* reported, "capable of construction prohibiting the Scouts from wearing the uniform which they had come to consider their own." West sent a telegram to each committee member expressing his concern about the clause, following up with a letter including a picture of the Scout uniform. "You can see that this does not imitate or ape the regular army uniform, but under the phraseology of the bill it could possibly be construed that parts of the uniform are similar to the United States Army uniform," he told committee members. But its "general makeup . . . gives quite a different result from that secured by the regulation army uniform." Subsequently the committee included a provision specifically granting an exception to the Boy Scouts of America.[5]

"Congratulations!" Beard wrote to West upon hearing this news. "You have certainly built up a powerful Boy Scout political machine. I am very much interested in what the future will develop. Hastily yours."[6]

Seton remained a sore point for West, who earlier that month wrote to Beard noting a *New York Herald* report on a rally organized by BSA's Brooklyn council. The *Herald* article reported that "Mr. Seton will be received with special honors and will be among the speakers." West had taken up the matter up informally with the council's president, who agreed Seton's engagement was unfortunate. "It will not do at all for anyone to get the idea" that Brooklyn differed with headquarters "on the issues presented in the action with reference to Mr. Seton," West said.[7]

His longtime rival vanquished, Beard assumed an increasingly prominent role in the Scouts. Despite the genial persona Beard cultivated, his communications to West and other executives often reflected resentment at perceived slights, and an eagerness for recognition. Even before Seton's differences with the BSA pointed to a breach, Beard had written to board member Presbrey in early 1914 suggesting it was "about time that they put me in as Chief Scout," an office Seton still held. This, Beard reasoned, "will not do any injury to Mr. Seton, it will not cast any reflection upon his reputation, it will only be doing what we do in all other organizations; put new blood in the institution and make a change in the office. Seton has had all the glory due him and I have tried to do my duty as a member of the Board." He urged Presbrey to "quietly talk the matter up and see what can be done" at a forthcoming BSA annual meeting. His appointment would be "a tardy justice recognition to which I am entitled."[8] This was not to be: West following Seton's departure would incorporate the title into his own to become chief scout executive.[9]

Though Beard recognized West's role in the survival and success of BSA, he would become increasingly critical of the administrator. Even in June 1916 Beard was taking aim at him over what he saw as BSA's insufficient attention to matters of patriotism. West sent Beard a note concerning a letter received by the staff of *Boys' Life* which, though unsigned, appeared to have come from Beard. "Oh yes! Hear ye! Hear ye! Listen all ye timid ones . . . even the women are bold in their Americanism, and only the opportunist [*sic*] at Headquarters are timid." West enclosed a clipping of an article published in *Scouting,* another publication of the organization, entitled "My Country," telling Beard that if he were to look through the publication's back issues, "you will see that we have not been one bit timid here about Americanism and Patriotism." Beard had told a BSA staff member that he didn't read *Scouting,* which "may account for your point of view."[10]

By January 1917, Beard was expressing outright animosity toward West, telling Presbrey in a bitter letter that like others who had left the movement, Seton "was in the way, he was dropped for a disloyalty known to everybody ever since the organization started, but this disloyalty was not considered important until he was in the way of our executive." Wherever Beard went, he informed Presbrey, he was "followed by spies from headquarters and there isn't the slightest doubt that charges would be brought against him . . . had there been the slightest shadow of a foundation upon which to build them, but failing in this other means of taking away the honor would be sought."

What West did to inspire such hostility is not clear, though he had blocked efforts by Beard to create a staff of his own. Echoing Seton's grievances, Beard charged that West "has never put one original idea in the organization" and was an "absolute failure" when it came to engaging the interest of boys. "He has not their sympathy nor [their] affection. That is his misfortune, not his fault, he never was a boy himself, but out of the original popularity of the Scout movement he built up a wonderful organization, he has made himself a power in the land."

West was "an astute politician and accomplished diplomat, but a movement of this kind needs something else . . . you MUST interest young people to make them listen and to interest them you must give them something new; and to give them something new you have got to have some man connected with the organization who will furnish new and novel ideas."[11] That man, of course, was Beard.

Nor had Beard lost his appetite for jousting with Seton. "Thank you for the copy of the manual sent me," he wrote him in February 1917. "I see that you have adopted my tramp signs and various other suggestions from my writings which is complimentary but it would have been more courteous had you consulted me before publishing them in your book. I also note a tendency to reform your former ideas of America and loyalty to 'Old Glory.'" In years past, he noted, he had impressed on Seton "the bad effect of your denunciation of our country, our flag and our government would have upon the American public, and I sincerely hope that this book will do much to reinstate you in the position which you so rashly sacrificed for the sake of loyalty to an alien form of government.

"Stick to the Stars and Stripes, under its protection you have made your fame and fortune. Under its protection you found your wife, under its banner your child was born! Don't ever go back on it again in word, action or speech. And I for one will try and forget the disloyal words you used in my presence and the presence of . . . West and others at that time on the editorial board."[12]

Seton turned to board member Edmund Seymour in exasperation, noting that he had inserted some of Beard's material in his latest *Handbook* giving him full credit "in the interest of peace and good fellowship," with the disconcerting result that followed. "I need hardly say that there is not an atom of foundation for any of his statements or innuendos."[13] Seton told Beard: "I never intentionally in my life used any man's stuff without giving him credit for it. I was not aware that you had ever written anything on Tramp Signs. In the *Manual* reference is made to the only three articles I ever saw on the subject and credit given for their assistance. If you will show that any use has been made of your stuff without credit, it will be corrected in the next issue."[14] Seymour urged Beard to withdraw his letter, and he wrote to Seton doing so. "I have no desire to inaugurate a dispute of any kind, and if you will kindly return that letter, we can call the incident closed."[15] Seton sent it back, declaring himself "very glad indeed to call the incident closed."[16]

Such differences faded into the background with the U.S. declaration of war on Germany in April 1917. Beard, increasingly identified with Scouting through his regular monthly articles in *Boys' Life,* took a prominent role in the Boy Scout home front effort, particularly in the sale of war bonds. The Scouts sold some 2.3 million bonds to raise $147,876,902, bringing in another $53 million through the sale of stamps.[17] "I wish it were possible for me to personally grasp your hand and . . . evidence the appreciation of all of us here at headquarters for your splendid co-operation with that of every other man in the field in making the Boy Scout Liberty Loan campaign a tremendous success," West told Beard in October 1917, at a point when Scouts had already sold some $50 million in bonds.[18]

West was no doubt also relieved that Beard had redirected his fits of pique from BSA management to the Kaiser. One Beard biographer concludes that he "provided a major impetus toward the increasingly nationalistic emphasis of the Boy Scouts of America." When the United States entered the war, BSA marshaled a larger force than the standing U.S. Army of 200,000. This "helped to create, as well as to reflect, the heightened nationalism of the World War era."[19]

Such nationalism was understandable, and perhaps inevitable, but Beard like others was at times carried away by patriotic fervor verging on xenophobia. His untrammeled patriotism corresponded with what intellectuals would later term American exceptionalism. "I love America; I think our history is grand," Beard told Edmund Seymour. "I think we have done more for the world at large in the matter of freedom . . . and manhood than any nation on the face of the earth."[20]

Even before the United States declared war, Beard was gravitating away from isolationism under the influence of those who charged that the U.S. reluctance to enter the war was unbecoming. In early 1917, Beard wrote to a Scouting official in Astoria, Queens, to inform him of a local brewer who "I am told sends checks to the Kaiser," and to advocate formation of a "secret service of boys in Queens, and reports made of every case, and kept on record in the office, open to the inspection of no one, but the Mayor or Governor."[21]

Around the same time, Beard joined the Vigilantes, a group of writers and artists who offered their services to the government to help encourage patriotism and loyalty. He drafted a "Message . . . to the Boys of America" denouncing the "degrading, disgusting and loathsome disease" of "Kaiserism" whose effects were to "stifle all manly aspirations, to kill all the higher thoughts, to strangle religious emotions, to rob the victim of chivalry, to take away from him his heart, and in the end to make a malicious ogre of him like his master." Beard contrasted what he denounced as German malignity with the big-heartedness of American heroes like Daniel Boone, whose advice, "Be sure you are right, then go ahead," he had taken as his personal motto.[22] Beard formed ties with the American Protective League, volunteers bent on rooting out sedition, writing to *Mothers' Magazine* editor and League official S. Keith Evans, concerning a "buzzing noise" on his telephone that he suspected came from a two-way radio operated by a spy in the German immigrant community spread through Whitestone, Bayside, and College Point. He

informed Evans of "a certain grocer by the name of John Fick in
Whitestone who is outspoken in his German talk."[23]

Though fully engaged in the Scout war effort, West was also
waging a final offensive against the American Boy Scouts, since renamed the U.S. Boy Scouts. In January 1918, West briefed Beard on
a meeting he had at headquarters with a certain Frank Winch, former
brigadier-general of the U.S. Boy Scouts, who told West he had been
"completely converted to the fact that the Boy Scouts . . . was what
was most needed by the boys of our country." Winch said he and others had been "grossly misinformed and deceived" as to his organization's condition and activities. Although "it was very humiliating, it
was his duty to come to our office and tender his services" to the Boy
Scouts of America. Since the BSA lawsuit had been brought against
USBS, Winch told West, the latter organization had become "seriously embarrassed financially," and it would be a "generous and gracious thing if the whole suit could be settled and an end brought to
the unfortunate situation." Winch insisted his "fundamental interest
was in boys and in serving his country patriotically." But he "made
it known that he would like to be employed by the Boy Scouts of
America if there were an opening available to him."[24]

One year later, West met with a lawyer for USBS who was eager
to settle the case. If BSA would cover $1,200 in outstanding bills, the
U.S. Boy Scouts would disband, said Victor Stockel, but he wanted
the lawsuit to be withdrawn without a court ruling. West replied that
it would be "of much help to us to have a decision in the matter. If
we go to court, I have no question as to the decision."

Their discussions resulted in a consent decree stipulating that
"the right to the name 'Boy Scout' is peculiarly that of the Boy Scouts
of America."[25] In March West informed Beard that the court had
given BSA exclusive use of the words "Boy Scout" or variations there-

upon, binding on the members and officers of the U.S. Boy Scouts.[26] West had finally locked up the Boy Scout franchise.

Dan Beard's nativism flared again in late November 1918, soon after the end of the war, objecting to a book for which West had supplied a foreword, charging that it gave "full credit for Scouting" to Baden-Powell. As a good American, said Beard, he could "have no sympathy with monarchical forms of government." He was not the enemy of any nationality, but protested "the snobbishness with which our organization is constantly licking the boots of a foreign gentleman, who himself is too big a man to accept the credit our organization gives him."

Referring to a Canadian newspaper article on Scouting which failed to make any mention of the U.S. movement, Beard charged that West had "never seemed to realize the really terrible responsibility of your position in this matter. You do not seem to understand the American spirit and what history will do to those of us who have tried to rob Uncle Sam of the credit due him, and fawningly placed the laurels on the head of a man, however worthy he may be of honors [who] is not entitled to the credit for the inception as he himself has said." This referred to Baden-Powell's 1910 description of himself as being no more than the "uncle" of Scouting.

"In this war America has proved to the world that her ideals are right, that her ideals will win and today she is looked up to for advice by every nation on Earth, and yet our organization is still licking the boots of a foreign nobleman. Shame on us all! Is this due to the fact that we have so many foreigners in the Movement?" Beard exhorted West to "try to understand the importance of making this Scout Movement unequivocally emphatically an American institution." Otherwise, "it will go the way of all weak-kneed half-baked sentimental things that are launched, bloom and wither and die within a few years."[27]

Apparently sensing he had gone too far, Beard wrote to West a few days later to apologize. "Recently I sent you a letter without censoring it, that is, a letter off the bat as I felt it, but it is not necessary to keep that letter on your file and if you will return it I will replace it with one couched in self-contained and diplomatic phraseology." All he wanted was "to record a protest as emphatically as is consistent with dignity. It is not my desire to offend you."[28]

West wrote back: "I have your two letters and from the bottom of my heart, I want to say how sorry I am that you feel called upon to write as you have.

"I don't believe that you can establish that I have consciously been guilty of any injustice or inaccurate statement at any time. Certainly if I have, I want to make amends. I see no reason for me to bother you to write a new letter to substitute for the one of November 9th. I am quite willing to accept the spirit which your letter of December 4th, makes clear you intended.

"I shall be very happy some time after we get over the present burdens of the Influenza [epidemic of 1918] and financial embarrassment to go into this matter thoroughly with you in a friendly conference and see if we can't reach some definite conclusion."[29]

Beard was amenable. "We had better have a personal conference first and decide what we want to advocate, then we will have something concrete to put up before the other men, after which I have no doubt that we will come to an understanding," he told West. "The greatest difficulty will be to undo the harm already done by a propaganda based on the wrong assumption of acts, but this may be done gradually without offending anyone and without making anyone retract simply by substituting new statements and forgetting the old."[30]

Commenting on the frequently stormy relationship between Beard and West, Beard's son would later offer the view that, "West was a dynamic, ambitious man. So was my father. West was a conformist. My father was an iconoclast in dress, in living, in thinking. West was a successful executive." Beard resented that he was paid $250 a month for his articles in *Boys' Life* while West and other headquarters officials drew full salaries (though the Beards were financially comfortable due to the real estate holdings of his wife's family). West made BSA a modern organization with national reach, but to Beard it often seemed to have lost its soul. "My father wore a halo, West wore a grey flannel suit," concluded Daniel Bartlett Beard. "They never were able to play their parts without butting heads."[31]

The conflict between Seton and Beard shifted to the confines of the Camp Fire Club. Seton wrote to Seymour in December 1918 to complain that Beard, "never loses a chance to injure me behind my back. Of this I have been warned by many members of the Club, and have again and again found printed and other evidence of his attitude." Seton had confronted Beard, "but received only evasive answers." Seton suggested a Camp Fire Club committee might look into the matter.[32]

Some such discussion apparently ensued, based on another letter from Seton to Seymour on January 11, 1919. "I was never more astonished in my life than when I learned from you that D. Beard accuses me of stealing his stuff. I challenge him to appear before any competent tribunal and if he proves that I have every used a hint or suggestion from him without credit I will pay him $100." He warmed to his subject. "For nearly twenty years I have had the painful experience of being blood-sucked by D.B. As each of my books appears it has been followed by some kind of an imitation by D.B. always without credit." Seton detailed some instances of alleged purloining of material. "I do not see how anyone can pretend that his actions are those of an honorable man. Yet he meets me regularly at the Club, professes friendship and never loses a chance to malign me."[33]

Seton, meanwhile, was struggling with his Woodcraft League, which he had in spite of his pacifist sentiments placed at the disposal of the war effort. But the minutes of the September 1918 meeting of his

Council of Guidance are those of a marginal organization. Its accounts showed unpaid bills of some $1,690, though $900 in revenues were hoped for soon. Against a proposed annual budget of about $12,000, revenues to date in 1918 had amounted to just $8,800, leaving a fairly hefty shortfall. But, "When we consider the conditions through which the Country has passed and the youth of the Woodcraft League," a Woodcraft official noted, "we have every reason to congratulate ourselves on having been able to carry on our work." Membership fees of $5 a year suggest a national membership of about 800—hardly a threat to the Scouts.[34] The Council's November minutes showed even more straitened circumstances: a "temporary financial statement" read to those present by Seton's daughter Ann noted cash on hand of $5.39 as of the beginning of November. Since then, $1,655.95 had been received, including a $175 loan from two members to cover "urgent expenditures." But $1,648.25 had flowed out again for a balance of $13.09 with unpaid bills totaling $928.78.[35] Seton wanted to put his organization on a self-sustaining footing, but when it came to administration it seemed he needed a James West of his own.

Seton in this period was shifting his focus in other ways. He sold his Cos Cob estate around the beginning of the war, commissioning a design from an English architect for the Tudor-styled home he built in Greenwich, giving it the name of DeWinton, after the town in Manitoba where he had homesteaded with his brother Arthur in the 1880s—and, no doubt, for the ancestral Seton title to which he laid claimed. The Greenwich property included an artificial lake that he called Little Peequo. Grace Seton threw herself into the war, raising funds to purchase several Ford trucks to establish an ambulance service from Paris to the trenches, all the while continuing to campaign for women's suffrage. But the couple had grown apart, and Seton's attention turned to Julia Moss Buttree, a younger woman he met in summer 1918 at a Woodcraft function in Connecticut.

Buttree was much taken with Seton, describing him later as "a tall, handsome, robust man with a vigorous, aggressive personality. His shock of heavy black hair was worn conspicuously long. His piercing black eyes darted this way and that as he gauged his audience before he began to speak." Even then, she recalled, "my interest was not aroused, but when the first words came from his lips, an electric thrill went through me."[36] The twenty-nine-year-old (to Seton's fifty-eight) was married to an impecunious and complacent Englishman named Ted, who raised no objections as his wife became Seton's secretary, helping him complete a new book on game animals, and before long his mistress. Grace Seton was traveling on writing projects, and Seton rented DeWinton, moving into a cottage across Little Peequo Lake. The Setons briefly reconciled in 1923, but by then Ernest was fully involved with his *Lives of Game Animals*—and with Julia, who was traveling with him on his business trips. Upon her return from the Far East in July 1924, Seton told his wife that he felt their marriage had run its course, though there was no traumatic breach and they would remain legally wedded for years to come.

Seton's *Lives of Game Animals* represented a return to his first professional path as a naturalist expressing himself in text and line—as indeed Hornaday had once urged him to do well before his five-year involvement with Scouting ended. Hornaday wrote Seton in December 1912 to congratulate him on the latest edition of *Woodcraft* following the second edition of the Scout *Manual*. "Now that these two books are out, I wish to take them as text for *a sermon*," Hornaday told him. "Let us consider that you have now reached the end of the trail, both in woodcraft and in boy-scouting. Truly I see nothing else remaining for you to pursue in either of these directions. While you have been on these trails . . . you have wandered so far from the field of natural history that your friends who do not know the '*Life Histories*' now think that you have abandoned this field forever. This must not be!" he chided. "I am absolutely and aggressively unwilling that you should give up either your art or your natural history for any scouting or woodcraft that possibly can be named. Don't give up talents of the greatest rarity for the sake of any work which can be done by others!!!" It was time for an "about face," said Hornaday. "For Heaven's sake do write SOMETHING in aid of the cause of wildlife protection! In that particular line you have been horribly remiss, and you have before you a work to do, which, as a conscientious naturalist, you can not ignore. The technical zoologists are perfectly able to set at their comfortable desks and tables, with their compound differential microscopes, and spend their time in play-work investigations, while the Army of Destruction is slaughtering all kinds of wild live [*sic*] all around them! Are *you* going to follow that plan, also? The time has come for active, aggressive, personal work, all along the line; for nothing else will call a halt to the Army of Destruction, and save the remnant."[37]

But Seton was also motivated by personal considerations. He had published his *Life Histories of Northern Animals* in answer to the "nature faker" charges—Roosevelt had urged him to provide evidence his animal stories were founded on scientific observation. Now, in his early sixties, Seton saw *Game Animals* as the capstone of his life's work. "This is my attempt to set out on paper everything that I know . . . about the home life of the wild animals, their joys, their sorrows, their domestic ways, their social games, their love-makings, their marriage ceremonies, their ideas of property, their methods of communicating," he told his old friend Frank Doubleday. To make his work "bomb-proof," he told the publisher, he was submitting every chapter to the Smithsonian Institution, the American Museum of Natural History, and other institutions.[38] Doubleday brought out the four-volume set in installments from 1925 to 1928—though not without a fight between Seton and editors over whimsical "synoptic drawings" he proposed for the table of contents, which brought out the unique traits or personalities of animals as he saw them. The editors' concerns were unfounded: in 1927 the John Burroughs Association honored Seton with a medal for his *Lives of Game Animals,* calling it a "magnum opus which has no peer either in text or in illustrations."[39]

BSA managers were to remain very much on their guard where Seton was concerned, however, as he retained a tendency to revive old disputes and grievances. In 1924, for instance, Seton wrote to Colin Livingstone proposing to write a history of the Boy Scouts, leading the Scouting executive to sent a confidential note to West. "I do not think that we want to develop a history over the signature of Seton. I am loath to get into a renewed controversy with him over the many points that he is liable to dispute."[40] In a further exchange on the subject, Livingstone expanded: "I sincerely hope that we may never become mixed up with our friend Seton again, who is unfortunately enrapt with a corona of self conceit through which blaze shafts of personal ambition not warranted by what he has done in Scouting, or by what he ever could do for Scouting. He practices fantastic idealism of which the boys soon tire, and which has no more place in our program of Scouting than the Tom Tom of the Indians would have in the tune of 'Home Sweet Home,'" he told West. "Mr. Seton is evidently making an effort to climb in over some low point in our barricade against demoralizing influences."[41]

The fact was that Seton remained obsessed with the historical record, particularly as expressed in BSA publications, writing to Livingstone in April 1926 to register his objection to some passages in a recently released manual for Scoutmasters. "Baden-Powell's history of the Boy Scout movement is so flatly contradicted by documents, and so wholly unfair to everybody but himself, that I feel bound to write the facts," he said, demanding to meet with "some acceptable member of the Boy Scout board" before going public with his objections.[42] Livingstone referred the matter to West. "I think it is important that some conference ought to be had as it is evident that he is going to raise a question of veracity somewhere and if it gets as it surely will into the press, it will be at least harassing."

The matter took on greater urgency for BSA than it might have had not Sir Robert Baden-Powell been due in the United States the following month to attend the annual meeting of the organization in Washington. Board member Milton McCrae weighed in to suggest that West as chief scout executive and Murray as editorial committee chairman meet with Seton to discuss the points in the history to which he objected, "but the matter should, of course, rest until after the departure of Sir Robert, who will undoubtedly never visit America again" given his advanced age. McRae urged West to prevail upon Seton to hold his peace in the matter until after Baden-Powell had left, as a personal favor to McRae.[43]

Finally, Livingstone appealed directly to Seton, referring to the forthcoming meeting in Washington "which would be attended by the President and a large number of Senators and Congressmen, that the controversy which you indicate may arise about the history of the Boy Scout movement be not developed until we have had an opportunity of sitting down quietly and discussing the whole question as it appears to you and to ourselves." Sweetening the proposition, he told Seton that the executive board at its annual meeting intended to confer on those who had been most instrumental in launching Scout in the United States a new honor, the Silver Buffalo medal.[44] Seton may not have been entirely pleased to be informed that this was modeled on Baden-Powell's English Silver Wolf award, and later took umbrage that he had received the Silver Buffalo designated number nine, while numbers one and two had gone to Baden-Powell and the Unknown Scout who according to official BSA history had come to the aid of the disoriented Boyce in London.[45]

Nonetheless, BSA management was relieved that the organization had avoided another unpleasant public dispute with Seton, and West appears to have made an effort to mend fences with the former chief Scout. Seton wrote to Beard in December 1926 indicating that he and West had had something of a reconciliation. "I had a pleasant visit from West the other day, and a long talk which I am sure will result in closer relations and better understanding than hitherto," Seton wrote Beard, with whom he was also gradually making peace. "There is no reason why the Woodcraft Indians should not collaborate with the Scouts everywhere."[46]

There was even discussion within BSA a few years later as to an amalgamation of Scouting and Woodcraft, following conversations between Seton and a Scouting official in Los Angeles along those lines. BSA Regional Executive C.J. Carlson wrote to West explaining the genesis of the idea, enclosing a memo he had requested from Seton and one of his own on the subject of a union between Woodcraft and Scouting. The first of Seton's sixteen points indicated that his sense of diplomacy had not developed much in the decade and a half since he parted company with BSA. "Although the Boy Scouts is larger in number, the Woodcraft is wider in influence and far superior in program." His fifth point stated: "E.T.S. [is] to be installed as Chief Scout, without salary or official duties, except a place and a vote on the Executive Board and on the Editorial Board, with a definite voice in the formulation of policies." Elsewhere he called for "a gradual elimination of all military features and ideals," and the "elimination of the names of blackguards and outlaws [as] heroes held up for boys to worship."[47] Carlson's memo toned this down quite a bit, proposing that Woodcraft should become a BSA department, while Seton, who would receive the title of Chief Woodcraft Scout, would be "liberal in the use of his Woodcraft writings . . . to aid the combined organization."[48]

The proposal was not enthusiastically received at Scouting headquarters, or even by some of Carlson's associates in California, one of whom, Los Angeles District Council Scout Executive E.B. DeGroot shared his thoughts with West in February 1930. "It may be true that Woodcraft is a richer out-door program than we have developed, but it is equally true that Woodcraft has its limitations. As I view it, Seaton's [*sic*] program may be perfectly calculated to develop appreciation of the virtues, habits and customs of a vanishing race—knowledge and practice of which might be regarded as a cultural attainment. Possession of that sort of culture has, however, in the last analysis, mighty little to do with fitting a boy for survival in this advanced civilization and present day society. Scouting on the other hand, with its civic service, organization, leadership training, pre-vocational experimentation, and great array of practical arts and crafts, is superior to Woodcraft for fitting a boy for survival and achievement in a world in which he must live and move and have his being. 'Woodcraft,' as such is too much an end in itself. Scouting, on the other hand, is always the means to an end—and the end is related most definitely to the battle of life as it is and henceforth must be lived by men in the United States of America." DeGroot added on a more personal note that, "Seton is offensively immodest when he exacts recognition for having given the United States of America its first and only lessons in Woodcraft and Indian lore."[49]

The proposal received some consideration at BSA headquarters, but West wrote to Carlson in March to tell him that "for many reasons it would be most unwise for us to encourage any further negotiations with Ernest Thompson Seton because of our experience in the past."[50] An appeal from Mortimer Schiff that April on a compassionate basis briefly revived the proposal and it was submitted to a special headquarters committee, which divided on the matter. Committee member E.S. Martin was positive on the idea. "If Mr. Seton's Woodcraft League could be purchased with all of the rights going with it, I would consider it very much worth while for the Boy Scouts of America to control it."[51] One member felt that BSA could benefit from the absorption of Woodcraft values by older boys and adult leaders—though he acknowledged that "the practical difficulties of working with Seton . . . might more than outweigh the values themselves."[52] Another panel member was dismissive. "I believe it would be a mistake do it to any degree whatever so long as it involves giving Seton a relationship to the organization or putting him in any position where he could talk to or for Scouts . . . Seton's best contribution to Scouting can be made after his death."[53]

The proposed Woodcaft-Scouting union was set aside.

While Seton fretted at a distance, Beard was becoming the grand old man of American Scouting. This suited his ego though at times affronted his dignity as some in the organization took the liberty of calling him "Uncle Dan." By one account the epithet was bestowed upon him by Scouting management, and it was at least initially not to his liking.[54] "I am a Democrat," he told West, "but there are certain lines of decorum which . . . should be observed even by those connected with our great work." It was "disconcerting in the extreme" to have been introduced to strangers as "Uncle Dan" by someone he did not know. "It was most undignified and woefully bad taste," he said, urging that Scouting officials be "coached to prevent the mortification incident to such breaks."[55]

Three months later, Beard again exhibited tetchiness. "I was humiliated and mortified by the neglect of the dinner committee in properly seating the National Scout Commissioner, one of the founders of the Organization," he complained. "This thing has occurred so often of late that out of respect to the office I hold I must decline to attend any similar functions."[56] West apologized, while adding, "Certainly it was unfortunate that it was not made clear to you that somebody made a mistake."[57] Beard accepted, but noted another slight by headquarters in the creation of field national Scout commissioners, thereby "confusing the title as to make mistakes in my position very universal," not least in *Scouting,* which had in effect demoted him. He demanded a correction.[58] West passed word down the line and one was drafted indicating that *Scouting* was "happy to state that there is only one National Scout Commissioner—Daniel Carter Beard."[59]

By this point, understandably, West was losing patience. "I think it most unfortunate that you should apparently insist in your determination to misunderstand and feel slighted. Certainly I am doing all in my power to prevent any justification for this." He noted that the field commissioners were provided for under BSA's constitution and by-laws. "I sincerely hope that you will overlook anything which might appear as a slight, as I assure you that such a thing is not our desire or intention. It will help very much if you will assume this attitude."[60]

One fellow illustrator who came to know Beard in his latter years admired his "inspiration," while acknowledging his self-regarding tendencies. He was "an egotist who could be petty on rare occasions. An opportunist. Colorful, romantic and dramatic."[61] Despite such shortcomings, West and other BSA managers recognized Beard's immense marketing value and consequently the need to mollify him. West wrote to Presbrey and another board member that December concerning plans to organize a dinner in honor of Dan Beard, National Scout Commissioner, telling them: "I shall be honored to have my name used in the manner suggested."[62] Such attention gratified Beard and reconciled him to the name of Uncle Dan.

He had by then established the Dan Beard Outdoor School for Boys on property he owned in Pike County, Pennsylvania, on Lake Teedyuskung or Big Tink. A 1919 brochure describes Beard as the "George Washington of the Boy Scouts . . . who has done more for the wholesome, moral and physical training of the American boys than any other man who has lived."[63]

The Outdoor School gave Beard a standing of his own, independent of the Boy Scouts—though *Boys' Life* ran advertisements for the camp at no cost to Beard. Board member and confidant Frank Presbrey made an investment of $500 in the camp, though it is doubtful there was ever a monetary return from what would always be a marginal—however vigorous—proposition.[64]

"Ours is the Pioneer School in real Pioneer work," declared the brochure. "We are not teaching our boys to be executives waited on by others, but are teaching them to be doers of things themselves." But it made clear that Beard was aiming at the carriage trade of the time "Not only has our mess been unexcelled by any other camp or school, but there are few high-class summer hotels which could compete with it," boasted the pamphlet. "The tables are furnished with linen, china and silver; the waiters are uniformed in white duck, giving them a neat and pleasant appearance." Yet it assured parents that, "This is a band of Spartans, a chosen lot of boys of character and will-power." Reminiscent of his Sons of Daniel Boone, Beard organized his campers in "stockades." Campers aspired to win a buckskin badge branded with a Boone powder horn, proof the boy was "absolutely truthful [and] thoroughly reliable."[65]

The camp's main selling point was of course Dan Beard himself. "Clad in buckskin, skillfully describing natural wonders, dramatically recounting the lives of American pioneers, and encouraging individual development, the Commissioner inspired affection, devotion and awe among his charges," relates a biographer. Among his campers was the adolescent Howard Hughes, later to become an eccentric titan of American industry. During one of the camp's eight-week sessions, Hughes is said to have returned his Buckskin Badge to Beard, having violated the Buckskin Oath by eating candy, which was forbidden to the campers during their stay.[66]

But it was mainly through his monthly *Boys' Life* columns that Beard became a living legend to American boys. His essays "blended personal anecdotes, handicraft instruction, and strident 'Americanism.' Their conversational tone suggested that the venerable sage was chatting with each youthful reader in front of a glowing campfire. The articles wove a didactic, moralistic pattern of piety, patriotism, and purity. At the same time, the author did not write condescendingly to his audience nor forget their yearning for fun and adventure."[67] Beard fielded questions from Scouts ranging from the feeding of bullfrogs to whether membership in Scouting entailed obligatory later military service. Through his columns he "served as a personal channel" to an increasingly "bureaucratized, impersonal" BSA.[68]

Visits by Beard became important events for communities around the United States. Following a visit to Lenoir City, Tennessee, a local reporter wrote that the local Scouts would "long cherish" their memories of the day. An editorial in that same *Lenoir City News* noted: "That aged philosopher stood before the boys, calling upon them to emulate the spirit of the pioneers who helped make this nation the great united Republic which it is today."[69]

In 1929, Beard traveled to England for an international jamboree, giving him an opportunity to express his ardent Americanism and lingering anglophobia. His son Bartlett (named for a pioneer scout) later related the typically expansive tale his father told on his return. At one point he found himself on a reviewing stand at the jamboree, dressed in buckskins with a flintlock rifle in his arms. Standing near him was the Duke of York. "Who is that man carrying that gun?" demanded the irascible aristocrat. "Get him out of here!" The irreverent Beard reassured his antagonist: "Don't worry, Duke, this rifle hasn't been fired since 1776."[70] Apocryphal, perhaps—but classic Beard.

The trip offered occasion for reconciliation with Baden-Powell, so often the target of Beard's anti-British outbursts. Upon his return to America, he wrote the old soldier to express "a real affection for the bully set of men I met in England." Beard the illustrator declared himself "delighted" with Baden-Powell's studio and sketches. "It explained many delightful things in your character which up to that time I had not fully understood. I congratulate you upon the fact that the present government and the people so thoroughly appreciate your work. At the same time, I know that recognition and honors are not the object of your work, but that you are working for the elevation of that sacred thing we call boyhood."[71]

In time Beard would acquire the status of an American folk hero, described in press accounts as the "patron saint of boyhood" and the nation's "First Scout," among other honorifics. When a St. Louis newspaper polled 1,200 schoolchildren in 1932 as to the greatest living men, they collectively nominated Colonel Charles Lindbergh, President Herbert Hoover, Henry Ford, General George Pershing, Albert Einstein, Admiral Richard Byrd, wrestler Ed "Strangler" Lewis, Benito Mussolini, cowboy star Hoot Gibson, Guglielmo Marconi, and Uncle Dan Beard.[72]

The aging Beard relished the part. "He enjoyed attention, often visiting the Scout office in New York dressed in a light colored buckskin suit with coat and trouser seams fringed and a broad brimmed hat" recalled one BSA administrator.[73] Yet Beard truly was an American original. He took a cold bath every morning, then woke up his household loudly singing: "It's a mighty pretty morning, good

Lord, good Lord. The devil's mad and I am glad. He missed a soul he thought he had, good Lord, good Lord."[74] He neither drank nor smoked, and kept the poems of Robert W. Service on his nightstand.

Upon Beard's eightieth birthday in June 1930, the *New York Times* offered readers his special "recipe" for Scouting. "Take a bowl full of unbounded love for boys, one pint of absolute faith in American institutions, two teacups of American pioneer blood, one tablespoon of thrills, one tablespoon of romance, two heaping tablespoons of adventure, a teaspoon of Indian traditions, a teacup of vigor and grit of the Puritans, a teacup of the chivalry of the Cavaliers, a quart of the idealism of Thoreau, John Burroughs and Henry van Dyke, whole seasoned well with patriotism and character and stirred up with the Golden Rule, after which sprinkle well with the Stars and Stripes and serve red hot."[75]

July 1937 brought the ultimate stamp of national approval for the Boy Scouts: *Time* magazine put the uniformed James West on its cover in connection with the organization's first National Jamboree in Washington. Some 25 thousand Scouts pitched tents on the Mall and nearby open spaces, and across the Potomac. On the first evening, those scouts and three thousand scoutmasters assembled at the base of the Washington Monument to light the official fire. "Up stepped wizened little Daniel Carter Beard with trusty flint and steel, struck the spark which lit a torch which ignited two big campfires. Old Dan Beard had every right to that honor. He has worn out more deerskin shirts and done more for boys than any magazine illustrator now alive," *Time* stated. The magazine noted that at 87 years of age, Beard remained vigorous and alert, and "throws hatchets for exercise."[76]

Seton, meanwhile, was turning his focus to the West. He had traveled there on a number of occasions, beginning with the wolf-hunting assignment during which he captured Lobo, continuing with expeditions to Yellowstone, where he found inspiration for Johnny Bear, spoiled to death by tourists, and other wild parts. Lummis, back in Los Angeles as city librarian and a Southwest preservationist, noted a typical Seton flying visit in his journal. "Seton called to say he had just gotten back from the desert and wanted to meet" at a rail station in Los Angeles or in Pasadena, where he would pick up a train to Chicago. Lummis rushed to Santa Fe Station from which he embarked with Seton for "a bully half hour talk on the way to Pasadena" and another hour and a half waiting for the Chicago train. "And he is as full of life and ginger and wisdom and hard work as ever."

Seton had been investigating prairie dogs. He showed Lummis "a painful map he had made the day before of the underground works of the Prairie Rat after 6 hours hard work with a spade and a boy to help him." Seton had "fallen violently in love with the Mojave desert."[77]

In a letter to Lummis dated "Woodchuck day, Hunger moon, 1922," Seton urged him to attend the upcoming Grand Council of the Woodcraft Folk to be held in Los Angeles at Blanchard Hall, the city's first art gallery. Lummis should be "prepared above all things to give us a 1-minute Scout Report on the *Message of the Desert,* or the *Spirit of the Mesas,* or perhaps that adventure of yours when you *walked alone with the Puma in Mexico* some 40 years ago."[78] Lummis turned out for the gathering. "The Chautauqua-minded Mayor [George] Cryer and wife were there, and he quite swelled himself up in several speeches which Seton turned him loose on. The tables were very well decorated in Indian fashion—each 'Lodge' having a table of its own and its own scheme. Our head table was Hopi; and our place-cards were granite stones the size of a goose egg. Pretty fair dinner," Lummis recorded. "Then the Wood-craft boys cleared the tables off their trestles and we made a grand circle They had expected 160, and there were 285; but it was very well managed. Seton had the Sand-Painting effect on a rug; and his fire altar, and knelt and made the fire in very short order with his rubbing sticks, to the great admiration of the multitude."[79]

But New Mexico became Seton's ultimate destination. As of 1927, Seton and Julia Buttree traveled twice a year to Santa Fe to scout out land on which to make their "final home."[80] In July of that year, Seton traveled to the Grand Canyon with a group including a curator of the American Museum of Natural History, Clyde Fisher, and his wife. A Lummis correspondent in the East offered a candid view of Seton and his domestic arrangements. "I don't know how well Seton knows the Southwest," she wrote, "but not so well but that he can afford to put his self-feeling in his pockets, and learn from you. And since his high and mighty wife is not to be along, I fancy he will be more amenable to advice. His clever secretary is to go, however, and she will never let Seton's light be hid under a bushel."[81]

Seton was very fond of Lummis, and upon his death in December 1928 sent a note of condolence to his family in Los Angeles. "Charles Fletcher Lummis has crossed the Great Divide," Seton wrote. "We can find comfort in this—he lived his life, he finished his work. He left an undying name and died triumphant, blest with the love and appreciation of the world who knew him."[82]

After much deliberation, Seton in 1930 purchased 2,500 acres of land on the so-called Sebastian de Vargas Grant made by the King of Spain to a *caballero* of that name in 1728. The property offered "unspeakable views into the Sandias, the Jemez, the Nacimientos, the Cerrillo, the Manzanos, the Sangre de Cristos, and other lesser ranges," his secretary-companion later wrote. "But, above all, there is a spiritual quality about the place that is felt by every visitor." Seton had in mind to establish an institution that would provide "spiritual refreshment for millions between the ages of four and ninety-four."[83] As Seton remade his organization, he deepened its ethnological and philosophical basis, taking as its logo the buffalo horn, symbol of the Plains Indians, incorporating Indian songs and dances from scholarly sources.[84] He was answering the "Buffalo Wind," a mystical force he would eventually describe as his life's primary guiding influence.

In the early 1930s, as the Great Depression took hold, Seton and Julia Buttree (with husband Ted who had tagged along to New Mexico) raised buildings on the property, including a museum to house Seton's collections. In 1932 the College of Indian Wisdom, accredited by the American Association of Colleges, opened its doors.

Students were housed in an improvised Indian village of "tepees, wickiups, a few log cabins, a dining hall, a Pueblo kiva, and a Navajo Hogan" that served as an auditorium.[85] A faculty of forty-two academics taught classes outdoors in July-August sessions, with frequent field trips to Indian sites.[86] College dean Julia Buttree marked the end of each day with an Indian song. Seton became a kind of shaman, performing weddings and funerals at the request of followers.

Buttree finally dissolved her marriage with Ted, and Seton set about unwinding his marital and financial relationship with Grace, involving lawyers in New York, New Mexico and Arizona, where his legal spouse was now spending winters. Ernest deeded Grace the Connecticut property, DeWinton, and most of the copyrights to his earlier writings with the particular exception of his *Lives of Game Animals*. It was a rather complicated divorce proceeding, but amicable between the Setons—though the legal papers revealed some animus on the part of Grace where Julia was concerned.

In the end, though, Seton reveled in his life out West, as indicated in some follow-up correspondence between Bethuel M. Webster, Jr., Grace Seton's New York lawyer, and New Mexico attorney Francis C. Wilson, not long after the divorce was finalized and Ernest and Julia were married on January 2, 1935, in Texas. "I was amused this morning to read a dispatch from El Paso announcing the marriage of the 'Chief' and Mrs. Buttree," Webster told Wilson. "It will amuse you to learn that after I said goodbye to you at the hotel [in Santa Fe] I was seized by the 'Chief,' Mrs. Buttree and Ted and spent the evening with them in the bar at the LaFonda. The President of the College of Indian Wisdom was pretty well pickled on Tequila cocktails when he left for Seton Village at about 10:30 p.m."[87]

Seton then began building yet another mansion, this time a 30-room pueblo-style structure, which became known as Seton Castle.[88] The couple took to the road again and Julia, dressed in Indian regalia, added singing and dancing to Seton's lectures as they traveled the States that year before their honeymoon in Europe. However rusticated he might have become in New Mexico, Seton maintained a wide acquaintance and remained a man of some means, disposing at the time of his divorce of financial assets worth about $200,000, still quite a respectable portfolio in those post-Crash days.[89]

In the late 1930s, with the footsteps of time growing louder, Beard and Seton returned to the controversies surrounding the origins of the Boy Scouts, spurred by BSA's publication in 1937 of *The History of the Boy Scout of America.* This was written by longtime board member William Murray with the close oversight of West. As drafts circulated, objections piled up from the YMCA, which felt it had been given short shrift, and others concerned. Even West was unhappy with portions, telling insurance executive Walter Head, a successor to Livingstone as BSA president, that, "The inaccuracy regarding me . . . is ridiculous, but nevertheless it hurts, and where anyone found basis for the statement as given, and how it was permitted to stand after review by a score or more people, I cannot understand."[90]

But the most strident objections, not surprisingly, came from Beard and Seton. Beard complained that the history was "ungenerous," saying it "should be burned and a new history written by an historian, not by a lawyer or by a member of headquarters with biased fixed beliefs and purposes."[91] Robinson sent Seton some extracts with the judgment that Murray "has tried to do you justice."[92] But Seton did not agree, informing Robinson that West had initially instructed E.S. Martin, his assistant, to write the history, but after Martin "came out flatfooted and said there is no question that the fundamental idea [was] supplied by Seton long before Baden-Powell," a furious West "took the whole thing out of Martin's hands" and gave it to Murray, "who has always been hostile to me."

He continued: "There is not at present a satisfactory history of the American Boy Scouts. It must be written in the near future. I am not the proper person to write it. Nevertheless, I have more valuable material about the origin, maybe, than anyone else. Will you write it?" Robinson never did take up the project.[93]

Seton noted in passing that, "James E. West cannot possibly live two years longer. He went recently to Rochester, Minnesota, to the famous Mayo Clinic. He got little encouragement from them. It was chiefly a warning to prepare for the finish. I do not know who will take West's place, but it will be one of three men, I am told, every one of them favorable to my views; that is, they want more of my thought and activities in their program." Seton could not let go. Moreover, he was misinformed as to the health of his onetime nemesis: West was to continue in office as BSA chief scout executive until 1942, when he stepped down under pressure from a board concerned at his autocratic management style and his compensation. West somewhat ironically received Seton's former title, Chief Scout, and an office in the Chrysler Building, near BSA headquarters, with little to do. He died on May 15, 1948, isolated from those he had worked with for many years.[94]

Eventually Beard and Seton would both bring out autobiographies in which, in the initial drafts at least, they proposed to set the historical record straight. But neither, in its published version, comprehensively addressed their roles in Scouting. In 1939 Doubleday published Beards's *Hardly a Man Is Now Alive,* a colorful account of his life and times, its title taken from Henry Wadsworth Longfellow's poem "Paul Revere's Ride."

But its publication followed extended consultations within BSA and between West and Beard's editor at Doubleday, Theodore Roosevelt, Jr., a member of the BSA board. The late president's son brought Beard's manuscript to West's attention. "The other day I spent some time in Colonel Roosevelt's office reviewing the chapter in Dan Beard's autobiography concerning Scouting and while Ted, of course, has asked me to keep this very confidential, which I shall. I do think I should say to you, as I have said to him, that the material as written by Dan Beard and revised and now in proof form is about as horrible as it possibly could be," West told Head in May 1939.[95]

Beard's account gave to understand that Scouting arose directly from his efforts. "My life of hard work, exposure, privations, jollity, fun, frivolity, study, and play was but the kindergarten, grammar school, high school, and university necessary to educate me for my real life's work as a Scout leader," Beard wrote. "The launching of the Boy Scouts of America was my graduating diploma." He liberally reconstructed his conversations with *Recreation* publisher William Annis about starting a boys organization. "'Annis, I think I have a great idea,'" Beard recalled telling him. "'We will form a Society of Boy Scouts and identify it with the greatest of Scouts by calling the boys, "The Sons of Daniel Boone."'" Annis was immediately enthusiastic. "He cried, 'Mr. Beard, we'll sweep the country with it.' He little knew that we were going to sweep the world."[96]

James West and others were aghast. The manuscript was "awful, indeed dreadful, because it is misleading and inaccurate in its implications, to say the least, and does not do credit to either the author or the Boy Scouts of America, or the cause of Scouting, or for that matter anyone concerned," he informed Head.[97] Others at BSA were less charitable. "This is the vaporing of a jealous old man whose envy and hate have soured many years of his life," BSA staffer George Ehler told West in a memo. "It is an insult to [Baden-Powell] and should be disowned by the B.S.A."[98]

West and Head prevailed on Roosevelt to judiciously edit the book so that it would at the very least not contradict the BSA official history in circulation, and Roosevelt deftly brought Uncle Dan around, arguing that unless the book were revised, BSA would never endorse or promote the book. Beard agreed, under protest. "I am wondering if it is right for us to allow an antagonistic party to dictate what we must publish and what we should not. Of course, as a publisher, you must, to a certain degree, consider the commercial end, but personally I would rather not have the thing published at all than to cravenly submit to intimidation." He added, reproachfully: "The great man you called Father never allowed anyone to bulldog him, and maybe that is one reason I loved him."

In August 1939 bound copies of *Hardly a Man* made the rounds of headquarters. "It is milder than I had expected," concluded West aide E.S. Martin. The book said "nothing that indicates that Baden-Powell was or was not the founder, or that Daniel Carter Beard was or was not the founder."[99] M.R. Greene remarked that "we are very lucky, because Mr. Beard might have said a great deal more than he has said here. I had the feeling he was holding his punches all the time." Beard implied that Baden-Powell lifted his Scouting idea, but "there is not a sentence that definitely says that." The author "might almost have had a legal mind in constructing some of these paragraphs," Greene noted, pointing to the offending statement about Beard's Scouting sweeping the world. "And yet he has never said that he started the Boy Scouts himself."[100]

Around the same time BSA got wind of another revisionist history in the making, this time from the pen of Ernest Seton, who at the age of seventy-nine was still determined to set down his version of events. Following his objections in 1926 to the history contained in the Scouting manual published that year, Seton had drafted a *History of Woodcraft* which similarly perplexed BSA managers. This time, Seton directly called on Baden-Powell to correct the historical record, once again maintaining that Scouting in its essential ingredients was drawn from his *Birch-Bark Roll.* "These facts, of course, are well known to you, and abundantly attested by your numerous letters to me," he told the aging general. "I think I need hardly do more than call your attention to this, and you will gladly supply the missing statements of credit. Of course, it would be simple for me to publish your letters, but that, I think, is hardly necessary."[101]

One can almost hear Baden-Powell sighing as he responded. He could not agree that he had gotten the main idea for Scouting from Seton. "If, however, you are anxious to claim authorship of the Boy Scout movement by all means do so. I have no objection, though I don't understand why, if you invented it, you have not carried it on."[102] Baden-Powell referred the matter back to West, who exercised his powers of persuasion—directly with Seton and indirectly through those who might influence the Woodcraft founder—to convince him to let the old controversy rest. As things worked out, Seton's Wood-craft text was never published in the United States and appeared as an innocuous monograph in Britain.[103]

Though prone to occasional venting of old grievances, Beard, ten years older than Seton, was coming to terms with the past. "My idea is to avoid any clash or fight," he wrote Seton when drafts of William Murray's history of BSA were being circulated amid much distress. "Gosh! I have had my belly full of that sort of thing, and I am clamoring for a peaceful old age. Let the historians do the fighting." He advised Seton: "Don't let's have a scrap with Baden-Powell or anybody else. We may both be full of spunk and full of pluck, but let us hope we are also full of wisdom. Such being the case, and time being short, without weakening, let us avoid all danger signs."[104]

But Seton found some encouragement for his point of view from Robinson, whose advice to him was not to attack Baden-Powell, which could only create bad feeling. In correspondence with Murray, however, he defended Seton's point of view. "The more I go into the matter the more I am convinced that Ernest Thompson Seton has a just cause for his dissatisfaction with the lack of expressed appreciation for his contribution both to Baden-Powell and to the Boy Scout movement in this country," he told the lawyer and official Scouting historian. Baden-Powell, he maintained, "leaned hard on Seton in the early days, in trying to adapt his Scouting movement to the needs of the boys." Still, he acknowledged, "It is a matter of opinion which contributed the most to the Boy Scouts the world over. Personally, I would like to see each of them get all the credit that each deserves. Their contributions, it seems to me, were as different and as necessary . . . as the contributions of a tailor and a weaver of cloth in the making of a suit of clothes."[105]

To Black Wolf he offered sound advice. "Regarding history, I think what is needed is not so much another history of the Boy Scout movement, as a history of the Seton Indians. The less said about the

Boy Scouts in it the better. *Focus the attention* of the public on your
creation and not any people that may have pilfered from it, or diluted
it, or changed terminology and claimed originality. Don't let the big
idea of your blue sky method be obscured by the dust of any squabble
about anyone who may have poached on your preserves," he counseled
Black Wolf. "It seems to me that the most valuable items of your program are still unknown. Only the spectacular items have been copied,
not the real thing. The public does not see behind the war paint and
feathers, the coups and achievements and the eternal values . . . does
not yet know or imagine the real values of your program, and there is
not the slightest danger of any organization stealing the real thing. All
that they will take will be what they understand and can display."[106]

But Gitchee Saka's wise counsel was in vain—Seton was determined to set the record straight and in 1939 word reached BSA that he
was again mustering his facts. Baden-Powell wrote to West informing
him of the receipt of a letter from Seton "in which he says that 'owing
to a strong and growing demand for a full accurate history of the Boy
Scout movement' he is now writing one." Seton sought permission
to quote from letters Baden-Powell had sent him over the years, to
which the British Scouting founder replied asking Seton to send him
the specific extracts he proposed to publish, before he could give permission.[107] At Baden-Powell's request, West agreed to represent him
in all such dealings with Seton, and in June 1940 the Scouting executive reported to Baden-Powell, then in retirement in Kenya, that BSA
managers "have just been permitted, confidentially, to see [a] copy of a
section which is to appear in the biography he is now having published
by Charles Scribners Sons." West assured Baden-Powell that he and his
associates at BSA would make "a sincere effort to have the publishers
convinced that Seton's statements are in many instances without foundation and in conflict with" official BSA history.[108]

Beyond this, West intimated to Scribners Vice President Whitney Darrow that failure to address such concerns might result in ligi-
tation. He offered his "fullest cooperation in any effort that might be
made to have such books as might be published by you, as nearly as

possible harmonize with the actual facts and justify our enthusiastic cooperation, rather than an antagonistic attitude or even formal action on our part."[109] It was understood that such an action would respond to statements about Baden-Powell that might be construed as libelous. West shared the letter with Baden-Powell, who complimented the lawyer on "the convincing way you have stated our case and in most charming and friendly terms . . . You have put Mr. Scribner in an awful quandary!"[110]

By the end of August 1940, West was able to cable Baden-Powell: "Happy report that publishers have agreed eliminate all reference to Scouting from Setons biography. Cordial greetings."

In fact, Grace Seton, still involved in her ex-husband's publishing affairs, had written to Scribner's editor Maxwell Perkins in May, shortly before West sent his deftly worded threat to the publishing firm, to tell him that "after long consideration, we feel that it will be better to omit the history of the Boy Scouts from the present volume." The book, to be entitled *Trail of an Artist-Naturalist,* would summarize that period, "and we will reserve the fuller history for some other presentation."[111]

Replying, Perkins assured her that the Scouting material had been excised, "leaving only the account of how Mr. Seton first began to work with the boys and organize them." All that concerned his dealings with Baden-Powell was removed.[112]

Perkins revisited the matter in a communication to Seton in April 1941, after Baden-Powell's death in Kenya that January, reporting that shortly before his autobiography went to press, "two of the Boy Scout people approached me with warnings on account of Baden Powell [*sic*], as I remember it. I told them we were not in the least worried as to libel, that there was nothing in the book that exception could be taken to. I don't know how the matter would stand now, that Baden Powell is dead."[113]

There is no indication Seton ever reconciled with Baden-Powell. But he did come to terms with Beard, the revival of their friendship in part nurtured by their shared grievances against West—though a genuine fondness is evident in their correspondence. "You and I have hit the same trail together for a long time. It has been rough in places but nearly always exhilarating," Seton told his onetime rival in a December 1930 note. "Now we are descending the western slope of the mountain together. We can see the sunset; and when we are called to the place beyond, let me hope for you, as for myself, that it will be, not to a land of harps and clouds, not to a place of slushy sentiment and thin wine gush—but to the Happy Hunting Ground that is the dream home of every red-blooded man of whatsoever race.

"Keep on, old man! Keep the trail high, and blaze it clear. A million boys are following after." Seton signed the note, "Your ancient friend," with his trademark pawprint.[114]

In similar spirit, Beard wrote to West in April 1935 taking a (temporarily, at least) philosophical attitude as to where credit should go for Scouting, and the inadequacies of the historical accounts. "I would like to see a real, unbiased history of the evolution and growth of the Movement itself, written by some outside party. Such a history is bound to be written sooner or later, by someone who will not be influenced by the personal claims of Ernest Thompson, Baden-Powell or Dan Beard. This will probably be done when you and I have the grass growing over our coverlid, and when we cannot make much of a kick, so why worry? All three of us have fought our fight, and we have fought a good fight, and the three of us have left our marks. And all three of us have reached the point where years have mellowed our characters. We can now smile at things that used to irritate us, and now laugh at things that used to make us angry.

"God bless you, old man, and good luck to you."[115]

Yet Beard could not resist, in May 1939, passing along a bit of gossip to his former foe. Board member Frank Seaman had told him that West, "fearing that Seton and Beard were too strong a combination . . . started a whispering campaign, which told Seton that Dan Beard had said thus and so, and incited his ire; and told Dan Beard that Seton had said this and that, angering him," Beard conspiratorially told Seton. "In the end he put you out of Scouting, but thank the

Good Lord, I was not there and took no part in that, and also thank the Good Lord, I have tumbled to the scheme and since have refused to quarrel with anybody else."[116]

Dan Beard died of heart failure induced by bronchitis on June 11, 1941, on the 14-acre property in Suffern, New York, above the Hudson River, to which he had moved when Flushing, Queens, became too urbanized for his taste. Eleven days later Beard would have turned 91. "Uncle Dan sublimated boyhood and in doing so became a hero to this country's youth," reported the Associated Press. "Often he said he would rather be an American boy than president, or a Boy Scout than a king."[117]

Scouting magazine that July quoted from a recent Beard column. "Old age is stepping on my heels, but why be downhearted. Life and death are what we make them. Joy and sorrow, heaven and hell are in our hearts. Then let's go through life with a song on our lips and when we cross the Great Divide, don't allow old kill-joy Charon to put gloom in our hearts, but sing him a jolly sailor's chantey song, keeping time with the stroke of the oars. It stands to reason we will be gladly welcomed by the waiting ones on the shining shores of Infinity."[118]

Beard himself had the last word, though. His final *Boys' Life* column appeared posthumously that July. "Uncle Dan realizes that he is close to the end of the trail, but it is a modern trail and he wants you boys to feel that whatever happens to him, he will still be with you in your camps, in your homes, and you may know he is whispering in your ears his confidence in you and his faith in your ability to carry on your grand work of Scouting wherever you may be."[119]

Through the 1930s, Seton continued with his College of Indian Wisdom while also contributing to the Indian Rights movement of the New Deal. He developed a working relationship with John Collier, appointed commissioner of Indian Affairs in the administration of President Franklin D. Roosevelt. Seton and Collier shared friends and Collier had been a leading figure in the Indian Rights movement since the early 1920s. As Indian Affairs commissioner, Collier pressed for passage of the Indian Reorganization Act of 1934 which shifted federal policy 180 degrees from assimilation to the encouragement of Native American self-determination, in particular through the restoration of communal lands. Collier recalled a speech by Seton in 1924 in New York deploring U.S. official treatment of the Indians. "His was the first voice to speak of the ill effects . . . of our victimization of the U.S. Indians," Collier once declared.[120] The Bureau of Indian Affairs sent some of its employees to study at Seton's College of Indian Wisdom so they could better promote the re-emergence of authentic Indian art forms. Ernest and Julia Seton made their own contributions to the effort to foster an Indian renaissance through books and lectures, one of the latter entitled "The Message of the Redman." In it, Seton condemned white society as a materialistic failure—this during the height of the Depression—compared with Indian values of service to the tribe. In 1936 the Setons developed this message in *The Gospel of the Redman,* which set the lessons of the Bible alongside Indian religious and philosophical beliefs. Seton had come full circle to the *Birch-Bark Roll,* albeit on higher plane. The book became a best seller and reinvigorated Seton's lecture tours, the College of Indian Wisdom hummed and thrived under the New Deal, and the Woodcraft League's national membership soared to an estimated 80,000.

In 1938, Seton marked his seventy-eighth birthday by christening as Beulah the two-month-old infant he and Julia had adopted; her Indian name was Payo Pai, or Summer Flower. In her honor, Seton published *Buffalo Wind,* a book of reflections on his life and the magnetic attraction of the wilderness, printed in a limited edition of two hundred copies with a buffalo hide binding. The Setons continued to travel, lecture, perform, and spread their message, though the 1941 session of the College of Indian Wisdom was to be its last, between Ernest's advancing age, and the dislocations of a widening global conflict.

The couple resumed their speaking tours after the war, driving their Chevrolet throughout the region to California and Colorado. Ernest remained active well into his eighties, writing and painting and putting a new roof on his library in 1945. They planned a lecture tour late the following year, but Seton died on October 23, 1946, the cause of death given as circulatory failure, though an autopsy showed pancreatic cancer.

As Seton had instructed, his body was cremated.[121] One imagines that his mourners recited or recalled his contribution to a Seton Village Poets collection, "My Prayer":

> *Great Spirit of my fathers,*
> *This is my prayer:*
> *Help me to feel thine urge and thy message;*
> *Help me to be a man, a man physically,*
> *thoughtfully, bravely and kindly.*
> *Help me to be just even to those who hate me,*
> *But above all things, help me to be kind.*[122]

Seton's passing marked the end of an era—all three Scouting founders had reached the end of the figurative trail, though not without blazing some enduring marks for the generations to follow. Despite their rivalries and quarrels over which of them had led the way to Scouting, the truth was that the Boy Scouts of America could not have emerged in the form it took had Seton not fatefully communicated his vision to Baden-Powell when he did, and had Beard not added his "tablespoon of romance" and "two heaping tablespoons of adventure" along with his effervescent personality. And without a James West to place the organization on a solid footing it might not have lasted through the critical first decade and become a particularly American institution tasked with shaping the nation's youth for service.

Still, it is worth wondering what the Boy Scouts of America might have been or become in the present day if Seton had been better able to put his stamp on BSA so that it embraced not only the legacy of the pioneer and the patriot but also his vision of the oneness of man and nature as expressed in the legacy of Native American culture. Though the Scouting Party briefly existed in those early days, it was quickly overtaken by events in the form of the First World War, which gave BSA a prominent role on the home front and ensured its success at the price of narrowing its vision. One hundred years after BSA's founding it does not seem too late, and may be an opportune moment, to reconsider and reintegrate some of the unconventional and idiosyncratic values that Seton—and Beard too—brought to the Scouting Party, making it so irresistible to American boys and the nation as a whole. Revisiting its origins in this way might provide the Boy Scouts of America with a useful touchstone for its next century.

BIBLIOGRAPHY

"Along Came the Astoria," *Old and Sold Antiques Digest,* originally published in 1931, http://www.oldandsold.com/articles08/waldorf-astoria-7.shtml.

Anderson, H. Allen. *The Chief: Ernest Thompson Seton and the Changing West.* College Station, Texas: A&M University Press, 1986.

_____. "Ernest Thompson Seton's First Visit to New Mexico, 1893–1894." *New Mexico Historical Review,* October 1981.

Baden-Powell, Donald. "Recollections of the Earliest Camps," *The Daily Arrow,* August 12, 1929.

Baden-Powell, Robert S.S. *Aids to Scouting for NCOs and Men.* London: Gale & Polden, 1899.

_____. *Boy Scouts Beyond the Seas: "My World Tour."* London: C. Arthur Pearson, 1913.

_____. "The Boy Scouts," *Boys of the Empire,* October 27, 1900.

_____. "Boy Scouts: A Suggestion," May 1907. Pamphlet.

_____. *The Downfall of Prempeh: A Diary of the Native Levy in Ashanti 1895–1896.* London: Methuen, 1896.

_____. "How I Started Scouting," *The Scout,* April 18, 1908.

_____. *Lessons from the Varsity of Life.* London: C. Arthur Pearson, 1934.

_____. Letters. Standish Museum and Unitarian Church, East Bridgewater, Massachusetts.

_____. *Life's Snags and How to Meet Them: Talks to Young Men.* London: C. Arthur Pearson, 1927.

_____. *The Matabele Campaign 1896.* London: Methuen, 1897.

_____. "My World Tour," *The Scout,* January 27, 1912.

_____. "My World Tour," *The Scout,* March 23, 1912.

_____. "My World Tour," *The Scout,* March 30, 1912.

_____. "My World Tour," *The Scout,* April 6, 1912.

_____. "My World Tour," *The Scout,* April 13, 1912.

_____. "My World Tour," *The Scout,* April 27, 1912.

_____. "My World Tour," *The Scout,* May 4, 1912.

_____. "My World Tour," *The Scout,* May 11, 1912.

_____. "My World Tour," *The Scout,* August 31, 1912.

_____. *Pigsticking or Hoghunting: A Complete Account for Sportsmen, and Others.* London: Harrison & Sons, 1889.

_____. *Reconnaissance and Scouting.* London: William Clowes & Sons, 1884.

_____. *Scouting for Boys, Installment 1.* London: Horace Cox, 1908.

_____. *Scouting for Boys.* Rev. ed. London: C. Arthur Pearson, June 1909.

_____. "The Woodcraft Indians and Boy Scouts," *The Scout,* February 5, 1910.

Baillie, Frederick David. *Mafeking: A Diary of a Siege.* Westminster, England: Archibald Constable, 1900.

Barrus, Clara. *The Life and Letters of John Burroughs, Vol II.* Boston: Houghton Mifflin, 1925.

Barton, Allen H. *The Wabanaki School and Seton's Indians: Transcript of Oral History Interview with Edith Hoisington.* Greenwich, CT: The Greenwich Library, 1981.

Beard, Daniel Carter. *The American Boy's Handy Book.* New York: Charles Scribner & Sons, 1882.

_____. *The Boy Pioneers: Sons of Daniel Boone.* London: Simkin, Marshall & Co., 1909.

_____. "The Boy Scouts," *The Outlook,* August 1910.

_____. "The Boy Scouts of America," *Review of Reviews,* October 1911.

_____. *Hardly a Man Is Now Alive.* New York: Doubleday, Doran, 1939.

_____. Papers, Library of Congress, Washington, DC.

_____. "The Scout: Boy and Man," *The Mentor,* August, 1927.

_____. "Sister Your Blind Is Disarranged," *The Arena,* July 1904.

_____. "The Sons of Daniel Boone," *Recreation,* July 1905.

Blumenfeld, Ralph D. "The Boy Scouts," *The Outlook,* July 23, 1910.

"Boers and Britons Camping Together," *The Brooklyn Daily Eagle,* March 28, 1901.

The Boer War: Ladysmith and Mafeking 1900. London: The Stationery Office, 1999.

Bok, Edward. *The Americanization of Edward Bok.* New York: Charles Scribner's Sons, 1921.

Boone, Daniel. "The Adventures of Colonel Daniel Boon [*sic*]," [1784], *Archiving Early America,* http://www.earlyamerica.com/lives/boone/.

"Boy Scout Founder Called an Authority in Scouting Tactics," *The Christian Science Monitor,* January 27, 1912.

Boy Scouts of America. National Archives, Irving, Texas.

Boy Scouts of America, *Second Annual Report.* New York: Boy Scouts of America, 1912.

Boy Scouts of America, *Fourth Annual Report.* New York: Boy Scouts of America, 1914.

Bradford, Mary and Richard, eds. *An American Family on the African Frontier: The Burnham Family Letters 1893–1896.* Niwot, CO: Roberts Rinehart, 1993.

Brendon, Piers. *Eminent Edwardians.* New York: Houghton Mifflin, 1980.

Brinkley, Douglas. *The Wilderness Warrior: Theodore Roosevelt and the Crusade for America.* New York: HarperCollins, 2009.

Brooklyn Daily Eagle Archive, Brooklyn Public Library, Brooklyn, New York.

Burnham, Frederick Russell. Papers, Yale University, New Haven, Connecticut.

Burroughs, John. "The Literary Treatment of Nature," *The Atlantic Monthly,* July 1904.

_____. "Real and Sham Natural History," *The Atlantic Monthly,* March 1903.

Carnegie, Andrew. "Mr. Carnegie's Word to Boys About War," *Boys' Life,* November 1914.

Carr, William H. "Daniel Carter Beard, Great Scout," *The Conservationist,* August–September 1973.

Cartwright, Thomas. *Why Boys Should Not Smoke.* London: T.C. & E.C. Jack, 1904.

Carver, Lord. *National Army Museum Book of the Boer War.* London: Sidgwick & Jackson, 2000.

Cooper, James Fenimore. *The Last of the Mohicans.* New York: Penguin, 1986.

Crenson, Matthew A. *Building the Invisible Orphanage: A Pre-History of the American Welfare System.* Cambridge, MA: Harvard University Press, 1998.

Daily Reports. National Meterological Library & Archives, Exeter, England.

Dalton, Kathleen. *Theodore Roosevelt: A Strenuous Life.* New York: Knopf, 2002.

Dizer, John T. "The Birth and Boyhood of Boys' Life," *Scouting,* November–December 1994.

_____. "*Boys' Life:* The Real Beginnings," *Dime Novel Round-up,* April 1996.

Easton, Robert, and Mackenzie Brown. *Lord of the Beasts: The Saga of Buffalo Jones.* Phoenix, AZ: The University of Arizona Press, 1961.

Ellis, Griffith Ogden. "Notable Boy Scouts Conference" *American Boy,* November 1910.

Ernest Thompson Seton Archive, Academy for the Love of Learning, Santa Fe, New Mexico.

Everett, Sir Percy. *The First Ten Years.* Ipswitch, England: The East Anglian Daily Times, 1948.

Farwell, Byron. *The Great Anglo-Boer War.* New York: W.W. Norton, 1976.

_____. "Taking Sides in the Boer War," *American Heritage,* April 1976, at http://www.ihr.org/jhr/v18/v18n3p14_Weber.html.

Fellows, Dexter W., and Andrew A. Freeman. *This Way to the Big Show: The Life of Dexter Fellows.* New York: The Viking Press, 1936.

Fisk, Chuck and Doug Bearce. *Collecting Scout Literature: A Collector's Guide to Boy Scout Fiction and Non-Fiction.* Salem, OR: The Bearce's Scouting Collectibles, 1990.

Flower-Smith, Malcolm, and Edmund Yorke. *Mafeking!: The Story of a Siege.* Weltevredenpark, South Africa: Covos-Day Books, 2000.

Forbush, William V. Letters. Riveredge Foundation, Glenbow Museum & Archives, Calgary.

Francis, Daniel. *The Imaginary Indian: The Image of the Indian in Canadian Culture.* Vancouver: Arsenal Pulp Press, 1992.

Freedman, Russell. *Scouting with Baden-Powell.* New York: Holiday House, 1967.

Fussell, Paul. *The Boy Scout Handbook and Other Observations.* New York: Oxford University Press, 1982.

Gardner, Brian. *Mafeking: A Victorian Legend.* New York: Harcourt, Brace & World, 1967.

Garland, Hamlin. *Companions on the Trail: A Literary Chronicle.* New York: Macmillan, 1931.

Garland, Hamlin. Papers. University of Southern California, Los Angeles, California.

_____. *Roadside Meetings.* New York: Macmillan 1930.

George, Henry. *Progress and Poverty.* New York: D. Appleton, 1879.

George, Henry Jr., *Life of Henry George.* New York: Doubleday and McClure, 1900.

Gibson, H.W. "The History of Organized Camping: The Early Days," *The Camping Magazine,* January 1936.

_____. "The History of Organized Camping: Establishment of Institutional Camps," *The Camping Magazine,* March 1936.

_____. "The History of Organized Camping: Genesis of a Camp Literature," *The Camping Magazine,* June 1936.

_____. "The History of Organized Camping: Leadership Training Conferences and Courses," *The Camping Magazine,* November 1936.

_____. "The History of Organized Camping: Origins of Conferences and Association Work," *The Camping Magazine,* May 1936.

_____. "The History of Organized Camping: Pioneer Camp Personalities," *The Camping Magazine,* February 1936.

_____. "The History of Organized Camping: The Private Camps," *The Camping Magazine,* April 1936.

_____. "The History of Organized Camping: Spread of the American Camp to Other Lands," *The Camping Magazine,* December 1936.

Gilbert, Bil. "Black Wolf," *Smithsonian,* July 1997.

Goodnight, Charles. Papers, Panhandle-Plains Historical Museum, Canyon, Texas.

Grey, Zane. *The Last of the Plainsmen.* New York: The Outing Company, 1908.

_____. "The Man Who Influenced Me Most," *American Magazine,* August (year unknown).

Gulick, Luther Halsey. *A Philosophy of Play.* New York: Charles Scribner's Sons, 1920.

Haines, Aubrey L. *The Yellowstone Story: A History of Our First National Park.* Yellowstone National Park: Colorado Associated University Press, 1977.

Haley, J. Evetts. *Charles Goodnight, Cowman and Plainsman.* Boston: Houghton Mifflin, 1936.

Halsey, Francis Whiting, ed. *American Authors and Their Homes.* New York: James Potts, 1901.

Hamilton, J. Angus. *The Siege of Mafeking*. London: Methuen, 1900.

Hargrave, John. *Lone Scouting*. London: Constable, 1913.

Harold, Williams, J. *Scout Trail 1910–1962: History of the Boy Scout Movement in Rhode Island*. Providence, RI: Rhode Island Boy Scouts and the Narragansett Council of the Boy Scouts of America, 1964.

Hillcourt, William. *Baden-Powell: Two Lives of a Hero*. New York: G.P. Putnam & Sons, 1964.

_____. "Go Camping Brownsea Style," *Scouting*, July–August 1967.

Hofstadter, Richard. "American Policy Favored the Allies," reproduced in *America's Entry into World I,* Donald Murphy, ed., Farmington Hills, MI: Greenhaven Press, 2004.

Hoover Institute, Stanford University, Palo Alto, California.

Hopkins, C. Howard. *History of the YMCA in North America*. New York: Association Press, 1951.

Hornaday, William T. "The Extermination of the American Bison," *Annual Report of the Board of Regents of the Smithsonian Institution*. Washington, DC: Smithsonian Institution Press, 1890.

Hornaday, William T. *Wild Life Conservation in Theory and Practice*. New Haven, Yale University Press, 1914.

Houston, C. Stuart. *Ernest Thompson Seton in Manitoba 1882–1892*. Winnipeg: Premium Ventures, 1980.

Hungerford, Edward. *The Story of the Waldorf-Astoria*. New York: G.P. Putnam's Sons, 1925.

Ineson, John. Collection, East Anglia, England.

Jeal, Tim. *The Boy-Man: The Life of Lord Baden-Powell*. New York: William Morrow, 1990.

Jensen, Kirsten M., "Grace Thompson Seton at the Helm of the Look-See," *Greenwich History,* 2002.

Jordan, David Starr. "A Challenge: Do You Want to Fight?" *Boys' Life*, November 1914.

Jordan, David Starr. Papers, Stanford University Archives, Palo Alto, California.

Kahler, William V. *An Historical Analysis of the Professional Career of Daniel Carter Beard, 1850–1941*. PhD diss., Texas A&M University, 1975.

Kahler, William V. Collection, Millersville, Pennsylvania.

Kaplan, Justin. *Mr. Clemens and Mark Twain*. New York: Simon & Schuster, 1966.

Kavee, Donna. *Bush-Holley House and Other Recollections of Greenwich: Transcript of Oral History Interview with Anya Seton*. Greenwich, CT: The Greenwich Library, 1975.

Keller, Betty. *Black Wolf: The Life of Ernest Thompson Seton*. Vancouver: Douglas & McIntyre, 1984.

Lepley, John G. and Sue, eds. *The Vanishing West: Hornaday's Buffalo*. Fort Benton, Montana: The River and Plains Society, 1992.

Levy, Harold P. *Building a Popular Movement: The Public Relations of the Boy Scouts of America.* New York: Russell Sage Foundation, 1944.

Lipton, Dan. "Where Scouting Began," *Scouting,* May–June 1983.

Lummis, Charles Fletcher. Papers. Autry National Center, Los Angeles, California.

Lutts, Ralph H. *The Nature Fakers: Wildlife, Science & Sentiment.* Golden, CO: Fulcrum, 1990.

MacLeod, David Irving. *Good Boys Made Better: The Boy Scouts of America, Boys' Brigades and the YMCA Boys' Work 1880–1920.* Diss., University of Wisconsin, 1973.

"Major Burnham, Chief of Scouts," from Richard Harding Davis, "Real Soldiers of Fortune, 1910," *The Pine Tree Web,* http://www.pinetreeweb.com/burnham-davis-soldier.htm.

Mark Twain Project, University of California, Berkeley, California.

Mathiews, Franklin K. "The Influence of the Boy Scout Movement in Directing the Reading of Boys," *Bulletin of the American Library Association,* July 1914.

Millis, Walter. *Road to War–America 1914–1917,* Boston: Houghton Mifflin, 1935.

"Minutes of Hearing Before the Committee on Education, House of Representatives, concerning H.R. 24747." Washington, DC: GPO, Sixty-First Congress, 1910.

Monroe, Keith. "Ernest Thompson Seton: Scouting's First Spellbinder," *Scouting,* October 1971.

_____. *Other Men's Sons,* manuscript.

_____. "The Way it Was: The Month the Money Stopped," *Scouting,* March–April 1984.

Morris, Brian. *Ecology and Anarchism: Essays and Reviews on Contemporary Thought.* Malvern Wells: Images, 1996.

Morris, Edmund. *The Rise of Theodore Roosevelt.* New York: Ballantine Books, 1980.

Morrison, Elting E. *Roosevelt Letters: Volume 7.* Cambridge, MA: Harvard University Press, 1954.

_____. *Roosevelt Letters: Volume 8.* Cambridge, MA: Harvard University Press, 1954.

Murphy, Donald, ed. *America's Entry into World I.* Farmington Hills, MI: Greenhaven Press, 2004.

Murray, William D. *The History of the Boy Scouts of America.* New York: The Boy Scouts of America, 1937.

_____. *As He Journeyed: The Autobiography of William D. Murray.* New York: Association Press, 1929.

Myatt, James Allen. *William Randolph Hearst and the Progressive Era, 1900–1912.* PhD diss., University of Florida, 1960.

Newlin, Keith, and Joseph B. McCullough, eds. an except from "Selected Letters of Hamlin Garland," http://people.uncw.edu/newlink/garland_letters.htm.

New York Journal-American Archive, Harry Ransom Center, The University of Texas, Austin, Texas.

Niethammer, Carolyn. "Sincerely Yours, C.J. Buffalo Jones," *Arizona Highways,* September 1978.

Nolte, Jeanne McQuarrie. *Growing Up in Cos Cob 1907–1923: Oral History Interview with Charles A. Clark.* Greenwich CT: Greenwich Library, 1976.

O'Toole, Patricia. *When Trumpets Call: Theodore Roosevelt after the White House.* New York: Simon & Schuster, 2005.

Packenham, Thomas. *The Boer War.* New York: Random House, 1979.

Paine, Albert Bigelow, *Mark Twain: A Biography.* 2 vols. New York: Harper & Brothers, 1912.

Paine, Albert Bigelow, et al. " 'Moonblight': Appreciations and Criticisms," *The Arena,* July 1904.

Peterson, Robert W. *The Boy Scouts: An American Adventure.* New York: American Heritage, 1984.

Peterson, Robert W. Collection, Macungie, Pennsylvania.

Petterchak, Janice A. *Lone Scout: W. D. Boyce and American Boy Scouting.* Rochester, IL: Legacy Press, 2003.

Phillips, John Calvin. *Selling America: The Boy Scouts of America in the Progressive Era, 1910–1921.* Master's thesis, University of Maine, 2001.

Price, Joe. *Kahunas Katalog of Boy Scout Handbooks.* Upland, CA: Joe Price, 1989.

Redekop, Magdalene. *Ernest Thompson Seton.* Don Mills, Ontario: Fitzhenry & Whiteside, 1979.

Renehan, Edward J. Jr., "The Half More Satisfying than the Whole: John Burroughs and the Hudson," *Catskill Archive,* http://www.catskillarchive.com/jb/jb-eh.htm.

Resek, Carl, ed., *The Progressives.* Indianapolis: Bobbs-Merrill, 1967.

Reynolds, E. E. *Baden-Powell: A Biography of Lord Baden-Powell of Gilwell.* London: Oxford University Press, 1942.

_____. *The Scout Movement.* London: Oxford University Press, 1950.

Richards, Paul, ed. *The Founding of the Boy Scouts as Seen Through the Letters of Lord Baden-Powell, October 1907–October 1908.* East Bridgewater, MA, The Standish Museums and Unitarian Church, 1973.

Roberts, Charles G. D. "Ernest Thompson Seton," *The Bookman,* December 1913.

_____. "The Home of a Naturalist," *Country Life in America,* December 1903.

Robinson, Edgar M. "Black Wolf in Camp with Boys," *The American Boy,* June 1911.

Robinson, Ronald, et al., *Africa and the Victorians: The Climax of Imperialism in the Dark Continent.* New York: St. Martins Press, 1961.

Roosevelt, Theodore. *America and the World War, 1916,* found at: http://www.trthegreatnewyorker.com/chronology/chronology.htm.

_____. *Hunting Trips of a Ranchman & The Wilderness Hunter.* New York: Modern Library, 1998.

_____. "Peace Insurance by Preparedness Against War," *The Metropolitan,* August 1915.

Rosenthal, Michael. *Character Factory.* New York: Pantheon, 1986.

Rosenthal, Michael. "Knights and Retainers: The Earliest Version of Baden-Powell's Boy Scout Scheme," *Journal of Contemporary History,* October 1980.

Rowan, Edward L. Collection, Exeter, New Hampshire.

Rowan, Edward L. *To Do My Best: James E. West and the History of the Boy Scouts of America.* Las Vegas, NV: International Scouting Museum, 2005.

Salomon, Julian Harris. *Three Great Scouts and a Lady,* unpublished manuscript, 1976.

Scanlon, Katherine. *Years Ago in Glenville: Oral History Interview with Frances Chmielowiec Geraghty.* Greenwich, CT: The Greenwich Library, 1977.

Schmitt, Peter J. *Back to Nature: The Arcadian Myth in Urban America.* New York: Oxford University Press, 1969.

Schroeder, Cindy and Andrea Tortora. "Neglected Civil War Site Defended with Shovels," *Cincinnati Inquirer,* August 30, 1998, http://www.enquirer.com/editions/1998/08/30/loc_kycivil30.html.

Scott, David C. Collection, Dallas, Texas.

Scull, Guy H. *Lassoing Wild Animals in Africa.* New York: Frederick A. Stokes, 1911.

Sell, Henry Blackman, and Victor Weybright. *Buffalo Bill and the Wild West.* New York: Oxford University Press, 1955.

Seton, Anya. Papers. Greenwich Historical Society, Greenwich, Connecticut.

Seton, Ernest Thompson. *The American Boy Scout: The Official Hand-Book of Woodcraft for the Boy Scouts of America.* c. April or May 1910.

_____. "The Boy Scouts in America," *The Outlook,* July 23, 1910.

_____. "The Boy Scouts in America" *The Outlook,* August 1910.

_____. *The Boy Scouts of America Official Handbook.* New York: Doubleday, Page, 1910.

_____. *Birch-Bark Roll of the Outdoor Life.* Garden City, NY: Doubleday, Page, 1908.

_____. *Birch-Bark Roll of the Woodcraft Indians.* New York: Doubleday, Page, 1906.

_____. *Buffalo Wind,* Santa Fe, NM: Seton Village Press, 1938.

_____. "Ernest Thompson Seton's Boys," Parts 1–7, *Ladies' Home Journal,* May–November 1902.

_____. *History of Scouting,* unpublished manuscript.

_____. Papers. Library and Archives, Ottawa, Canada.

_____. *The Plan of My Life,* unpublished manuscript, March 7, 1881.

_____. "The Story of Wyndygoul," *Country Life in America,* August 1909.

_____. *Trail of an Artist-Naturalist.* New York: Scribner's, 1939.

_____. "The Twelve Secrets of the Woods," *Craftsman,* June 1916.

_____. "Two Little Savages" serialized in *Ladies' Home Journal,* January–August 1903.

_____. *Wild Animals I Have Known.* New York: Charles Scribner's Sons, 1898.

Seton, Ernest Thompson, and Julia M. Seton. *Gospel of the Redman.* London: Methuen, 1937.

Seton, Ernest Thompson, and Robert S.S. Baden-Powell, *Boy Scouts of America: Official Handbook.* New York: Doubleday, Page, 1910.

Seton, Julia M. *By a Thousand Fires, Nature Notes and Extracts from the Life and Unpublished Journals of Ernest Thompson Seton.* Garden City, New York: Doubleday, 1967.

_____. *Trail and Campfire Stories.* San Gabriel, CA: Willing, 1940.

Seton Memorial Library, Philmont Scout Ranch, Cimarron, New Mexico.

Seton Village Poets. *Pictographs of the Southwest.* Cedar Rapids, IA: The Parnassian Press, 1937.

Shell, Hanna Rose. Introduction to *The Extermination of the American Bison,* by William T. Hornaday. Washington. DC: Smithsonian Institution Press, 2002.

Smith, Henry Nash. *Mark Twain's Fable of Progress—Political and Economic Ideas in A Connecticut Yankee.* New Brunswick, NJ: Rutgers University Press, 1964.

Smith, Phillip Thurmond, ed. *Mafeking Memories by Frederick Saunders (1883–1964).* London: Associated University Presses, 1996.

The Statutes at Large of the United States of America From December 1915 to March 1917. Washington, DC: GPO, 1917.

Steffens, Lincoln. *The Autobiography of Lincoln Steffens.* New York: Harcourt, Brace & World, 1958.

Storms, W. W. "The Woodcraft Indians," *Holiday Magazine,* October, 1904.

Sullivan, John F. *W.D. Boyce: Honoring the Man who Brought Scouting to America.* Ottawa, IL: John F. Sullivan, 1985.

Sullivan, Mark. *Our Times.* New York: Scribner, 1996.

Thomas, Phillip Drennon. *Buffalo Jones: Citizen of the Kansas Frontier.* Garden City, Kansas: Finney County Historical Society, 2004.

Thompson, Ernest E. "The King of the Currumpaw: A Wolf Story." *Scribner's,* November 1894.

Turner, Frederick Jackson. *The Frontier in American History.* New York: Dover, 1996.

Twain, Mark. *A Connecticut Yankee in King Arthur's Court.* New York: Charles L. Webster, 1889.

U.S. Congress. House of Representatives. "Incorporation of the Boy Scouts of America, Hearing Before the Committee on Education," H.R. 24747, May 10, 1910.

U.S. Congress. House of Representatives. "Report No. 130." 64th Congress, 1st sess., February 7, 1916.

Wadland, John Henry. *Ernest Thompson Seton: Man in Nature and the Progressive Era, 1880–1915.* New York: Arno Press, 1978.

_____. "Indians at Wyndygoul," *Greenwich News,* October 23, 1903.

_____. Papers. Trent University Archives, Trent University, Peterborough, Ontario, Canada.

Wagner, Carol Ditte. *The Boy Scouts of America: A Model and a Mirror of American Society.* Ph.D. Diss., Johns Hopkins University, 1979.

Wakefield, W.B. " 'Be Prepared': That is the Motto of the Boy Scouts," *The American Boy,* November 1910.

Walker, Colin R. "Aids to Scouting: Scouting for Men." http://www.scoutingmilestones. freeserve.co.uk/.

_____. "Beaulieu: The Third B-P Camp." http://www.scoutingmilestones.freeserve. co.uk/.

_____. "Brownsea and Its Significance." http://www.scoutingmilestones.freeserve.co.uk/.

_____. "Humshaugh: The Second B-P Camp." http://www.scoutingmilestones.freeserve. co.uk/.

Wetmore, Helen Cody. *The Last of the Great Scouts: The Life Story of 'Buffalo Bill'.* Lincoln: University of Nebraska Press, 2003.

Whitmore, Allan Richard. *Beard, Boys, and Buckskins: Daniel Carter Beard and the Preservation of the American Pioneer Tradition.* Diss., Northwestern University, 1970.

Wiley, Farida A., ed. *Ernest Thompson Seton's America.* New York: Devin-Adair, 1954.

Willan, Brian P., ed. *Edward Ross: The Diary of the Siege of Mafeking October 1899 to May 1900.* Cape Town: Van Riebeeck Society, 1980.

Wills, Chuck. *Boy Scouts of America: A Centennial History.* New York: DK Publishing, 2009.

Wilson, Sarah, Lady. *South African Memories: Social, Warlike, & Sporting. From Diaries Written at the Time.* London: Edward Arnold, 1909.

Witt, David L. *Ernest Thompson Seton: The Life and Legacy of an Artist and Conservationist.* Layton, UT: Gibbs-Smith Publishers, 2010.

Wooley, Edmund D. Papers. Gerald R. Sherratt Library, Southern Utah University, Cedar City, Utah.

Yellowstone National Park, First Letters, YNP Archives, Yellowstone National Park, Wyoming.

YMCA Papers. Babson Library, Springfield College, Springfield, Massachusetts.

NOTES

List of Abbreviations Used in Notes

ALL	Ernest Thompson Seton Papers, Academy for the Love of Learning, Santa Fe, New Mexico
ASP	Anya Seton Papers, Greenwich Historical Society, Greenwich, Connecticut
BDE	*Brooklyn Daily Eagle* Archive, Brooklyn Public Library, Brooklyn, New York
BPL	Baden-Powell Letters, Standish Museum and Unitarian Church, East Bridgewater, Massachusetts
BSA	Boy Scouts of America, National Archives, Irving, Texas. Direct quotations by permission of the Boy Scouts of America.
CFL	Charles Fletcher Lummis Papers, Autry National Center, Los Angeles, California
CGP	Charles Goodnight Papers, Panhandle-Plains Historical Museum, Canyon, Texas
DCB	Daniel Carter Beard Papers, Library of Congress, Washington
DCS	David C. Scott Collection, Dallas, Texas
DSJ	David Starr Jordan Papers, Hoover Institute, Stanford University Archives, Palo Alto, California
ELR	Edward L. Rowan Collection, Exeter, New Hampshire
ESP	Ernest Thompson Seton Papers, Library and Archives, Ottawa, Canada
EWP	Edmund D. Wooley Papers, Gerald R. Sherratt Library, Southern Utah University, Cedar City, Utah
FRB	Frank Russell Burnham Papers, Yale University
HGP	Hamlin Garland Papers, University of Southern California
HRC	*New York Journal-American* Archive, Harry Ransom Center, University of Texas, Austin, Texas
JHW	John Henry Wadland Papers, Trent University Archives, Trent University, Peterborough, Ontario, Canada
JIC	John Ineson Collection, East Anglia, England
MTP	Mark Twain Project, University of California at Berkeley

NML   Daily Reports, National Meterological Library & Archives, Exeter, England

RWP   Robert W. Peterson Collection, Macungie, Pennsylvania

SML   Seton Memorial Library, Philmont Scout Ranch, Cimarron, New Mexico

WFL   William V. Forbush Letters, Riveredge Foundation, Glenbow Museum &
          Archives, Calgary, Alberta, Canada

WVK   William V. Kahler Collection, Millersville, Pennsylvania

YPA   First Letters, Yellowstone National Park Archives, Yellowstone National Park,
          Wyoming

YMN   Kautz Family YMCA Archives, University of Minnesota, Minneapolis,
          Minnesota

YBL   YMCA Papers, Babson Library, Springfield College, Springfield,
          Massachusetts

Introduction—At the Waldorf-Astoria

1. This was the original Waldorf-Astoria Hotel on Fifth Avenue between Thirty-
   third and Thirty-fourth Streets on the future site of the Empire State Building.
   The hotel was born of a feud between William Waldorf Astor and his aunt and
   neighbor, Caroline Webster Schermerhorn Astor, doyenne of New York society.
   On the death of his father, John Jacob Astor III, William challenged her right to
   this title, arguing that it rightfully went to his wife, Mary Dahlgren Paul. But his
   aunt was immovable, perhaps contributing to his decision to emigrate to England
   in 1891, having concluded America was no longer "a fit place for a gentleman
   to live." William ordered his mansion at 350 Fifth Avenue to be torn down to
   make room for the Waldorf Hotel. The Astors in time settled their differences
   and in 1895, Caroline and her son, John Jacob Astor IV, tore down their mansion
   and commissioned architect Henry J. Hardenbergh, designer of the Waldorf, to
   create the Astoria Hotel. A 300-foot corridor connected the two hotels, renamed
   the Waldorf=Astoria. The mathematical symbol signified parity between the
   institutions and family branches (though it was quickly replaced by a simple
   hyphen). The long corridor became known as "Peacock Alley" for its displays
   of pomp and finery, and the Waldorf-Astoria synonymous with elegance and
   influence; "Along Came the Astoria."

2. *The New Yorker,* 25 February 1903, pp. 20–21. Hungerford, *Story of the Waldorf-
   Astoria.*

3. Salomon, *Three Great Scouts,* p. 119, ELR. "The men were seated at tables on the
   ballroom floor; women and scouts were in the balcony."

4. Mafeking would in modern times become known as Mafikeng—the capital of
   modern South Africa's North-West Province.

5. Hillcourt, *Baden-Powell: Baden-Powell: Two Lives,* p. 54.

6. In addition to supporting the YMCA and BSA, Carnegie funded the New York Public Library system. In 2005 dollars, his philanthropy equaled some $82 billion.

7. Brinkley, *The Wilderness Warrior,* pp. 7–19.

8. O'Toole, *When Trumpets Call,* p. 93.

9. Sullivan, *Our Times,* p. 298.

10. Dalton, *Theodore Roosevelt,* pp. 362–363.

11. Ibid.

12. Theodore Roosevelt to Ernest Thompson Seton, 23 September 1910, BSA.

13. Turner, *The Frontier in American History,* p. 1. Turner took note of an 1890 bulletin issued by the U.S. Superintendent of the Census stating that, "Up to and including 1880 the country had a frontier of settlement, but at present . . . there can hardly be said to be a frontier line."

14. From "A Souvenir of 'The Camp Fire Club,' Buckskin Night, December 4, 1909, at Hotel Astor, New York, Ernest Thompson Seton, President," DCS.

15. "Buffalo Bill's Wild West and Congress of Rough Riders of the World, Historical Sketches and Programme," c. 1900.

16. Boone, "The Adventures of Colonel Daniel Boon [*sic*]," chapter 1.

17. Cooper, *The Last of the Mohicans,* Chapter 6, p. 52.

18. Sell and Weybright, *Buffalo Bill and the Wild West,* pp. 59–60.

19. Fellows and Freeman, *This Way to the Big Show,* p. 80; "Boers and Britons Camping Together," p. 3, BDE. Cody included soldiers from both sides of the trenches from the Siege of Mafeking in his 1902 program.

20. Fellows and Freeman, *This Way to the Big Show,* p. 152; "Boy Scout Founder Called an Authority in Scouting Tactics," *The Christian Science Monitor,* January 27, 1912.

21. "Major Burnham, Chief of Scouts," from Richard Harding Davis, "*Real Soldiers of Fortune,* 1910."

22. Ibid.

23. Baden-Powell, *The Matabele Campaign,* pp. 70–71.

24. Baden-Powell, *Aids to Scouting,* p. 31.

25. Forerunner of the present-day Bronx Zoo.

26. As recorded by the expedition's manager and scribe, Scull, in *Lassoing Wild Animals.*

27. Thomas, *Buffalo Jones,* p. 48. Another flyer quoted Baden-Powell saying: "Teach the boys to be like Buffalo Jones, the Ideal Scout of the World."

28. Thomas, *Buffalo Jones,* p. 48, 56.

29. Haley, *Charles Goodnight,* p. 453.

30. Jones to Edmund D. Wooley, 21 August 1910, EWP.

31. *The Kansas City Star,* 1897, quoted in Haines, *The Yellowstone Story,* p. 72.

32. Niethammer, "Sincerely Yours," p. 35.

33. Easton and Brown, *Lord of the Beasts*, pp. 30–35.

34. Niethammer, "Sincerely Yours," p. 36.

35. Fellow cattleman Charles Goodnight, a longtime Jones rival, called Jones's cattalo efforts "foolish baby talk." "Notes," CGP.

36. Jones to unknown business contact, 27 June 1891, YPA.

37. Major John Pitcher to the Military Secretary of the Department of Dakota, Saint Paul, Minnesota, 28 November 1906, YPA.

38. Grey, *The Last of the Plainsmen*; Grey, "The Man Who Influenced Me Most."

39. Wetmore, *Last of the Great Scouts*, p. xix.

40. T. Roosevelt, *Hunting Trips*, pp. 236–243.

41. Lepley and Lepley, eds., *The Vanishing West*, pp. 60–61.

42. Shell, Introduction to Hornaday, *The Extermination*, p. xvii.

43. Hornaday, "*The Extermination*," p. 529.

44. Ibid.

45. Ibid.

46. Ibid., pp. 530–531.

47. Ibid., p. 533.

48. Ibid.

49. Hornaday to Seton, 22 May 1889, ESP.

50. Hornaday to Seton, 22 December 1896, ESP.

51. "Baden Powell's Boy Scout Plan Invades America," *New York Times*, April 24, 1910.

52. Baden-Powell to Seton, 24 September 1910, ESP.

53. "Baden Powell's Boy Scout Plan Invades America," *New York Times*, April 24, 1910.

Chapter 1—Black Wolf

1. Morris, *Rise of Theodore Roosevelt*, pp. 551–553.

2. Brinkley, *Wilderness Warrior*, pp. 207–208. Remington had illustrated Roosevelt articles on conservation published in *Century* and provided illustrations for his book *Ranch Life and the Hunting-Trail* (Philadelphia: Gebbie, 1903).

3. Newlin and McCullough, eds., an excerpt from "Selected Letters of Hamlin Garland."

4. Garland, *Roadside Meetings*, p. 371.

5. Seton, *Trail of an Artist-Naturalist*, p. 351.

6. In a letter to Roosevelt dated 5 December 1896, Seton confessed to a "slight attack of 'rattle' that hampered me."

7. Seton, *Trail of an Artist-Naturalist,* p. 351.

8. Roosevelt to Anderson, 15 March 1897, YPA, Document 2906.

9. Keller, *Black Wolf,* pp. 95–96.

10. Ibid., p. 96.

11. Seton, *Trail of an Artist-Naturalist,* pp. 303–305.

12. Ibid., pp. 305, 331–339; Thompson, "The King of the Currumpaw" *Scribner's,* November 1894; Seton, *Wild Animals I Have Known,* pp. 17–54. For a detailed account of Seton's time in New Mexico, see Anderson, "Ernest Thompson Seton's First Visit to New Mexico, 1893–1894," *New Mexico Historical Review,* October 1981, pp. 369–386.

13. Seton, *Trail of an Artist-Naturalist,* p. 331. Lobo's pelt has been preserved by the Seton Museum at the Philmont Scout Reservation in Cimarron, New Mexico.

14. http://freepages.genealogy.rootsweb.ancestry.com/~npmelton/sfbgalla.htm. The State of California ultimately purchased the house in Sacramento in which Grace was born and made it the governor's mansion; Kavee, *Bush-Holley House,* p. 16.

15. Seton, *Trail of an Artist-Naturalist,* pp. 343–344.

16. Ibid., p. 343. Journalist Lincoln Steffens observed that Grace Seton had more business acumen than Seton. "When she married him in Paris she saw . . . that Seton Thompson (as he then was) had possibilities, and she undertook his management. She raised his prices, widened his market, and set him talking and lecturing as well as writing." Steffens, *Autobiography,* p. 440.

17. After Scribner's magazine published Seton's story of Johnny Bear, a cub "spoiled to death" by Yellowstone hotel employees, Bryn Mawr students commissioned stuffed likenesses from F.A.O. Schwartz in New York. Their "Johnny Bear" was supplanted in 1902 by the "Teddy Bear," after President Theodore Roosevelt on a hunting trip in Mississippi declined to open fire on a bear that his hosts had secured to a tree for his convenience. A cartoonist at the Washington Post seized on the episode to illustrate a political dispute of the day, inspiring Brooklyn merchant Morris Michtom to bring out "Teddy's Bear" with the president's permission.

18. "Memorandum Agreement between Ernest Seton Thompson and Charles Scribner's Sons," July 1, 1898. ESP; Garland, *Companions,* p. 99.

19. Seton, *Wild Animals I Have Known.*

20. Ibid., pp. 9–13.

21. Redekop, *Ernest Thompson Seton,* p. 46.

22. Charles G.D. Roberts, "Ernest Thompson Seton," *The Bookman,* December 1913.

23. Wadland, *Ernest Thompson Seton: Man in Nature,* pp. 170, 177–178; Burroughs, "Real and Sham."

24. Wadland, *Ernest Thompson Seton: Man in Nature,* pp. 178–179.

25. Garland, *Companions,* p. 224. Long was "a tall, fervid, rather boyish clergyman, just the type to imagine things which could not happen . . . while he may have convinced himself that a bird bandages its own leg, he can't convince John Burroughs."

26. Wadland, *Ernest Thompson Seton: Man in Nature,* p. 180; Burroughs, "Real and Sham," pp. 303–309.

27. Burroughs, "Real and Sham," pp. 298–301; Lutts, *The Nature Faker,* pp. 37–55; Hamlin Garland commented: "I am on Burrough's side in this controversy, although I think John is too hard and fast in his generalizations. There are animal heroes." Garland, *Companions,* p. 224.

28. Burroughs, "Real and Sham," p. 298.

29. Renehan, "The Half More Satisfying than the Whole."

30. Burroughs, "Real and Sham," p. 298.

31. Seton, *Trail of an Artist-Naturalist,* pp. 367–371.

32. Keller, *Black Wolf,* pp. 155–156; Burroughs, "The Literary Treatment of Nature."

33. Barrus, *The Life and Letters of John Burroughs, Vol. II,* pp. 49–50; Anderson, *The Chief,* p. 121.

34. Garland, *Companions,* p. 205.

35. Garland, *Companions,* p. 206; Anderson, *The Chief,* p. 122; *New York World,* May 24, 1907; J. M. Seton, *By a Thousand Fires,* pp. 222–223.

36. Seton, *Wild Animals,* p. 1; Gilbert, "Black Wolf."

37. "Three Years with Nature," *Toronto Globe,* February 11, 1893; C. Stuart Houston, *Ernest Thompson Seton in Manitoba 1882–1892,* Introduction. Similar descriptions abound in Cos Cob memoirs. "He was absolutely magnificent; out of the ordinary with his chamois trappings and his long, flowing hair and his moustache and his moccasined feet." Scanlon, *Years Ago in Glenville,* p. 75; "Mr. Seton had charm. I don't know what else to say. Everybody liked him almost immediately. He had a terrific charm and he was a very interesting man beside his Indian lore and he was a very marvelous painter and artist, of course." Barton, *The Wabanaki School and Seton's Indians,* p. 8.

38. Keller, *Black Wolf,* pp. 146–147.

39. Ibid., pp. 143, 149; Garland, *Companions,* p. 99.

40. "Alhambra in the Rough," *Brooklyn Daily Eagle,* August 23, 1902.

41. Seton, "The Story of Wyndygoul"; Keller, *Black Wolf,* p. 149; Roberts, "The Home of a Naturalist"; Garland, *Companions,* pp. 111–112.

42. Seton, *The Plan of My Life,* ESP.

43. Seton, *Trail of an Artist-Naturalist,* pp. 5–7.

44. Ibid.

45. Ibid., p. 10.

46. Ibid., pp. 97–99.

47. Seton, *Trail of an Artist-Naturalist,* pp. 126–130.

48. Ibid., pp. 139–140.

49. Ibid., pp. 152–153.

50. Ibid., pp. 155–156. For a detailed look at Seton's years in Manitoba, see the Introduction to *Ernest Thompson Seton in Manitoba 1882–1892* by Houston.

51. Seton, *Buffalo Wind,* p. 3.

52. Seton, *Trail of an Artist-Naturalist,* pp. 240–242.

53. Ibid., pp. 391–393.

54. Seton sometimes rendered his name as Seton-Thompson, but this was not the only variation. In 1885 he signed a pen-and-ink drawing of a panther and cubs as Ernest E.T. Seton.

55. Seton, *Trail of an Artist-Naturalist,* pp. 250–258.

56. Ibid., pp. 261–262.

57. Ibid., p. 279; Keller, *Black Wolf,* p. 113.

58. Seton, *Trail of an Artist-Naturalist,* pp. 282–283.

59. Anderson, *The Chief,* pp. 106–108; Halsey, ed., *American Authors and Their Homes,* pp. 281–292. The town was a well-known artists colony, giving rise to the Cos Cob School; Steffens, *Autobiography,* pp. 436–437, p. 440. Seton advised Lincoln Steffens that he should not buy in nearby Greenwich because only the very rich lived there and land cost $1,000 per acre whereas land in Cos Cob went for no more than $25 an acre.

60. Seton, *Trail* of an Artist-Naturalist, pp. 374–377.

61. Ibid., pp. 376–385.

62. Seton, "The Boy Scouts in America," *The Outlook,* July 23 1910, pp. 630–635; Wiley, *Seton's America,* pp. 344–354.

63. Wadland, *Ernest Thompson Seton: Man in Nature,* p. 114; Keller, *Black Wolf,* pp. 163–164.

64. Seton and Seton, *Gospel of the Redman,* pp. 26–30; Anderson, *The Chief,* p. 136; Wadland, *Ernest Thompson Seton: Man in Nature,* pp. 316–319; Seton to Garland, 15 May 1897, HGP.

65. Wadland, *Ernest Thompson Seton: Man in Nature,* pp. 321–324.

66. Ibid., pp. 328–329.

67. Seton and Seton, *Gospel,* pp. 64–65; Wadland, *Ernest Thompson Seton: Man in Nature,* p. 331; Seton to the Editor, *New York Herald,* 27 November 1912.

68. The *Ladies' Home Journal* had a monthly circulation of about 1 million copies.

69. Seton, *History of Scouting,* pp. 21–22, ESP; Bok to Seton, 18 July 1901 and 29 July 1901, ESP; Bok, *Americanization of Edward Bok,* pp. 166–180; Seton, "The Boy Scouts in America"; Seton, "Ernest Thompson Seton's Boys."

70. Hall, *Adolescence,* as quoted by Wadland, *Ernest Thompson Seton: Man in Nature,* p. 335; Gulick, *A Philosophy of Play,* pp. 205–210. Gulick considered Seton's Indians one of "the most interesting examples of the intelligent use and direction of play instinct feelings . . . to make use of the instinctive desires of the boy in reinforcing the traditions and standards which he wishes to impress. He has learned the proper method of play control."

71. Seton told his Woodcraft Indians: "You're absolutely never lost in the woods. You always know where you are. What's lost is your teepee. So your job is to find your teepee." Nolte, *Growing Up in Cos Cob 1907–1923,* p. 41; Francis, *The Imaginary Indian,* pp. 145–158.

72. Seton called it the "Village of the Standing Rock on Lake Wyndygoul." Seton to "The Chief," The 10th Sun of the Rose Moon (June 10), 1906, quoted in Wadland, *Ernest Thompson Seton: Man in Nature.*

73. Wadland, *Ernest Thompson Seton: Man in Nature,* p. 341.

74. Seton, Draft of "The League of Seton Indians" By-Laws, undated c. 1903, ESP; Wadland, *Ernest Thompson Seton: Man in Nature,* p. 343.

75. Robert W. Peterson, interview with Julian Salomon, c. 1983, Suffern, New York.

76. Ibid.

77. Seton, "Two Little Savages."

78. Wadland, "Indians at Wyndygoul," *Greenwich News,* October 23, 1903; "Are You a Seton Indian? Whoop!" *New York Herald,* October 11, 1903; Storms, "The Woodcraft Indians"; Wadland, *Ernest Thompson Seton: Man in Nature,* p. 344.

79. Lummis's fellow guest may have been Frederic C. Walcott, a businessman, investment banker and later U.S. Senator for Connecticut, as well a conservationist, big-game hunter and competent amateur photographer. He contributed a chapter on private wildlife preserves to a book published by Hornaday in 1914, *Wild Life Conservation in Theory and Practice,* based on a series of lectures delivered at Yale University.

80. Charles Fletcher Lummis, journal entries for July 12 and 24, 1908, CFL

81. Burroughs to Roosevelt, undated July 1906, quoted in Barrus, *Life of John Burroughs, Vol. II,* p. 97.

82. Seton, "The Twelve Secrets of the Woods," *Craftsman,* June 1916, cited by Wadland, *Man in Nature,* p. 354.

83. Ibid.

Chapter 2—Sons of Daniel Boone

1. Gibson, "The History of Organized Camping: The Early Days."

2. Ibid.

3. *McClure's Magazine,* August 1893, quoted in Gibson, "The History of Organized Camping: Pioneer Camp Personalities."

4. Hopkins, *History of the YMCA in North America,* p. 203. Hopkins notes that although "rescue missions were available for the neglected boy," the YMCA publication The Watchdog argued that it was "more strategic to attempt to reach the lower class of boys by means of the upper class than to try the opposite." This reasoned shift away from troubled urban youth to those of the middle class "was to trouble the YMCA conscience from then on." Hopkins continues, "Many Associations did maintain work for boys from distressed areas and classes, but this received relatively minor emphasis."

5. Ibid., p. 469.

6. Edgar M. Robinson, "One of the Most Unforgettable Personalities I Have Ever Known," unpublished, undated typescript, p. 1, YPA.

7. Ibid., p. 2.

8. Ibid., p. 15.

9. See also, John Henry Wadland, "Indians at Wyndygoul," *Greenwich News,* October 23, 1903, JHW.

10. Daniel Carter Beard, *Hardly a Man is Now Alive,* unpublished draft manuscript, p. 38, DCB; Beard to Cyril Clemens, 2 April 1940, DCB.

11. Beard to Alexander, undated, DCB.

12. Beard to Presbrey, 22 March 1934. DCB.

13. Beard to Boy Pioneers, "Exhibit A," Recreation, 1905. DCB. Beard, *Hardly a Man is Now Alive,* unpublished draft manuscript, pp. 10–11, DCB.

14. Whitmore, *Buckskins,* p. x; Carr, "Daniel Carter Beard, Great Scout."

15. Beard, "The Scout: Boy and Man," p. 15; James H. Beard, *Autobiography,* manuscript, DCB.

16. Beard, "The Scout: Boy and Man," pp. 15–22.

17. Beard, *Hardly a Man Is Now Alive,* pp. 1–11.

18. "San Jacinto Battle Flag," http://www.tfaoi.com/aa/1aa/1aa4g.htm; "Flags of the Texas Revolution," http://www.lsjunction.com/facts/flags.htm.

19. Daniel Carter Beard's Reflections of Abraham Lincoln, April 16, 1929, DCS; Beard to Cyril Clemens, 21 January 1938, DCB; Beard, *Hardly a Man Is Now Alive,* pp. 124–126.

20. Cindy Schroeder and Andrea Tortora, "Neglected Civil War Site Defended with Shovels," *Cincinnati Inquirer,* August 30, 1998, http://www.enquirer.com/editions/1998/08/30/loc_kycivil30.html.

21. Kahler, *Professional Career of Daniel Carter Beard, 1850–1941,* pp. 67–68.

22. William Beard's best-known work was "Bulls and Bears in the Market," depicting a street battle on Wall Street. It was purchased in 1971 by the New York Historical Society.

23. Whitmore, *Buckskins,* p. 72.

24. Frank Beard to Beard, 22 August 1869, DCB.

25. Beard, *Hardly a Man Is Now Alive,* pp. 225–230.

26. Kahler, *Professional Career of Daniel Carter Beard, 1850–1941,* p. 95.

27. Beard, *Hardly a Man Is Now Alive,* pp. 274–280; Seton, *Trail of an Artist-Naturalist,* pp. 247, 358; Whitmore, *Buckskins,* pp. 92–95.

28. Whitmore, *Buckskins,* pp. 95–97, 110.

29. Whitmore, *Buckskins,* p. 110; Beard's Address to Art Students League, 1891, DCB.

30. George, *Progress and Poverty,* title page.

31. Resek, *The Progressives,* pp. xx–xxiii.

32. Whitmore, *Buckskins,* p. 145; Certificate of Appointment as Poll Watcher, 8 November 1887, DCB; Beard to Earle Locker, 22 March 1933, DCB.

33. George, *The Life of Henry George,* pp. 473–485.

34. Illustration for "Wu Chih Tien, The Celestial Empress," *Cosmopolitan Magazine,* March 1889.

35. Kaplan, *Mr. Clemens and Mark Twain,* pp. 290–293.

36. Paine, *Mark Twain: A Biography,* pp. 887–889; Twain, *Connecticut Yankee.*

37. Smith, *Mark Twain's Fable of Progress,* pp. 4–7.

38. Mark Twain to Fred J. Hall, 24 July 1889, DCB.

39. Smith, *Mark Twain's Fable of Progress,* p. 74.

40. Beard, "Sister Your Blind Is Disarranged," *The Arena,* July 1904.

41. *New York Times,* December 10, 1889; Twain to Beard, August 28, 1889, DCB.

42. Twain to Beard, 11 November 1889, DCB.

43. *New Orleans Picayune,* April 11, 1893.

44. Beard to Cyril Clemens, 15 October 1940, WVK, from the now-defunct Standish Museums in East Bridgewater, Massachusetts.

45. "Sherman's Last Portrait," *New York Times,* April 1893.

46. Daniel Bartlett Beard to William V. Kahler, 4 August 1974, WVK; Beard, *Hardly a Man Is Now Alive,* p. 295; Kahler, *Professional Career of Daniel Carter Beard, 1850–1941,* pp. 129–135.

47. Positive reviews of Moonblight were printed in *The Arena,* one by Hamlin Garland, who wrote that "the sturdy Americanism which Dan Beard loves is in this book, and its effect cannot fail to be of great value to the reader . . . Long live Dan Beard and his unconquerable soul! His pen as well as his pencil is always on the side of right."; Garland, *Roadside Meetings,* p. 175; Albert Bigelow Paine et al. " 'Moonblight': Appreciations and Criticisms."

48. The editor of St. Nicholas sent the original drawings of Huck, Tom, and Jim back to Beard to re-draw with shoes; bare feet were deemed "excessively coarse and vulgar." Beard, *Hardly a Man Is Now Alive,* p. 344.

49. George, *Life of Henry George,* pp. 600–604.

50. Ibid., pp. 605–606.

51. Beard to CC, 11 April 1936, DCB.

52. Whitmore, *Buckskins,* pp. 165–166.

53. Whitmore, *Buckskins,* pp. 177–178; Dan Beard, "The Sons of Daniel Boone," *Recreation,* July 1905.

54. Whitmore, *Buckskins,* pp. 177–178; Draft of the Constitution of the Sons of Daniel Boone, undated, DCB.

55. "The Sons of Daniel Boone: How to Organize and How to Conduct a Fort," pamphlet, c. 1905, DCS; "Constitution of the Sons of Daniel Boone," c. 1905, DCB; Beard added that: "In creating the Sons of Daniel Boone, I confined myself to the United States for my inspiration . . . In place of the lance and buckler, is the American long rifle and buckskinned clothes . . . I tried to put into the organization the joyousness of the blue sky with its fleeting clouds, the 'rectitude of the cliff,' the reality and stability of the earth beneath our feet, and the natural democracy of Daniel Boone himself—in other words, to make the difference as great as that of Oliver Cromwell from Charles I, or Thomas Jefferson from Charles II." Beard, *Hardly a Man is Now Alive,* unpublished draft manuscript, p. 6, DCB.

56. Draft of the Constitution of the Sons of Daniel Boone, June 30, 1905, DCB.

57. Whitmore, *Buckskins,* pp. 180–181; Arthur Mead to Beard, 9 February 1906, DCB.

58. Whitmore, *Buckskins,* pp. 183–184.

59. Vance to Beard, undated, DCB; Beard to Vance, 7 March 1906, 24 April 1906, DCB; Vance to Beard, 20 April 1906, 10 May 1906, DCB; Whitmore, *Buckskins,* p. 184; Beard to H. J. Fisher, 28 December 1908, DCB; Beard to William D. Murray, 16, November 1934, YPA, ESP.

60. William F. Cody to Beard, 8 April 1907, DCB; Beard, "Buffalo Bill 'Notch' " memo, DCB.

61. Beard to Twain, 10 April 1907, DCB; Lyon to Beard, 10 April 1907, DCB; Mark Twain Project Papers, MTP; Beard, Drafts of "Mark Twain Top-Notch," DCB.

62. Beard Papers, DCB.

63. Seton to Baden-Powell, 10 December 1909, ESP; Baden-Powell to Seton, 1 August 1906, ESP.

Chapter 3—The Hero of Mafeking

1. G.W. Stevens, *From Cape Town to Ladysmith,* p. 21, quoted in Farwell, *Anglo-Boer War,* p. 46.

2. Farwell, *Anglo-Boer War,* pp. 43–45.

3. Ibid., pp. 76–147.

4. *New York Journal,* January 7, 1900, quoted in Farwell, *Anglo-Boer War,* p. 142.

5. Farwell, *Anglo-Boer War*, p. 54. Kipling turned his literary talents to canvassing support for his Soldiers' Families' Fund with a poem published in the *Daily Mail* on October 31, 1899, that began:

> When you've shouted "Rule Britannia," when you've sung "God Save the Queen,"
> When you've finished killing Kruger with your mouth,
> Will you kindly drop a shilling in my little tambourine,
> For a gentleman in khaki ordered south?

6. Seton to Kipling, 5 February 1900, ESP.

7. "Mafeking," *The Outlook*, May 26, 1900, pp. 185–186; "The Relief of Mafeking," *The American Monthly Review of Reviews,* June 1900; Farwell, "Taking Sides in the Boer War"; Myatt, *William Randolph Hearst,* p. 173.

8. Robinson et al., *Africa and the Victorians,* passim.

9. Farwell, *Anglo-Boer War;* Jeal, *Boy-Man,* pp. 213–215.

10. Flower-Smith and Yorke, *Mafeking!: The Story of a Siege,* pp. 1–5.

11. Hillcourt, *Baden-Powell: Two Lives,* pp. 3–18.

12. Baden-Powell, *Life's Snags and How to Meet Them,* p. 25; Baden-Powell, *Lessons from the Varsity of Life,* pp. 24–26.

13. Baden-Powell scored so highly in the military exams that he was excused from studies at Sandhurst, giving him two years seniority among other contemporary officers.

14. Hillcourt, *Baden-Powell: Two Lives,* pp. 33–35.

15. Baden-Powell, *Pigsticking or Hoghunting,* pp. 2, 21.

16. Baden-Powell, *Reconnaissance and Scouting,* p. 3.

17. Hillcourt, *Baden-Powell: Two Lives,* pp. 78, 92.

18. Ibid., pp. 102–104.

19. Baden-Powell, *Downfall of Prempeh.*

20. Hillcourt, *Baden-Powell: Two Lives,* p. 121.

21. Ibid., p. 145.

22. *The Boer War: Ladysmith and Mafeking 1900,* pp. 150–152.

23. Flower-Smith and York, *Mafeking!: The Story of a Siege,* pp. 39–40; Jeal, *Boy-Man,* p. 226.

24. Jeal, *Boy-Man,* p. 228; Willan, *Edward Ross: The Diary,* p. 9.

25. Hamilton, *Siege of Mafeking,* pp. 192–195.

26. Gardner, *Mafeking: A Victorian Legend,* p. 62; Neilly as quoted in Gardner, *Mafeking: A Victorian Legend,* p. 62.

27. As quoted in Gardner, *Mafeking: A Victorian Legend,* p. 67; *New York Times,* October 25, 1899.

28. Hillcourt, *Baden-Powell: Two Lives,* pp. 174–175; Wilson, *South African Memories,* p. 91; Baillie, *Mafeking,* p. 21; Smith, *Mefeking Memories,* p. 56; Willan, *Edward Ross: The Diary,* p. 21.

29. Packenham, *Boer War,* p. 423.

30. Ibid.; Baden-Powell, *Lessons from the Varsity of Life,* pp. 204–207.

31. "Notice," The Mafeking Mail Special Siege Slip, January 1, 1900; "General Orders," *The Mail,* February 15, 1900; *The Boer War: Ladysmith and Mafeking 1900,* p. 152; Flower-Smith and Yorke, *Mafeking!: The Story of a Siege,* p. 89; "Notice," *The Mail,* January 11, 1900.

32. Jeal, *The Boy-Man,* p. 76.

33. Hillcourt, *Baden-Powell: Two Lives,* pp. 198–199.

34. Ibid.

35. Willan, *Edward Ross: The Diary,* pp. 65, 233–234.

36. One reliever, Patrick Maxwell, recalled that, "Baden-Powell was there & looks just the smart little man one would expect him to be." Quoted in Carver, *National Army Museum Book,* p. 155.

37. Freedman, *Scouting with Baden-Powell,* p. 134. The final casualty totals were: whites, 71 killed and 123 wounded; coloureds, 25 and 68; natives, 65 and 117; Baralong, 264 killed. 53 whites had died from other various other causes. Quoted in Carver, *National Army Museum Book,* p. 155.

38. Baden-Powell responded, "Your Majesty's most gracious message amply repays anything we may have suffered and heartens up to renewed efforts to uphold the honour of our Queen." "Congratulations," *The Mail,* May 29, 1900.

39. "The Relief of Mafeking: Scenes in London," *The Times* (London), May 19, 1900.

40. "Imperial Rejoicings," *The Times* (London), May 21, 1900; "March of Col. Mahon's Column: The Final Boer Assault," *The Times* (London), May 22, 1900; Gardner, *Mafeking: A Victorian Legend,* pp. 199–203; *The Outlook,* May 26, 1900, pp. 185–188.

41. Gardner, *Mafeking: A Victorian Legend,* p. 198; Pakenham, *Boer War,* p. 440.

42. Hillcourt, *Baden-Powell: Two Lives,* pp. 202–206.

43. E. Russell Polden to Baden-Powell, 6 September 1899, BSA; Hillcourt, *Baden-Powell: Two Lives,* p. 166.

44. Baden-Powell, *Aids to Scouting,* p. xi; Walker, "Aids to Scouting."

45. "Mems," *The Mail,* May 1, 1900.

46. Cartwright, *Why Boys Should Not Smoke,* pp. 5–7; Baden-Powell to Mrs. Vaughn, 22 November 1906, DCS; Jeal, *Boy-Man,* p. 364.

47. Walker, "Aids to Scouting"; Baden-Powell, "The Boy Scouts."

48. Baden-Powell, *Aids to Scouting,* pp. 14–15.

49. Ibid., p. 18.

50. Baden-Powell, "The Boy Scouts."

51. Ibid., pp. 330–332.

52. Hillcourt, *Baden-Powell: Two Lives,* pp. 221–222.

53. Rosenthal, *Character Factory,* pp. 46–47; Hillcourt, *Baden-Powell: Two Lives,* p. 228; Freedman, *Scouting with Baden-Powell,* pp. 144–145.

54. Jeal, *Boy-Man,* p. 342

55. Hillcourt, *Baden-Powell: Two Lives,* p. 232; Baden-Powell to Henrietta Baden-Powell, 27 June 1900, BSA; Baden-Powell to Henrietta Baden-Powell, 21 July 1902, BSA; Jeal, *Boy-Man,* pp. 305–306.

56. Hillcourt, *Baden-Powell: Two Lives,* pp. 247–249.

57. *Glasgow Evening Citizen,* May 2, 1904; Rosenthal, *Character Factory,* pp. 52–53.

58. Jeal, *Boy-Man,* p. 361.

59. Hillcourt, *Baden-Powell: Two Lives,* p. 249; *Boys' Brigade Gazette,* June 1, 1904; Baden-Powell, *Lessons from the Varsity,* pp. 274–275.

60. Rosenthal, *Character Factory,* pp. 56–57; Baden-Powell, *Eton College Chronicle,* December 22, 1904.

61. Jeal, *Boy-Man,* p. 365.

Chapter 4—Scouting for Boys

1. Seton, *Birch-Bark Roll of the Woodcraft Indians,* p. 1.

2. Baden-Powell, *The Eton College Chronicle,* December 22, 1904; Rosenthal, "Knights," pp. 603–617.

3. Baden-Powell to Seton, 1 August 1906, SML.

4. Baden-Powell to Seton, 15 September 1906, SML.

5. Baden-Powell Diary, 30 October 1906, BSA.

6. Baden-Powell to Seton, 31 October 1906, ESP.

7. Seton to Baden-Powell, 3 November 1906, SML.

8. Baden-Powell to Seton, 6 and 7 November 1906, SML.

9. Baden-Powell to Seton, 10 and 12 November 1906, SML.

10. Baden-Powell to Seton, 23 November 1906, SML.

11. Baden-Powell to Seton, 4 December 1906, SML.

12. Seton to Lord Roberts, 8 December 1906, SML.

13. Ibid.

14. Baden-Powell to Col. Herbert, 21 February 1907, DCS; Baden-Powell to Lord Mayor & Lady Mayoress, 26 February 1907, DCS; Baden-Powell to Major Fryer, 3 March 1907, DCS; Jeal, *Boy-Man,* pp. 367–368; Everett, *The First Ten Years,* p. 10.

15. Baden-Powell to Seton, 17 June 1907, ESP.

16. Jeal, *Boy-Man,* p. 383, quote attributed to George Wyndham, former chief secretary in Ireland.

17. Baden-Powell, "Boy Scouts: A Suggestion," (pamphlet, May 1907).

18. Hillcourt, *Baden-Powell: Two Lives,* p. 244; Brendon, *Eminent Edwardians,* p. 239; Baden-Powell to Seton, 17 June 1907, ESP; Draft of contract with C. Arthur Pearson, July 30, 1907, BSA; Pearson to Baden-Powell, 22 October, 1907, BSA.

19. Hillcourt, *Baden-Powell: Two Lives,* pp. 264–265; Lipton, "Where Scouting Began."

20. Jeal, *Boy-Man,* pp. 383–384; Walker, "Brownsea and Its Significance."

21. Hillcourt, "Go Camping Brownsea Style"; D. Baden-Powell, "Recollections of the Earliest Camps"; Reynolds, *Baden-Powell,* pp. 143–144.

22. Reynolds, *Scout Movement,* p. 17.

23. Ibid.

24. Reynolds, *Scout Movement,* p. 18.

25. Ibid., p. 19; Hillcourt, "Go Camping Brownsea Style," pp. 15–19; Seton and Baden-Powell, *Boy Scouts of America: Official Handbook* (1910), p. 25.

26. Hillcourt, *Baden-Powell: Two Lives,* pp. 270–271.

27. Hillcourt, *Baden-Powell: Two Lives,* p. 272.

28. Baden-Powell to Mrs. Langdale, 9 August 1907, JIC; Walker, "Brownsea."

29. Baden-Powell Diary, December 26, 1908, BSA; Baden-Powell to Peter Keary, 27 December 1907, BPL; Richards, *Founding of the Boy Scouts.*

30. Baden-Powell, *Scouting for Boys, Installment 1,* pp. 9–19.

31. Hillcourt, *Baden-Powell: Two Lives,* p. 286; Baden-Powell to Keary, 25 March, 1908, BPL; Richards, *Founding of the Boy Scouts;* Baden-Powell, "How I Started Scouting"; Baden-Powell to Keary, 29 March 1908, BPL; Pearson to Baden-Powell, 10 September 1907, BSA; Pearson to Baden-Powell, 15 October 1907, BSA; Contract with C. Arthur Pearson Ltd., 1 January 1908, BSA; Baden-Powell Diary, 7 February 1908, BSA; Baden-Powell to Seton, 13 February 1908, YBL; Baden-Powell Diary, 16 May 1908, BSA; Walker, "Humshaugh: The Second B-P Camp"; Walker, "Beaulieu: The Third B-P Camp."

32. Baden-Powell to Keary, 1 March 1908 and 9 September 1908, STMP; Richards, *Founding of the Boy Scouts;* Baden-Powell to Seton, 9 July 1908, SML; Baden-Powell to Frank N. Doubleday, 31 July 1910, ESP; Baden-Powell Diary, 24 September 1910, ESP; Baden-Powell to Seton, 24 September 1910, ESP.

33. *Scouting for Boys* was issued in 6 fortnightly parts between January 15 and March 26, 1908. Under Baden-Powell's contract with Pearson all proceeds were to be ploughed back into the "scheme" to repay Pearson's "contribution" of £1,000 to fund the London Scout Headquarters for the first year. Baden-Powell was to promote the program nationally, producing a weekly newspaper called *The Scout,*

whose profits would go directly to Pearson. The newspaper first appeared on April 18, 1908. Contract between Baden-Powell and C. Arthur Pearson, January 1, 1908, BSA.

34. Baden-Powell to Seton, 24 January 1908, ESP.

35. Baden-Powell to Seton, 24 February 1908, SML.

36. Baden-Powell Daily Diary, March 1, 1908, BSA.

37. Seton, "Open Letter to General Sir Robert Baden-Powell," 24 April 1910, ESP.

38. This letter is believed to have been lost, as it is not in any known archive of Setoniana.

39. Baden-Powell to Seton, 14 March 1908, ESP.

40. Seton, "Open Letter," ESP.

41. In his essay "The Truth About Baden-Powell and the Boy Scouts" from his book *Ecology and Anarchism* (1996), Brian Morris argues that Baden-Powell rejected Seton's aim of the pure promotion of "nature, conservation and wildlife and good fellowship" because he wanted to promote the British Empire and "capitalist hegemony." He also contends that Baden-Powell infused the concept of "good citizenship," with a military bent along with duty to God and country.

42. Rosenthal, *Character Factory,* p. 64; Baden-Powell to Burnham, 28 September 28, 1900, FRB. Baden-Powell clearly found inspiration in many sources for his concept of the Boy Scout Movement, his experiences with Burnham among them. Shortly after Mafeking, Baden-Powell wrote to Burnham seeking advice on army training. "I shall be very glad if you will at any time write me any further ideas that may strike you on the subject—not that I propose to suck your brains and use your ideas—but that we may act in unison and get this thing through."

43. Rosenthal, *Character Factory,* pp. 71–72.

44. Keller, *Black Wolf,* p. 167.

45. Jeal, *Boy-Man,* pp. 379–380.

46. Baden-Powell to Seton, June 24, 1908, SML.

47. Baden-Powell, "Preface to New Edition," *Scouting for Boys,* rev. ed., p. 5.

48. Richards, *Founding of the Boy Scouts*; Baden-Powell to Keary, 30 May 1908, STMP; Roosevelt to Baden-Powell, 1 August 1908, BSA.

49. McLaren to Baden-Powell, 12 March 1908, BSA: Kenneth McLaren, Baden-Powell's Scout Association office manager, resigned in March 1908, stating, "I cannot conscientiously continue as manager . . . I consider the joint arrangement with Pearson unsatisfactory and cannot get on with [Pearson agent Peter] Keary."

50. Baden-Powell to Seton, 24 June 1908, SML.

51. Baden-Powell to Seton, 9 July 1908, SML.

52. Seton to Baden-Powell, 10 August 1908, SML; Baden-Powell to Keary, 12 September 1908, STMP; Richards, *Founding of the Boy Scouts*; Seton, *Birch-Bark Roll of the Outdoor Life,* pp. 26–28.

53. Lanier to Seton, 11 August 1908, ESP.

54. Lanier to Seton, 25 August 1908, ESP.

55. Baden-Powell to H.C. Roberts, 3 September 1909, ESP.

56. Seton to Baden-Powell, 30 September 1909, ESP; Seton to Copper Eagle, 22 July 1908, ESP.

57. Seton to Baden-Powell, 10 December 1909, SML.

58. Bok to Seton, 1 December 1909, ESP.

59. Seton to Bok, 13 December 1909, ESP.

60. Baden-Powell to Seton, 17 January 1910, BSA.

61. Baden-Powell, "The Woodcraft Indians and Boy Scouts."

62. Seton to Baden-Powell, "Open Letter," ESP.

63. Ibid.

64. "Boy Scouts of America," memo, November 26, 1910, BSA: Patrols that sprang up without adult leadership were known as "monkey patrols" by the National Office and were not granted official badges.

65. Peterson, *The Boy Scouts,* pp. 28–29; Osage County (OK) Historical Society, http://www.osagecohistoricalmuseum.com/; See also: L. E. Jones to unknown, published letter on YMCA stationery from Fort Worth, Texas, 15 August 1910, YMN.

66. Peterson, *The Boy Scouts,* p. 30.

Chapter 5—The Boy Scouts of America

1. *Times of London,* December 17, 1909.

2. *Chicago Tribune,* June 13, 1909.

3. *Washington Herald,* April 21, 1910.

4. Ibid. Boyce is quoted as saying, "I never heard of the Boy Scouts until last December."

5. Boyce to West, 27 February 1928, BSA; "Memorandum Concerning How Scouting Came to America as Told by W.D. Boyce," undated, BSA; See also: Petterchak, *Lone Scout,* pp. 63–64; Wagner, *The Boy Scouts of America,* p. 60; Seymour to Boyce, 31 August, 1926, BSA.

6. Robert W. Peterson interview of William Hillcourt (typescript), c. 1984, RWP. Baden-Powell biographer William Hillcourt believed the Boyce story was fabricated. He told an interviewer that "Baden-Powell was out of town most of that period for his Inspector General's work. I don't think he ever met Baden-Powell." BSA historian Robert W. Peterson notes that Baden-Powell's diaries and appointment books, held in the BSA archives, contain "no mention of meeting Boyce."

7. "Summary of Observations," July–August 1909, NML. Boyce's account is also questioned in "W.D. Boyce: Honoring the Man Who Brought Scouting to America," a pamphlet published by the curator of the Boyce Scouting Hall of Fame in Ottawa, Illinois. John F. Sullivan writes: "In *Lone Scout* for February

1922, the fog story first appeared in an article about Baden-Powell . . . Unsigned and offered as straight reporting, written by editor G. N. Madison, it was here the Boy Scouts found material for legend. The myth seems to have been put into circulation about 1927, devised possibly by Henry Van Dyke, the famous allegorical and religious writer, named on the editorial board of the *Boy Scout Handbook For Boys* in that year, and following closely the Boyce award of the Silver Buffalo (the third person to be so honored, the Unknown Scout being the first).”; Sullivan, *W.D. Boyce: Honoring the Man,* p. 9. There were at least two letters to West from Boyce in the 1920s regarding this incident.

8. A certificate noting Boyce's entry at Ellis Island, New York, indicates his departure in the small hours of December 24 from Southampton on the steamship *New York* of the American Line arriving Cherbourg, France at 6 a.m., leaving immediately for Queenstown, Ireland, from which he departed that same day, arriving in New York on December 30.

9. Baden-Powell to Doubleday, 31 July 1910, SML.

10. Beard's son, Daniel Bartlett Beard, told a biographer in 1974: “Now ‘poor old Boyce,’ as my father called him in a letter (to) Seton, actually did incorporate the Boy Scouts of America, but right or wrong, my father told me that the story about Boyce being helped across the street by an English boy scout, then going to see Baden-Powell was a lot of bunk.” WVK.

11. William D. Boyce to James E. West, 27 February 1928, BSA; “Memorandum Concerning the Boy Scouts of America,” undated, c. 5 November 1910, BSA; James E. West, “The History of the Scout Movement in America,” c. April 1913, BSA.

12. “Minutes of Hearing Before the Committee on Education, House of Representatives, concerning H.R. 24747.”

13. Murray, *As He Journeyed,* pp. 46–47.

14. The two other incorporators were Edward S. Stewart and Stanley D. Willis; Boyce to West, 27 February 1928, BSA; “Memorandum Concerning the Boy Scouts of America,” undated, c. 5 November 1910, BSA; “The True Facts Concerning the Boy Scout Movement in America,” undated, BSA; West to Lloyd Shafer, 24 September 1935, BSA.

15. “W.D. Boyce is Heard From,” *Ottawa Fair Dealer,* March 4, 1910; Petterchek, *Lone Scout,* pp. 65–66.

16. From the archives of the Illinois Institute of Technology at: http://archives. iit.edu/history/armour/pg1.html. Boyce initially sought the help of Dr. Frank W. Gunsaulas, a clergyman whose work in Chicago's meatpacking district and sermons on education led meat-packing tycoon Philip D. Armour to give him a million dollars to start what became the Illinois Institute of Technology.

17. *Association Boys,* June 1909, pp. 162–164, YBL; Boyce to Seymour, 28 August 1926, BSA; Robinson, “Recollections,” p. 2, YBL; Seton to Robinson, 23 October 1934, ESP. For a discussion on the social problems surrounding the appearance of camping as training for boys, see Schmitt's *Back to Nature* and Gibson's “The History of Organized Camping.”

18. Baden-Powell to Dear Sir, 17 February 1910, BSA.

19. "Memorandum" from Robinson to West dated 7 November 1917 submitted in evidence in Boy Scouts of America v. United States Boy Scouts, 1917, BSA. The other YMCA officials were L.L Doggett and J.A. Van Dis; See also, Murray, *History,* pp. 20, 26; MacLeod, *Good Boys Made Better,* pp. 237–238; Whitmore, *Buckskins,* p. 212; Petterchak, *Lone Scout,* p. 67; Wagner, *Boy Scouts of America,* p. 64.

20. Robinson, "Recollections," pp. 2–3, YBL; "Memorandum: BSA v. United States Boy Scouts," p. 2, YBL; Robinson to E. W. Wakefield, 6 June 1910, YBL; Murray, *History,* pp. 20, 26.

21. Robinson, "Recollections," pp. 2–3, YBL; William Scarlett to Lorriland Spencer, 3 May 1910, BSA.

22. Untitled memo by Seton, "The Foundation of the Boy Scouts of America took place on Jan. 18, 1910, at Christ Church Auditorium etc.," undated, SML; Robinson to Wakefield, 8, 22, and 26 April 1910, 17 and 25 May 1910, 28 June 1910, YBL.

23. "Incorporation of the Boy Scouts of America, Hearing Before the Committee on Education."

24. Ibid.

25. MacGrath to Robinson, 6 May 1910, BSA. Robinson had been sent a formal invitation by James F. MacGrath, secretary of the American Boy Scouts.

26. Robinson to West, 7 November 1917, BSA; MacGrath to Robinson, 6 May 1910, BSA; "American Boy Scouts Movement Is Ably Launched," *New York American,* May 10, 1910, HRC; "Committee On Organization Report to the American Boy Scouts," May 26, 1910, BSA; Robinson to West, 7 November 1917, YBL.

27. "Summons and Complaint: Boy Scouts of America against United States Boy Scout," July 31, 1917; Robinson to Wakefield, 6 and 28 June 1910, YBL.

28. Verbeck to Seton Thompson [*sic*], 2 December 1910, ESP. Gen. Verbeck did not roll his organization straight into BSA: he initially asked Seton to provide his program with "the Indian part" as Grand Sachem of the National Scouts of America, with Verbeck providing military leadership.

29. Robinson, "Recollections," p. 4, YBL; Robinson to Boyce 17 May 1910 makes clear that Hearst's advance into the Scouting field provided an impetus for consolidation. Robinson said Bomus "expressed his entire willingness to resign and come in under the shadow of your wing, if that was the best thing to do." Bomus and his aides "explained that their action appointing a staff and publishing the names was to forestall the movement started by (Hearst), and as far as I can discover they are entirely altruistic in their movement but very military in their ideas." Robinson to Wakefield, May 17, 1910, YBL.

30. Robinson, "Recollections," p. 4, YBL; Robinson to Wakefield, May 25, 1910, YBL.

31. That same summer Gulick would launch the Camp Fire Girls with his wife Charlotte, Dan Beard's sister, Lina, and Ernest and Grace Seton. "Minutes of a Conference" June 6 and 7, 1911, ESP.

32. Boy Scouts of America, *Second Annual Report,* pp. 4–5.

33. Seton in April or May 1910 issued the eighth edition of his *Birch-Bark Roll* under the title of *The American Boy Scout: The Official Hand-Book of Woodcraft for the Boy Scouts of America* in an apparent effort to influence the direction of the American Scouting movement.

34. Robinson, "One of the Most Unforgettable Personalities," pp. 24–25, YBL.

35. Baden-Powell to W.T. Porter, 22 June 1908, SML; Seton to Baden-Powell, 24 April 1910, ESP, SML; Seton to Baden-Powell, 24 June 1910, ESP; Baden-Powell to Doubleday, 31 May 1910, SML. Specifics of Seton's letter dated March 3, 1910 are not known as this letter has not surfaced in any of the archives holding Seton or, more generally, Scouting materials. However, that Baden-Powell received a cable from Doubleday may be inferred from his May 31 response.

36. Baden-Powell to Seton, 31 May 1910, ESP.

37. Seton to Baden-Powell, 13 June 1910, ESP; That Baden-Powell took no royalties provides evidence that his first concern was to advance the movement.

38. Grace Seton to Ernest Seton, August 22, 1910, ESP. Though a prolific correspondent, Seton was so caught up in the program that he neglected to write to Grace for much of the two-week camp. "No letter today, no letter since you arrived at Silver Bay," she wrote. "You are being scolded—are you having a good time, a bad time or is there such a place?"

39. Robinson, "One of the Most Unforgettable Personalities," p. 26, YBL

40. "The Boy Scouts of America Meeting Minutes," 26 May 1910, BSA; Seton to Reverend Doctor William Forbush, 5 June 1910, WFL.

41. Alexander to Beard, 17 June 1910, BSA; Beard to Alexander, 19 June 1910, BSA.

42. Alexander to Beard, 22 June 1910, BSA.

43. *New York Times,* April 21, 1910.

44. Arthur Vance to Beard, 16 January 1909, DCB.

45. Beard to Vance, 15 August 1910, DCB; Vance to Beard, 15 August 1910, DCB; See also Beard, *The Boy Pioneers* and Beard, *The American Boy's Handy Book.*

46. Beard, "The Boy Scouts," pp. 696–697; Seton, "The Boy Scouts in America," pp. 630–635; Ralph D. Blumenfeld, "The Boy Scouts," pp. 617–629; Beard to Lyman Abbott, undated 1910, DCB.

47. Hornaday to Seton, 28 June 1910, ESP.

48. Beard, *Hardly a Man Is Now Alive,* unpublished draft manuscript, p. 13, DCB.

49. Seton to Robinson, 13 October 1934, ESP.

50. Seton, *The Boy Scouts of America Official Manual,* pp. 173–192; Alexander to George D. Pratt, 3 August 1910, BSA.

51. Seton, *Official Manual,* Preface; Verbeck to Seton, 21 July 1910, ESP; Seton to Verbeck, 23 July 1910, BSA.

52. Alexander to Robinson, 8 July 1910, BSA; Alexander to Pratt, 3 August 1910, BSA.

53. Boy Scouts of America, *Second Annual Report,* p. 5.

54. Alexander to Robinson, 8 July 1910, BSA; Seton to Edward Cave, 23 July 1910, ESP; Alexander to Seton, 24 September 1910, BSA.

55. Alexander to Beard, 3 August 1910, BSA; Whitmore, *Buckskins,* p. 219.

56. Beard to Alexander, undated c. 1910, DCB; Beard to Alexander, undated c. 1910, DCB.

57. Alexander to Beard, 10 August 1910, BSA.

58. Alexander to Seton, 10 August 1910, ESP.

59. Beard to Alexander, undated c. August 1910, BSA.

60. Seton to Beard, 7 September 1910, DCB.

61. Seton to Beard, 14 September 1910, DCB.

62. Ibid.

63. Seton to Robinson, 13 October 1934, ESP; Murray, *History,* p. 33; Murray, *As He Journeyed,* pp. 346–355.

64. Anderson, *The Chief,* p. 156.

65. Anderson, *The Chief,* pp. 156–159; Seton to Robinson, 13 October 1934, ESP.

66. Seton to C.A. Schenek, 8 September 1910, ESP.

67. Anderson, *The Chief,* pp. 158–159; Murray, *History,* p. 33; See also: E. M. Robinson, "Black Wolf in Camp with Boys," pp. 9, 30.

68. Robert W. Peterson, interview with William Edel, RWP.

69. Ibid.

70. Seton to Robinson, 3 October 1934, ESP; Anderson, *The Chief,* p. 159; "The Boy Scouts of America," *The Epworth Herald,* July 30, 1910, p. 974, YMN.

71. Alexander to Seton, 6 September 1910, BSA; Alexander to Verbeck, 6 September 1910, BSA; Alexander to Beard, 6 September 1910, BSA; Alexander to Livingstone, 6 September 1910, BSA.

72. Livingstone to Alexander, 10 September 1910, BSA; Roosevelt to Seton, 13 September 1910, ESP; Abbott to Seton, 13 September 1910, ESP; Livingstone to Roosevelt, 17 September 1910, BSA; Livingstone's secretary to Alexander, 20 September 1910, BSA; on Roosevelt attendance at Press Club premiere, Jones to Seton, 14 September 1910, ESP.

73. Robinson to Baden-Powell, 13 September 1910, BSA.

74. Seton was probably alerted by his wife Grace who wrote him at Silver Bay that, "Hearst is making a great effort to utilize Baden-Powell's presence in America for his own uses." Grace Seton to Ernest Seton, undated c. August 1910, ESP.

75. Seton to Baden-Powell, 17 September 1910, ESP.

76. Baden-Powell Diary, 22–23 September 1910, BSA; Seton to Robinson, 23 October 1934, ESP.

77. Roosevelt to Seton, 23 September 1910, ESP.

78. Baden-Powell Diary, 23 September 1910, BSA; Seton to Robinson, 23 October 1910, ESP; Ellis, "Notable Boy Scouts Conference," p. 10.

79. Seton to Beard, 22 December 1938, DCB, ESP.

80. "Boy Scouts Movement," *Brooklyn Daily Eagle,* September 24, 1910, BDE; "How Boy Scouts Began," *New York Tribune,* September 24, 1910; "Boy Scout Leaders Dine Baden-Powell," *New York Times,* September 24, 1910; "Roosevelt Joins the Boy Scouts," *New York Press,* September 24, 1910; Monroe, "Ernest Thompson Seton: Scouting's First Spellbinder," pp. 27–28, 70.

81. Beard, *Hardly* (Draft), pp. 17–18.

82. Transcript of Robert W. Peterson's interview with William Hillcourt for the book *The Boy Scouts: An American Adventure,* 1983, RWP. Baden-Powell biographer Hillcourt argues that Baden-Powell "committed one of his few real blunders" in describing Seton and Beard as the "fathers" of the movement because "from that moment, the two of them had a deadly fight between them, proving that they were the fathers of the Boy Scouts."

83. Ibid. For a review of the British Scout activities at the time, refer to Blumenfeld, "The Boy Scouts," pp. 617–629; "Boy Scout Organization," Informational Pamphlet, British Scout Association, January 1910, YMN; Wakefield, " 'Be Prepared'," p. 11.

84. Washington to Seton, 4 October 1910, ESP. The BSA printed a special edition of about 300 of the first Handbook in red leather. A copy was given to each attendee, one of whom wrote to Seton, "Let me thank you or your secretary very much for sending me a copy of the Souvenir edition of 'The Boy Scout,' which were given to the guests at the banquet for General Baden Powell. I was very careful with my own copy and also found two others which had been abandoned. And took them down and left them on the rack with my coat, but someone else valued them equally as highly and walked off with all three."

85. James E. West, "The Boy Scout Movement in America," Proceedings of the First Annual Meeting of the National Council of the Boy Scouts of America, February 14, 1911, p. 4, BSA.

86. Baden-Powell to Seton, 24 September 1910, ESP.

87. Alexander to Seton, 24 September 24, 1910, BSA.

88. Alexander to Seton, 29 September 1910, ESP.

Chapter 6—West Takes the Helm

1. Charles D. Morton to Hanmer, October 21, 1910, BSA; Charles D. Morton to Hanmer, November 3, 1910, BSA.

2. Murray, *History,* pp. 34–35.

3. John L. Alexander to the Board of Managers, 22 November 1910, BSA.

4. "Memorandum Concerning the Boy Scouts," undated, c. 5 November, 1910, BSA; Robinson to Boyce, 12 October 1910, BSA; Robinson to Murray, 3 October and 5 November 1934, YBL; "Boy Scouts of America v. United States Boy Scouts" Memorandum, undated, YBL; Monroe, "The Way it Was"; Seton to Beard, 22 December 1938, DCB.

5. Robinson to Murray, 3 October 1934, YBL; Robinson to Murray, 23 October 1934, ESP; Robinson to Murray, 5 November 1934, YBL; Livingstone to Boyce, 12 October 1910, BSA; Livingstone to Alexander, 14 October 1910, BSA.

6. "Memorandum Concerning the Boy Scouts of America," undated, c. 5 November 1910, BSA.

7. Ernest P. Bicknell to Gulick, 2 November 1910, BSA. The other candidate was Eugene T. Lies, the Secretary of the Associated Charities of Minneapolis, whose salary at the time was $265 a month.

8. Bicknell to Gulick, 2 November 1910, BSA; Robinson to Livingstone, 5 November 1910, BSA; Robinson noted that West was first suggested to him by a Mr. William Knowles Cooper, who may have mentioned West to Livingstone. Robinson to West, 4 October 1934, YBL.

9. Crenson, *Building the Invisible Orphanage,* p. 7–11.

10. Ibid.

11. Ibid., pp. 19–20.

12. Roosevelt to West, 31 January 1909, BSA.

13. "Research Notes on the Life of Dr. James West, 1876–1910," undated, BSA. It is unclear who compiled this document which it contains a wealth of information on West's early life, education, and career. It refers to documents not found in the BSA Archive, such as a "Scrapbook" and a "Letter Book," suggesting the entries were based on documentation.

14. "Research Notes," cites letter by YMCA Boys Department Chairman John B. Sleman.

15. West letter, apparently to Dreiser, quoted in "Research Notes," p. 22; Theodore Dreiser to West, 23 April 1909, cited in "Research Notes," pp. 22, 31.

16. West to Robinson, 27 December 1910, BSA. West seems to have thoroughly investigated BSA before deciding. A postscript to his letter states: "I am enclosing a memorandum of the expense of four trips to New York, one in November and three in December. You will note I am charging only for one half of one trip as I found it possible to have *The Delineator* pay for the other half."

17. West to Robinson, 15 December 1910, BSA.

18. West to Walter Head, 13 November 1939, BSA; West to Col. Theodore Roosevelt, 11 March 1939, BSA.

19. West to Theodore Roosevelt, Jr., 11 March 1939, BSA.

20. West to Beard, 3 January 1911, DCB.

21. Seton to Robinson, 4 November 1910, BSA.

22. Alexander to Beard, 19 November 1910, BSA.

23. Alexander to Beard, 20 December 1910, BSA.

24. Beard to Alexander, undated, probably December 1910, BSA.

25. Whitmore, *Buckskins,* p. 222; Beard to G. W. Emerson, 14 December 1910, DCB.

26. Whitmore, *Buckskins,* p. 225; West to Beard, 14 January 1911, DCB; See also, Seton and Baden-Powell, *Boy Scouts of America: Official Handbook.*

27. West to Beard, 8 February 1911, DCB.

28. Roosevelt to West, 10 February 1911, Morrison, *Roosevelt Letters: Volume 7,* pp. 729–730; Levy, *Building a Popular Movement,* pp. 20–21. The Russell Sage Foundation commissioned a study on the reasons for BSA's success, which found five. First, BSA "clothed its program with romance." Second, it emphasized the qualities of good citizenship. Third, BSA "adopted a point of view attuned to a democratically minded citizenry and opened its ranks freely to all creeds, races and classes." Fourth, its leaders were "men of national standing in business and industry, in public affairs, in letters, in natural science, and to a certain extent in social work." Last, "BSA's leadership aggressively" approached the task of expanding scouting on a national level.

29. "Tentative Program of the First Meeting of the Advisory Council of the Boy Scouts of America at Washington, DC, February 14 and 15, 1911," LC; "1st Annual Meeting Proceedings" February 14, 1911, BSA.

30. Lee F. Hanmer, "Introduction of the National Council," 1st Annual Meeting Proceedings: February 14, 1911; From BSA annual reports 1911–1920, BSA.

31. "Tentative Program," BSA.

32. Murray, *History,* p. 51. See also: West to Beard, 14 April, 1911, DCB; West to Beard, 28 April 1911, DCB; West to Beard, 1 May 1911, DCB; West to Beard, 11 May 1911, DCB.

33. "Minutes of Meeting of the Executive Board of the Boy Scouts of America," April 1, 1911, DCB; See also, Hanmer, "Introduction," February 14, 1911; "Memorandum Concerning the Boy Scouts of America," undated c. 5 November 1910, BSA; Alexander to Robinson, 29 July 1910, BSA; Alexander to Robinson, 8 July 1910, BSA.

34. Luther Gulick to Seton, 30 January 1911, BSA.

35. Seton to Murray, 12 April 1911, BSA.

36. Seton to Editing Committee, 12 April 1911, LC.

37. Ibid.; See also Seton to Editorial Board, 12 April 1911, BSA.

38. Seton, Draft of "A Message From the Chief," c. May 1911, DCB; This message was also known by the title "The Scouting Mind," undated, SML.

39. Ibid.

40. Beard to West, 15 May 1911, DCB; West to Beard, 18 May 1911, DCB.

41. Alexander, "Report to Executive Board," May 6, 1911, DCB.

42. West to Beard, 1 June 1911, DCB; See also: For a listing of the press run and printings, refer to Joe Price's *Kahunas Katalog* and Fisk and Bearce's, *Collecting Scout Literature.*

43. Seton to "The Boys of America" Draft, June 1, 1911, BSA.

44. Bicknell to West, undated, c. June 15, 1911, DCB.

45. James E. West, "Minutes of the Meeting of the Executive Board Held at the Office of the National Headquarters, June 13, 1911," DCB.

46. Baden-Powell to West, 16 September 1911, DCB; For an interesting contemporary essay on the *Boy Scout Handbook,* refer to Fussell's *The Boy Scout Handbook and Other Observations.*

47. Beard, "The Boy Scouts of America," pp. 429–438.

48. Seton to "My Dear Sir," 1 June 1911, BSA; Seton to West, 2 September 1911, BSA.

49. Beard to West, 14 September 1911, DCB.

50. Baden-Powell to West, 16 September 1911, DCB.

51. "Hearst, Dewey and Levy Quit the Boy Scouts," *New York Journal-American,* December 9, 1910, HRC.

52. Bicknell of the Red Cross to Gulick, 21 December 1910, BSA. "I have heard that Mr. Hearst has severed his connection with the American Boy Scouts and has charged the administration with certain shortcomings which are being, or will be, investigated." He suggested the BSA Executive might well "take advantage of the situation, so far as it may honorably do so, to remove the confusion which has been caused in the public mind by the existence of two societies."

53. "Information for Members of the Executive Board of the Boy Scouts of America Calling Attention to the Confusion Which Might Arise From the Fact That There is an Organization Known as the American Boy Scouts," BSA. This memo seems to have been drafted by West, and although undated, was probably circulated in late 1912. See Also, Livingstone to West, 14 October 1911, BSA; West to Baden-Powell, 8 March 1911, BSA; Baden-Powell to West, 31 March 1911, BSA.

54. Draft memorandum of agreement between "Mr. Lee Keedick of No. 150 Nassau Street, City of New York," and BSA, November 1911, BSA; West to E.S. Martin, 9 November 1911, BSA; Kenneth Gardener to Baden-Powell, 15 December 1911, BSA.

55. West to Beard, 1 June 1911, DCB.

56. Extract from Judge Ben B. Lindsay, Juvenile Court, Denver, Colorado, dated December 20, 1911. Correspondent unknown, DCB.

57. West to Beard, 30 December 1911, DCB.

58. Ibid.

59. "Baden-Powell Here Again," *New York Times,* February 3, 1912, p. 6; Attachment, West to Beard, 2 February 1912, DCB.

60. West to Beard, 6 January 1912, DCB; "Program for Meeting of Executive Board, Tuesday, November 28, 1911, 3:00 p.m., Office of Kuhn, Loeb & Company, New York City," DCB.

61. Seton to West, 19 May 1911, BSA; West to Seton, 20 May 1911, BSA.

62. "Boy to Greet Baden-Powell," *New York Times,* January 30, 1912, p. 5; Hillcourt, *Baden-Powell: Two Lives,* p. 335.

63. "Boy Scouts Greet Gen. Baden-Powell," *New York Times,* February 1, 1912, p. 9.

64. Baden-Powell, *Boy Scouts Beyond the Seas;* Baden-Powell, "My World Tour," *The Scout,* March 23, 1912, p. 682.

65. "Boy Scouts Guard Feast," *The New York Times,* February 10, 1912.

66. Baden-Powell, "My World Tour," *The Scout,* March 30, 1912, p. 700; Baden-Powell, "My World Tour," *The Scout,* April 6, 1912, p. 730; Baden-Powell, "My World Tour," *The Scout,* April 13, 1912, p. 754; Baden-Powell, "My World Tour," *The Scout,* April 27, 1912, p. 802; Baden-Powell, "My World Tour," *The Scout,* May 4, 1912, p. 826; Baden-Powell, "My World Tour," *The Scout,* May 11, 1912, p. 849; See also: Hillcourt, *Baden-Powell: Two Lives,* p. 326; "Baden-Powell in Headquarters'*Gazette,*" April 1912; Baden-Powell to Dr. Campbell, 11 March 1911, BSA.

67. "Memorandum Submitted by Lieutenant-General Sir Robert S.S. Baden-Powell Just Before Leaving America," March 1912, BSA; see also: Baden-Powell, "My World Tour," *The Scout,* August 31, 1912, p. 1234; Baden-Powell, "My World Tour," *The Scout,* January 27, 1912, p. 490.

68. Membership rose from some 61,000 at the end of 1911 to nearly 127,000 at the end of 1912, according to BSA records.

69. Livingstone to West, 14 October 1911, BSA.

Chapter 7—The Fork in the Trail

1. Seton to West, 12 October 1911, BSA.

2. Seton to BSA Editorial Board, 26 November 1911, BSA.

3. West to Beard, 4 December 1911, DCB.

4. Beard to West, 6 December 1911, DCB.

5. West to Beard, 4 December 1911, DCB.

6. Seton to Beard, 1 May 1912, DCB.

7. Beard to Seton, 6 May 1912, DCB.

8. Murray to West, 10 May 1912, DCB.

9. Hammer to West, 14 May 1912, BSA.

10. Beard to Murray (Marked "Not Sent"), 20 May 1912, DCB.

11. Whitmore, *Buckskins,* pp. 278–289.

12. Seton to Beard, 22 May 1912, DCB.

13. Beard to Seton, 27 May 1912, DCB.
14. Robert H. Peterson Interview with Julian Salomon, c. 1983, RWP.
15. Wadland, *Ernest Thompson Seton: Man in Nature,* p. 313.
16. West to Seton, 5 October 1911, DCB.
17. *Boys' Life Magazine,* March 1, 1911.
18. "The Boy Scouts: News and Notes," *Boys' Life,* March 1, 1911, p. 36
19. Harold, *Scout Trail 1910–1962,* p. 17. The official story from BSA was that as a boy, Lane founded the magazine. But Dr. John T. Dizer, an expert and author in the area of juvenile literature, conjectures that West himself originated this version of facts. Jack Dizer to D.C. Scott, 20 May 2005. In the November 1934 issue of *Scouting* magazine, West lays out the "Lane myth" as it was passed down through the years in the BSA's "*Boys' Life* Fact Sheet" through the 1980s. But due to Dizer's research and a report published in the November–December 1994 issue of *Scouting,* the fact sheets were changed to reflect Barton as the founder of *Boys' Life* and not Joseph Lane.
20. Dizer, "The Birth and Boyhood of *Boys' Life.*" Dizer notes that *Boys' Life* moved offices four times in 18 months, suggesting circulation gains. In the August 1911 issue, Barton announced that circulation had risen to from 25,000 to 35,000 copies a month, and eventually hit 65,000 with the January 1912 issue. Dizer, "*Boys' Life:* The Real Beginnings."
21. Ibid.
22. Glenister to West, 18 October 1911, DCB.
23. Ellis to West, 20 November 1911, DCB. Until June 1911, *American Boy* had been promoting its own organization, called the Order of the American Boy. Ellis was at the Waldorf-Astoria in September 1910 and wrote an account of the event for the November 1910 issue. Ellis commissioned a series of articles from Seton that ran from July 1911 through April 1912.
24. Morton Radhner to West, 19 December 1911, DCB.
25. Livingstone to Boyce, 27 March 1912, BSA.
26. Boyce to Livingstone, 29 March 1912, BSA; Even after this snub to Boyce, West approached the publisher for a contribution to the BSA funding drive later that year stating, "At the present time we are facing the necessity of raising $15,000 and I wondered if you would not be good enough to send us a contribution at this time." West to Boyce, 10 October 1912, BSA; Within three years, Boyce was to found a rural scout program called "Lone Scouts." Based on the 1913 book *Lone Scouting* by Englishman John Hargrave, a former stretcher-bearer at Gallipoli during World War I, Boyce envisioned a Scouting program that did not require youths to be in a troop. He encouraged many rural boys to pay their way in the program by selling subscriptions to his weekly newspaper, which eventually became a monthly called *Lone Scout.*
27. West to Joseph Lane, 22 April 1912, DCB.
28. George S. Barton to West, 23 April 1912, DCB.

29. W.P. McGuire to West, 11 May 1912, DCB.

30. West to McGuire, 15 May 1912, DCB; Mathiews, "The Influence of the Boy Scout Movement," p. 223. Chief Scout Librarian Franklin K. Mathiews added a second reason for buying *Boys' Life:* eliminating potential competition. Addressing the American Library Association annual meeting in May 1914, Mathiews said the purchase of *Boys' Life* "was deemed necessary to prevent the threatened exploitation of the boys of America by individuals using the name of our organization with incalculable harm to the movement."

31. Dizer notes that BSA bought the magazine based on 6,000 paid copies a month, whereas Barton claimed a monthly circulation of 65,000 copies. Dizer, *"Beginnings,"* p. 39.

32. Beard to West, 8 October 1913, DCB. A monthly column by Beard appeared in the magazine for the rest of his life, and a final missive appeared posthumously in July 1941. In "The Day That Made America," Beard closed: "Uncle Dan realizes that he is close to the end of the trail, but . . . he wants you boys to feel that whatever happens to him, he will still be with you in your camps, in your homes, and you may know he is whispering in your ears his confidence in you and his faith in your ability to carry on your grand work of Scouting wherever he may be."

33. West to Scoutmasters, 6 June 1912, DCB.

34. Seton to Chairman of the Editorial Board, 26 June 1912, BSA.

35. Editorial Board Memorandum of the Meeting of July 29 1912, BSA.

36. A.S. Moffat to West, 16 July 1912, entitled "Showing Points of Similarity Between the *Book of Woodcraft* and the *Handbook for Boys,"* BSA; unsigned memo, apparently by Moffat, 27 July 1912, "Comparing the last *Birch-Bark Roll* with the proposed *Book of Woodcraft,"* BSA.

37. William Murray, George Pratt, and A.A. Jameson to Seton, 15 August 1912, SML.

38. Seton to BSA Editorial Board, 25 August 1912, SML.

39. Beard to West, 16 September 1912, DCB.

40. Beard to West, undated, c. 1911, DCB.

41. Beard to West, 14 October 1912, DCB.

42. Seton to Alexander, 13 January 1913, SML.

43. Seton to Executive Board, 21 November 1912, SML; Seton to Editorial Board, 25 August 1912, SML.

44. West to Beard, 12 March 1913, DCB; "Staves aided Boy Scouts," *Washington Evening Star,* March 13, 1913, DCB.

45. Beard to West, 10 April 1913, DCB.

46. Seton to West, 5 January 1914, DCB. It is worth noting in Seton's defense that there in fact was a "gum trust" on Wall Street, which controlled trading in that commodity to its advantage.

47. Ibid.

48. Beard to West, 7 January 1914, DCB.

49. Beard to Frank Presbrey, 8 January 1914, DCB.

50. "Extract from the address by National Scout Commissioner Daniel Carter Beard at the Annual Meeting." Boy Scouts of America, *Fourth Annual Report.*

51. Beard to West, 4 May 1914, DCB.

52. Seton to BSA Executive Board, undated, BSA. Seton appears to have drafted and reworked this during 1914 and 1915. He alludes to it in a May 8, 1914 letter to Robinson.

53. West would eventually soften his position and approve the "Order of the Arrow," BSA's honor society. Inspired by Seton and based on the lore of the Lenne Lenape or Delaware Indians, the Order of the Arrow was founded in 1915 by Philadelphia scout executives E. Urner Goodman and Carroll A. Edson at the council's Treasure Island summer camp.

54. Seton to BSA Executive Board, undated, ESP.

55. Seton to Robinson, 8 May 1914, BSA.

56. Doubleday to Seton, 19 August 1914, ESP.

Chapter 8—Seton Takes Leave

1. Beard to West, 15 September 1914, DCB. He left England at midnight of the 23rd (turning to the 24th) from Southampton on the steam ship *New York* of the American Line arriving Cherbourg, France at 6 a.m. Same day departure for Queenstown, Ireland on the 24th and arrived same day after a 6 hour voyage. Left Ireland on the 24th and arrived NY on December 30 after 5 days, 20 hour voyage. Certificate for entry to Ellis Island issued on December 31, 1909.

2. Alexander to West, 22 September 1914, DCB.

3. Beard to West, 30 September 1914, DCB.

4. Jensen, "Grace Thompson Seton at the Helm," p. 53.

5. West to Alexander, 3 October 1914, DCB.

6. Beard to West, 9 November 1914, DCB.

7. West to Doubleday, 16 October 1914, DCB.

8. "Cannot Vote if They Win," *New York Times,* March 26, 1914, p. 1; "Where Mrs. Paul Will Vote," *New York Times,* March 27, 1914, p. 10.

9. Alexander to West, 27 October 1914, BSA.

10. Alexander to Seton, 7 December 1914, BSA.

11. George W.P. Hunt to West, 18 April 1916, BSA; Ernest Lister to West, 17 April 1916, BSA.

12. Boy Scouts of America v. the United States Boy Scouts, New York Supreme Court complaint, filed July 31, 1917.

13. Beard to West, 2 August 1914, BSA.

14. West to Beard, 4 August 1914, DCB.

15. Beard to Murray and West, 18 December 1914, DCB.

16. Seton to Livingstone, 28 December 1914, BSA.

17. Ibid.

18. Livingstone to Seton, 29 January 1915, BSA.

19. Ernest Seton to Grace Seton, 30 January 1915 (mistakenly dated 1914), ASP.

20. Ernest Seton to Grace Seton, 31 January 1915, ASP.

21. Seton to Livingstone, 10 May 1915, BSA. Seton refers to an enclosed "letter of resignation, written some time before I left for England" at the beginning of 1915.

22. Seton to BSA President and Executive Committee, 29 January 1915, DCS.

23. West to Baden-Powell, 26 September 1911, DCB.

24. "Memorandum For Mr. West" by John Price Jones, dated October 10, 1911, DCB.

25. Samuel Gompers to West, 15 December 1911, DCB.

26. Phillips, *Selling America,* p. 21.

27. West to Beard, 16 March 1911, DCB; William H. Short to West, 15 March 1911, DCB.

28. Baden-Powell to West, 14 April 1911, DCB.

29. Jordan, "Challenge" pp. 3–4.

30. West to David Starr Jordan, 18 July 1913, DSJ.

31. West to Jordan, 4 September 1914, DSJ.

32. West to Jordan, 21 and 29 September 1914, DSJ.

33. Jordan, "Challenge," pp. 3–4.

34. Carnegie, "Mr. Carnegie's Word to Boys About War." Carnegie's message read in part: "We have abolished slavery from civilized countries, the owning of man by man. The next great stop that the world should take is to abolish war . . . Men of all nations should learn that they are members of the brotherhood of man . . ."

35. West to Jordan, 27 October 1914, DSJ.

36. Hofstadter, "American Policy Favored the Allies," reproduced in *America's Entry into World I,* ed. Donald Murphy (Farmington Hills, MI: Greenhaven Press, 2004), p. 17.

37. Murphy, *America's Entry,* p. 11.

38. Roosevelt, *America and the World War, 1916,* found at: http://www.trthegreatnewyorker.com/chronology/chronology.htm.

39. Roosevelt to John Callan O'Laughlin, 6 May 1915, *Roosevelt Letters, Vol. 7,* pp. 921–922.

40. Roosevelt to Archibald Roosevelt, 19 May 1915, Morrison, *Roosevelt Letters, Vol. 7,* pp. 922–923.

41. Roosevelt to Albert Bushnell Hart, 1 June 1915, Morrison, *Roosevelt Letters, Vol. 7*, p. 927.

42. Roosevelt to Raymond Robins, 3 June 1915, Morrison, *Roosevelt Letters, Vol. 7*, p. 928.

43. Baden-Powell to West, 31 May 1915, BSA.

44. Beard to West, 5 June 1915, DCB.

45. Beard to West, 9 June 1915, DCB.

46. Roosevelt, "Peace Insurance by Preparedness Against War," pp. 10–12, 62–67.

47. Major General Leonard Wood, 1860–1927, http://www.wood.army.mil/MGLeonardwood.htm.

48. Millis, *Road to War*, pp. 93–97.

49. Millis, *Road to War*, pp. 148–149; Roosevelt, "to the Men . . .," 21 May 1917, Morrison, *Roosevelt Letters, Volume 8*, p. 1195.

50. Minutes of Meeting of the Executive Board Held at the Lawyer's Club, 115 Broadway, 1:00 p.m., October 4, 1915, DCB.

51. Roosevelt to West, 30 November 1915, DCB.

52. Seton to Canadian Minister of War, 16 September 1914. "Modern Literature: The Journals of Ernest Thompson Seton," (auction catalog, Parke-Bernet Galleries, New York, 4 May 1965, sale # 2350 lot #210PBG.37); Newton D. Baker to Seton, undated 1917. "Modern Literature: The Journals of Ernest Thompson Seton," (auction catalog, Parke-Bernet Galleries, New York, 4 May 1965, sale # 2350 lot #210PBG.37).

53. Livingstone to West, 5 March 1915; Paul Sleman to West, 5 March 1915, BSA.

54. Seton to Livingstone, 10 May 1915, BSA; Seton to Charles C. Jackson, 12 May 1915, ESP.

55. Murray to West, 13 May 1915, BSA.

56. Presbrey to West, 13 May 1915, BSA.

57. Livingstone to West, 22 May 1915, BSA.

58. "First statement in reply to Mr. Seton," issued by BSA, 5 December 1915, BSA.

59. "Seton Still Insists on Quitting Scouts" *New York Times*, December 6, 1915.

60. Ibid.

61. Ibid.

62. "First statement in reply to Mr. Seton," BSA.

63. "West Says Seton Is Not a Patriot," *New York Times*, December 7, 1915.

64. Ibid.

65. Hornaday to West, 8 December 1915, BSA.

66. J.C. Elsom to A.C. Olson, 10 December 1915, cited in Whitmore, *Buckskins*, p. 298.

67. Edward B. Groot to West, 28 December 1915, cited in Whitmore, *Buckskins,* p. 299.

68. West to Jordan, 28 December 1915, DSJ.

69. Ibid.

70. Olson to West, 8 December 1915, BSA.

71. Roosevelt to West, 15 December 1915, BSA.

72. Doubleday to Livingstone, 3 January 1916, BSA.

73. Keith Monroe, *Other Men's Sons,* manuscript, p. VII-19, DCS.

74. Ibid.

75. Livingstone to West, 14 December 1915, BSA.

76. Ibid.

Chapter 9—Into the Sunset

1. Livingstone to West, 21 December 1915, BSA.

2. House of Representatives, 64th Congress, 1st Session, Report No. 130, February 7, 1916.

3. West to Beard, 31 May 1916, DCB.

4. *The Statutes at Large of the United States of America From December 1915 to March 1917,* pp. 227–229.

5. "Army Bill Amended for the Boy Scouts," *New York Times,* June 18, 1916.

6. Beard to West, 21 June 1916, DCB.

7. West to Beard, 2 June 1916, DCB.

8. Beard to Presbrey, 7 February 1914, DCB.

9. Rowan, *To Do My Best,* p. 95.

10. West to Beard, 8 June 1916, DCB.

11. Beard to Presbrey, 15 January 1917, DCB.

12. Beard to Seton, 10 February 1917, DCB.

13. Seton to Seymour, 13 February 1917, DCB.

14. Seton to Beard, 17 February 1917, DCB.

15. Beard to Seton, 20 February 1917, DCB.

16. Seton to Beard, 2 March 1917, DCB.

17. Wills, *Centennial History,* pp. 73–77.

18. West to Beard, 2 October 1917, DCB.

19. Wills, *Centennial History,* pp. 73–77; Whitmore, *Buckskins,* p. 277.

20. Beard to Seymour, 11 September 1912, quoted in Whitmore, *Buckskins,* p. 283.

21. Beard to C.A. Worden, 22 February 1917, cited in Whitmore, *Buckskins,* pp. 305–306.

22. "Message From Dan Beard to the Boys of America," draft, c. 1917, cited by Whitmore, *Buckskins,* pp. 309–311.

23. Beard to L. Keith Evans, 14 February 1918, cited in Whitmore, *Buckskins,* p. 313.

24. West to Beard, 4 January 1918, DCB.

25. "Verbatim Report of End of a Conversation Between Mr. James E. West, Chief Scout Executive, Boy Scouts of America, and Mr. Victor H. Stockel, a Lawyer Representing the U.S. Boy Scouts (Reported by Mr. Olsen)," January 28, 1919, DCB.

26. West to Beard, 17 March 1919, DCB.

27. Beard to West, 29 November 1918, DCB.

28. Beard to West, 4 December 1918, DCB.

29. West to Beard, 7 December 1918, DCB.

30. Beard to West, 9 December 1918, DCB.

31. Daniel Bartlett Beard to William Kahler, 25 May 1974, WVK.

32. Seton to Seymour, 2 December 1918, ESP.

33. Seton to Seymour, 11 January 1919, ESP.

34. Minutes of Woodcraft League Council of Guidance, September 26, 1918, ESP.

35. Minutes of Woodcraft League Council of Guidance, November 14, 1918, ESP.

36. Keller, *Black Wolf,* p. 192, citing J. M. Seton, *Trail and Campfire Stories,* p. 1.

37. Hornaday to Seton, 9 December 1912, ESP.

38. Seton to Doubleday, 28 November 1923, ESP.

39. Keller, *Black Wolf,* p. 200.

40. Livingstone to West, 4 October 1924, BSA.

41. Livingstone to West, 13 October 1924, BSA.

42. Seton to Livingstone, 9 April 1926, ESP.

43. Milton McRae to West, 22 April 1926, BSA.

44. Livingstone to Seton, 23 April 1926, ESP.

45. Seton to Walter W. Head, 16 August 1926, ESP.

46. Seton to Beard, 17 December 1926, DCB.

47. "For Union of Woodcraft and Boy Scouts—No. 1," Seton, c. January 1930, ESP.

48. "Memorandum Regarding Woodcraft and Boy Scouts," C.J. Carlson, c. January 1930, ESP.

49. E.B. DeGroot to West, 28 January 1930, BSA.

50. West to Carlson, 4 March 1930, BSA.

51. E.S. Martin to West, 26 April 1930, BSA.

52. H.W. Hurt to West, 5 April 1930, BSA.

53. George W. Ehler to West, 26 April 1930, BSA.

54. Edward Dodd to William Kahler (Questionnaire), 12 June 1974, WVK. "I feel the 'brass' gave him this name. I mean the higher ups at National Scouting Headquarters. I believe it was condescending and he did not like it. He liked to be called 'The Chief.'?"

55. Beard to West, 31 January 1919, DCB.

56. Beard to West, 10 April 1919, DCB.

57. West to Beard, 12 April 1919, DCB.

58. Beard to West, 14 April 1919, DCB.

59. G.M. Murray to West, 16 April 1919, DCB.

60. West to Beard, 17 April 1919, DCB.

61. Dodd was the creator of the comic strip "Mark Trail," about the eponymous outdoorsman.

62. West to S. Keith Evans & Frank Presbrey, 27 December 1919, DCB.

63. Brochure, "The Dan Beard Outdoor School For Boys (Incorporated)," 1919, DCB.

64. Daniel Bartlett Beard to William Kahler, 5 August 1974, WVK. The camp operated from 1916 until 1933 or 1934.

65. Ibid.

66. Whitmore, *Buckskins,* p. 360.

67. Ibid., pp. 361–362.

68. Ibid., p. 363.

69. Ibid., pp. 367–368.

70. Bartlett Beard to William Kahler, 25 May 1974, WVK.

71. Beard to Baden-Powell, 5 September 1929, DCB.

72. Whitmore, *Buckskins,* pp. 373–374.

73. Fred C. Mills to William Kahler, 30 September 1974, WVK.

74. Daniel Bartlett Beard to William Kahler, 25 May 1974, WVK.

75. "Dan Beard, At 80, Gives Scout Ideal," *New York Times,* June 22, 1930.

76. "Scouts: National Jamboree," *Time,* July 12, 1937, pp. 14–16. The Boy Scouts of America at that date involved some 1,075,00 people, and an estimated total of 7,500,000 Scouts and Scout leaders had been associated with the organization over the previous 27 years, *Time* reported.

77. Lummis journal, April 7, 1919, CFL.

78. Seton to Lummis, "Woodchuck day, Hunger moon, 1922," c. 2 February 1922, CFL.

79. Lummis journal, January 26, 1922, CFL.

80. J. M. Seton, *By a Thousand Fires,* p. 251.

81. Clara Barrus to Lummis, 22 June 1927, CFL.

82. Seton to the Family of Charles F. Lummis, 6 December 1928, CFL.

83. Anderson, *The Chief,* p. 216.

84. Ibid., p. 187.

85. Ibid., p. 220.

86. Ibid., p. 221.

87. Bethuel M. Webster, Jr. to Francis C. Wilson, Esq., 23 January 1935, BSA.

88. Seton Castle caught fire and burned to the ground November 15, 2005 during renovations, though Seton's extensive collections housed there for many years had been removed.

89. Seton divorce documents, SML.

90. West to Walter H. Head, 19 November 1935, quoted by Salomon, *Three Great Scouts,* p. 250.

91. Beard to Presbrey, 18 February 1936, DCB. Quoted in Salomon, *Three Great Scouts,* p. 253.

92. Robinson to Seton, 17 January 1935, YBL.

93. Seton to Robinson, 8 March 1938, SML. The letter was on Seton Institute stationery.

94. Rowan, *To Do My Best,* pp. 193–199.

95. West to Head, 5 May 1939, BSA.

96. Beard, *Hardly a Man Is Now Alive, Part XII,* unpublished draft manuscript, DCB.

97. West to Head, 13 November 1939, BSA.

98. Memo from George Ehler to James West, 30 August 1939, BSA.

99. Memo from E.S. Martin to West, 28 August 1939, BSA.

100. Memo from M.R.Greene to E.S. Martin, 28 August 1939, BSA.

101. Seton to Baden-Powell, 26 September 1927, ESP.

102. Baden-Powell to Seton, 26 October 1927, ESP.

103. West to Seton, 27 October 1927, BSA; West to Robinson, 5 November 1927, BSA; Seton, Ernest Thompson, *Woodcraft,* pamphlet published by Godshill, Fordinggridge, Hants, England: The Order of Woodcraft Chivalry, 1927, pp. 3–12, DCS.

104. Beard to Seton, 27 March 1935, ESP.

105. Robinson to Murray, 24 October 1934, BSA.

106. Robinson to Seton, 12 March 1938, ESP.

107. Baden-Powell to West, 8 August 1939, BSA; Baden-Powell to Seton, 8 August 1939, BSA.

108. West to Baden-Powell, 4 June 1940, BSA.

109. West to Whitney Darrow, 8 May 1940, quoted in Salomon, *Three Great Scouts,* p. 256.

110. Baden-Powell to West, 18 June 1940, BSA.

111. Grace Seton to Maxwell Perkins, 7 May 1940, ESP.

112. Perkins to Grace Seton, 9 May 1940, ESP.

113. Maxwell Perkins to Seton, 7 April 1941, ESP.

114. Seton to Beard, 1 December 1930, DCB.

115. Beard to Seton, 13 April 1935, DCB.

116. Beard to Seton, 20 May 1939, DCB.

117. AP report in *Salt Lake Tribune,* June 12, 1941.

118. "Uncle Dan," *Scouting,* July 1941, pp. 7, 28.

119. Ibid.

120. Anderson, *The Chief,* p. 229.

121. Ibid., pp. 238–250; Keller, *Black Wolf,* p. 217. According to biographer Keller, Seton's ashes were kept by his family until August 14, 1960, 100 years after his birth, when they were scattered by his two grandsons over the place where he had ended his life.

PHOTO CREDITS

INDEX

Wild Animals I Have Known (Seton), 16, 25–26, 30
wilderness, 7, 8, 27
Wilson, Woodrow, 178, 179, 182, 185
Winch, Frank, 200
Wolseley, Garnet, 62, 63
wolves, 22–24
Wood, Leonard, 181, 182
Woodcraft Indians, 3, 17–18, 37–40, 43–44, 55–56, 79–80, 82–83, 85, 88, 100, 103–106, 134–135, 145–146, 208–210

Woodcraft League, 185, 193, 203–204
World War I, 19, 163, 170, 173–174, 176, 178–180, 182–183, 198–200

Y

Yellowstone National Park, 11, 23
Young Men's Christian Association (YMCA), 3, 42–44, 97–99, 105–106, 123–124
youth movement, 115

RED HONOR™
PRESS

About Red Honor Press

Red Honor Press is a special imprint of PenlandScott Publishers established in 2006 to unite timeless, engaging, and enriching subjects and themes with outstanding authors to create distinctive titles for all ages and interests. Red Honor has emerged as a resourceful publisher of quality educational, informative, and inspirational books and media. The Press also produces quality works for fraternal, faith-based, and service-oriented groups and organizations. The Red Honor mark of distinction—conceived by naturalist, artist, and author Ernest Thompson Seton—reflects the imagination and integrity that distinguish all Red Honor Press publications.

The eagle feather and three circles of brotherhood in the Red Honor Press colophon represent the commitment of the company to Scouting ideals and American values.

.